TWELVE YARDS

BEN LYTTLETON is a journalist and broadcaster who has written for *Sports Illustrated* and *Time International*, among others, and is Bloomberg TV's on-air soccer analyst. He is also a director of Soccernomics, the soccer consultancy. He lives in London. This is his first book.

Twelve Yards

The Art and Psychology of the Perfect Penalty Kick

Ben Lyttleton

PENGUIN BOOKS

PENGUIN BOOKS

An imprint of Penguin Random House LLC
375 Hudson Street
New York, New York 10014
penguin.com

First published in Great Britain by Bantam Press, an imprint of Transworld Publishers, 2014
Published in Penguin Books 2015

LIBRARY OF CONGRESS CATALOGING-IN-PUBLICATION DATA
    Lyttleton, Ben.
    Twelve yards : the art and psychology of the perfect penalty kick / Ben Lyttleton.
        pages cm
    ISBN 978-0-14-312730-7 (paperback)
    1. Passing (Soccer)   2. Soccer—Psychological aspects.   I. Title.
GV943.9.P37L98 2015
796.334—dc23
2014038915

Printed in the United States of America
10   9   8   7   6   5   4   3   2   1

Set in Chaparral Pro
Designed by Sabrina Bowers

CONTENTS

TO ABC, WITH LOVE

Twelve Yards

PROLOGUE

Shay Given is a man of few words, and when he was twenty, even fewer. The goalkeeper had just signed for Newcastle United when I went to Dublin to interview him before his debut for the club, a friendly against PSV Eindhoven. He was a little anxious about his first appearance, having spent the previous season on loan at Newcastle's rivals Sunderland. Celtic, his first club, were possible opponents in the final of this preseason tournament at Lansdowne Road.

I told him I was nervous too. His glove manufacturers had arranged for me to compete in a sudden-death penalty shoot-out at halftime with Packie Bonner in goal. Bonner was an Irish legend, still playing at Celtic (it was his presence that forced Given to look elsewhere for games) and immortalized for one save: a dive to his right that kept out Romanian defender Daniel Timofte's penalty kick in a shoot-out at the 1990 World Cup. That one moment changed Bonner's life: when David O'Leary scored, Ireland reached the quarterfinal for the first (and so far only) time in their history.

Given perked up. "Ah, you're taking a penalty against Packie. Good luck then—you'll need it."

I appeared to have taken his mind off his worries, but he had hardly helped mine.

"Give me some advice then," I said. "What should I do?"

"The first thing is, don't change your mind. Decide where you're going to kick it, and stick with it. And when Packie's in goal, don't play silly games. No use trying to psyche him out."

When game day arrived, I tried to remember Given's words. Newcastle were 2–1 up at halftime, but the game had barely registered. I was standing next to the tunnel as the players walked off and I tried to catch Given's eye. That didn't work. My mind had gone blank. Had he told me to change my mind or not to change my mind? Did he say I should try to psyche out Bonner, or not? My brain was turning to mush, and I was not yet on the pitch.

I consoled myself with the fact that, as it was preseason, there were only 25,000 fans at Lansdowne Road; and as it was halftime, most of them would be getting a cup of tea, nipping to the loo or reading the match program. I was wrong. Bonner, of course, was an Irish hero and as many fans had turned up to glimpse him as to watch the game. I was quite surprised when one of my penalty opponents (there were three of us competing) was booed when he placed the ball on the spot. Fans behind the goal tried to put him off by waving and jumping. One dropped his trousers and flashed his bottom. It didn't work: he kept his head down and, off a long run-up, hit the ball hard and low to Bonner's right. Goal.

I was next up. I also kept my head down, and slowly put the ball on the spot. I took three steps back, and looked up. Deep breath. The goal looked big. But so did Bonner. Another deep breath. I had recently rewatched the Ireland–Romania shoot-out and noticed that Bonner dived to his right when players took shorter run-ups. It made sense: to generate power off a short run-up, a player is more likely to strike the ball to his natural side (that is, a right-footed player would kick to the keeper's right).

One more breath, a little skip, and I was off. My first movement was a step to the left to widen the angle of my run-up. After three steps forward, I opened my body and struck the ball cleanly with my instep. I can still see the slight curl on the ball as it headed for the inside of the side-netting, the dream target for a striker. Bonner, whose first movement was a step to his right, was wrong-footed. I had wrong-footed Packie Bonner! On his home turf, no less! I wanted to tell Given what had happened. I wondered if he had been watching on a monitor in the dressing room.

The drama wasn't over. My last opponent had missed, and I was left with another kick to stay in the competition. My mentality was different now. Nervous tension had given way to confidence. Confidence had been supplanted by arrogance. I knew I was going to score this one. Bonner's legs had gone. He couldn't read me. I had him just where I wanted him. And this time, in front of his adoring fans, I was going to show him.

I chose a straighter run-up this time, slightly longer. It suggested power, and a kick to Bonner's right. Instead, I wanted to attempt a chip down the middle, known as a "Panenka" after Antonin Panenka, the Czech midfielder whose penalty won the 1976 European Championship final—the first and last time a German national side lost a shoot-out. I later discovered that Panenka had spent two years working on that one kick, on the disguise, the run-up, the contact and the pace of the shot. I had never even practiced it.

It showed. As I approached the ball, my feet got in a tangle. My left foot was too far from the ball for me to kick it, and when I took another step forward, I stumbled. I was leaning over the ball when my right foot made contact, and it rolled apologetically toward Bonner in the center of the goal. Had he not been there it might not even have crossed the line. It was my Icarus moment. I, not Bonner, had been humiliated. I could not even hear the crowd cheer, jeer or laugh; they must have felt sorry for me. That didn't help either.

In the space of five minutes I had endured the glory and the pain of penalties. There were more nuances behind the penalty battle between goalkeeper and striker than I realized: body language, how to spot the ball, eye contact, angle of run-up—and that's only what you see before the ball has been kicked. I had underestimated the mental battle, not so much with the goalkeeper but within myself; and of course, like a true Englishman, I had failed to practice correctly. Well, I was hardly going to be able to re-create the same atmosphere and pressure in my back garden, was I?

Not that I hadn't tried. The majority of my childhood soccer memories, from a playing point of view at least, involve penalty kicks. I would spend hours taking penalties at home, using a sponge-ball and a radiator for a goal. It was a form of fantasy soccer: I'd choose two teams in my head, pick five kickers from each team, and replicate a shoot-out. My response to those players every weekend was invariably based on how they had performed in my home-game shoot-outs. As I got older, I took the game to the park, and to friends' houses: the same rules, with imagined players, but this time a goalkeeper to get past. I thought my sponge-ball practice had given me the edge—but it was not quite enough to beat Bonner twice.

After the game I caught up briefly with Given, and congratulated him on his debut. (I'd seen even less of the second half, too busy replaying my moment of shame over and over again, but others had told me he'd done well. I had convinced myself that Bonner had let me score the first penalty, as the late change to my run-up was an obvious tell. I still think that's true, but no longer feel bad about it.) He asked how I got on, and I didn't miss a beat.

"Yeah, pretty good, thanks," I replied. "I scored one and Packie saved one, so fairly happy with that."

"Nice one," Given said.

I prayed he had not been watching on a monitor after all.

*

Thirteen years later, almost to the day, I watched the 2010 World Cup final unfold between Spain and Holland. Spain were the better side and deserved to win the match, but I was hoping that Holland would hold on and reach the end of extra time with a 0–0 draw. The reason? By this time I had cofounded a soccer consultancy business called Soccernomics and we were working with Ignacio Palacios-Huerta, a professor of game theory at the London School of Economics. Palacios-Huerta wrote a paper in 1999, "Professionals play minimax," which is still seen as the seminal academic work on penalty kicks.

Using regression analysis, Palacios-Huerta is able to detect trends and patterns in the penalty habits of kickers and goalkeepers. If the majority of penalties, say 70 percent of them, are struck to the kicker's natural side—right of the keeper for right-footed kickers, left for left-footed ones—he can detect the player who kicks his penalties only 60 percent to his natural side. That in itself is useful, but of even more value is his ability to spot patterns in players: Diego Forlán, a Copa America champion with Uruguay, kicks to the left, then the right, then the left again; Miroslav Klose, a two-time World Cup Golden Boot winner, always kicks to the same side if the score is goalless; Frank Lampard's penalty tactic is very different when faced with an English goalkeeper who may have trained with him during international meet-ups.

Soccernomics had been in touch with some teams in the build-up to the tournament; one took Palacios-Huerta's full analysis for a knockout match, but lost before they reached penalties (and there were no spot kicks in the game). Another team asked for a penalty report twenty-four hours before their knockout match, but Palacios-Huerta needs three days to pore over the data for new teams, so that wasn't possible. That team was eliminated inside ninety minutes.

Before the final we had made contact with the Dutch FA and they were interested in the penalty analysis. Palacios-Huerta, a

Spaniard, supplied a report on his compatriots and the Dutch were delighted. "We were highly impressed," said goalkeeping coach Ruud Hesp. "It gave us valuable additional information and analysis on each player."

Before the second period of extra time was up, Spain's two most regular penalty takers, Xabi Alonso and David Villa, had been substituted, and when the whistle went Spain had only one player on the pitch, Fernando Torres, who had taken more than five spot kicks in his career (but even then, Torres only took them for Atlético Madrid, not Liverpool, where he had been playing for three seasons). The report showed that players who rarely take penalties have a clear preference to kick to their natural side. On the other hand, Torres had a slight bias to kick to his nonnatural side. Iker Casillas, Spain's goalkeeper, dived more than average to his natural side, giving those kicking to his nonnatural side a greater chance of scoring. He also, in fifty-nine penalties faced, had never stayed in the middle before.

No wonder the Dutch bench was totally deflated when Andrés Iniesta scored four minutes before the end of extra time. After the game Holland, who for so long had been a byword for penalty failure—they remain the only team to miss five penalties in one tournament match, a ridiculous Euro 2000 semifinal against Italy—said they felt sure they would have won a penalty shoot-out, and a first ever World Cup.

For Holland at least, the penalty report became meaningless. For another team, in another big game, it might just make all the difference. Penalties have always been a part of soccer, but because of their apparent simplicity their significance is easily overlooked. After all, for professional soccer players who play and practice every day, it shouldn't be so hard to score from twelve yards. But it is, often, and that's what makes the penalty so fascinating.

This book tries to solve a simple question: how do you score—or save—from twelve yards? To answer that, you need to know why in the case of certain teams or individuals they have been failing in the first place. I have looked into the reasons behind the struggles of these teams and players and learned innovative solutions to avoid future failures. My biggest delight was that despite its inherent cruelty, everyone loves a penalty. Every player and fan has a penalty story to tell—the best one, the worst one, the one that wasn't given, the one that was. Let's be honest, we have all watched a match in extra time and hoped for no more goals so we can enjoy the drama of a penalty shoot-out. The penalty is soccer in its purest form: kicker, goalkeeper and ball. Nothing else. A test of technique and nerve. It's the essence of the game, soccer at its most elemental. And even then, it is far from simple.

The penalties I've written about in the following pages were included because they tell a story about the history, culture or tactics of the spot kick. If your favorite is not here, don't worry: just go to the Web site www.facebook.com/twelveyards and nominate the penalty that means the most to you. You can also watch all the penalties here.

I want to thank all the players, goalkeepers, coaches, academics and athletes from other sports who took time to speak to me, and helped me learn what taking penalties is all about. If I faced Packie Bonner again today, I don't think he would stand a chance.

CHAPTER 1

THE ENGLISH DISEASE

I have seen England win a penalty shoot-out. I was at Wembley that Saturday afternoon on June 22, 1996, when England beat Spain 4–2 on penalties in the quarterfinals of the European Championship.

If only I'd known then what I know now: that England would lose their next five shoot-outs; that players who never take penalties would miss, and players who regularly take penalties would miss; that high-status players would miss, and low-status players would miss; that defenders would miss, midfielders would miss and strikers would miss. Back then it was "just" a quarterfinal against Spain. But still, if only I'd known. If only any of us had known.

Instead, four days later, England lost to Germany, again, on penalties. At least the team had come closer this time: they scored their first five spot kicks, which made it nine in a row if you included the Spain game. Two years later, at the 1998 World Cup, Argentina beat England on penalties. At Euro 2004 and at the 2006 World Cup, it was Portugal. At Euro 2012, Italy beat England on penalties.

Every time a major tournament comes around, England now dread the penalty shoot-out. It has got to the point where some opponents play for penalties because they know they have a psychological advantage. Even though England have had different players in every tournament—four different goalkeepers have played in those last five losses—it's the same outcome. And the excuses . . . well, they don't often change either:

1990: "The important thing was that the team played well. In the end nobody could beat us in open play." (Bobby Robson)

1996: "I was surprised that the coach had picked me to take one. I had never practiced taking penalties and had only taken one in my life before that, which I'd missed." (Gareth Southgate)

1998: "You can never re-create on the training ground the circumstances of the shoot-out." (Glenn Hoddle)

2004: "It was as much down to the penalty spot as anything. When you get into that it is a lottery." (Gary Neville)

2006: "We practiced penalties so much, I really don't know what more we could do about it. We have trained so much—almost every day—but when it comes to the pressure we are not good." (Sven-Göran Eriksson)

2006: "You can practice all you like in training and we had, throughout the tournament, but it's never the same as real life." (Wayne Rooney)

2012: "The practicing didn't help us too much on this occasion. Maybe it's just fated at the moment that we don't win on penalties but . . . you can't reproduce the tired legs. You can't reproduce the pressure. You can't reproduce the nervous tension." (Roy Hodgson)

I'm fed up with England losing on penalties now. I'd rather England lost in normal time, or extra time.* I wanted to find out why England kept losing, and to see how they could improve their chances of success.

But first I needed to know what England had been doing wrong. I assumed they had been missing too many penalties and not saving enough. I looked into the penalty records of all major national teams that had participated in more than ten shoot-outs.[†]

Figure 1: All-time penalty shoot-outs—penalties scored/missed ratio

Country	P-W-L	Scored-Missed	Goal %	Win %
Germany	6–5–1	26–2	93%	83%
Paraguay	5–3–2	19–3	86%	60%
Brazil	11–7–4	39–14	74%	64%
Spain	7–4–3	25–8	76%	57%
Uruguay	9–5–4	38–7	84%	56%
Argentina	10–6–4	37–10	79%	60%
France	6–3–3	25–6	81%	50%
Mexico[‡]	7–3–4	18–11	62%	43%
Italy	8–3–5	30–12	71%	38%
Holland	7–2–5	22–10	69%	29%
England	7–1–6	23–12	66%	14%

* In "U-21 flameout more evidence of English stagnation" (ESPN.com, June 11, 2013), Rory Smith wrote: "There is a reason England secretly loves being knocked out of tournaments on penalties. It is because a narrative can then be constructed where English football has but one failing—an ability to kick the ball accurately from 12 yards—rather than many." This may well be true, but other narratives coexist alongside Smith's, including England as plucky losers who deserved better (Germany in 1990 and 1996, Portugal in 2004), or, when a man down, they are holding on in adversity (Argentina in 1998, Portugal in 2006).

[†] This table takes into account penalty records from World Cup, European Championship and Copa America matches. I have not included records from the African Nations Cup or the Asian Cup due to concerns over the reliability of data.

[‡] Mexico includes Gold Cup and Copa America as invited guest.

The table in Figure 1 suggests that the England coaches might have a point. England's goal conversion percentage, 66%, may be below the average conversion rate of around 78% (significantly, this figure drops in tournament shoot-outs) but their win percentage, 14%, is woeful. Mexico, for example, have a worse conversion record but their win ratio is 43%—a figure England can only dream about. France could also consider themselves unlucky, with a 50% win rate despite an 81% conversion record.

Figure 2: All-time penalty shoot-outs—penalties conceded/saved ratio*

Country	Conceded/Saved	Opp. Conversion %	Save %
Brazil	35/17	67%	33%
Germany	20/9	69%	31%
Paraguay	16/6	73%	27%
Argentina	37/12	76%	24%
Mexico	23/7	77%	23%
Italy	30/8	79%	21%
Spain	24/6	80%	20%
Uruguay	35/8	81%	19%
France	26/6	81%	19%
England	29/6	83%	17%
Holland	28/5	85%	15%

Figure 2 looks at the impact goalkeepers have on their teams' penalty chances and the saving records of these eleven teams in world and continental competitions. Winning a shoot-out is about stopping penalties as much as scoring them, and it's clear that England and Holland lag behind the rest. Brazil and Germany have an above-average (22%) save percentage which in part explains their positive records.

After every England defeat, the focus, naturally enough, is on the players who missed, or the coach who bemoans fate—the "lottery" of the shoot-out—or, in Eriksson's case, practicing

---

* "Saved" also includes missed penalties.

hard but still not *quite* so hard as to do it every day. But we never hear from the opposition, the winning side, the team that progressed to the next round because they were lucky enough to take England to penalties. So I set out to speak to one player from every team that has beaten England on penalties and find out where they think England have been going wrong. It might not bring me to the ultimate solution for England's penalty-spot problems, but if it shed some light on how to improve the team's chances, it was worth a go.

The man who has contributed most to England having the worst record from penalty shoot-outs of any country in international soccer is Ricardo Alexandre Martins Soares Pereira. Ricardo, as he is known, is the Portugal goalkeeper who in the 2004 European Championship quarterfinal ripped off his gloves before saving Darius Vassell's penalty, and then converted the winning penalty himself. Two years later, in the 2006 World Cup quarterfinal, he saved three England penalties—the first player ever to do so in a World Cup shoot-out. FIFA gave England midfielder Owen Hargreaves the Man of the Match award, Ricardo put it, "just because he was the only player able to score a penalty past me." The referee, Horacio Elizondo, gave Ricardo the match ball, with his signature on it, because he felt so bad about FIFA's decision.

England, as we know, already had an issue with shoot-outs by 2006. Against Ricardo across those two matches England took eleven penalties and only scored six. Ricardo's intervention turned England's problem into more than that. A complex. An obsession. A crisis. The upshot? England's next shoot-out, six years later in the 2012 European Championship quarterfinal against Italy, was yet another defeat waiting to happen.

There are not too many Portuguese golfers at the Oceanico Vitoria course in Vilamoura early on a Monday morning in spring. This is the time of year when serious golfers, after months of playing in the cold, flock to the Algarve to play two rounds a day. The clubhouse fills with the chatter of Irish, Swedish and German players; the sun-dappled putting green is a kaleidoscope of fashion disasters. Just beyond that, on the driving-range, one man stands out, not so much for his swing, which actually looks pretty good, but for his outfit: white shoes, lime-green trousers and navy T-shirt with lime trimming. You have to be decent at golf to get away with that. Or be one of the most successful goal-keepers in Portugal. Ricardo is both. He has been playing golf for five years, and already plays off a handicap of four. He said the game helped improve him as a goalkeeper, made him concentrate better and taught him to refocus quickly after making a mistake.

Ricardo was seeing out his soccer career at Olhanense in the Algarve when we met, mostly on the bench. He suggested the reasons were political, the coach threatened by his presence as a senior player "with status," but he did not seem too fussed. He has been able to improve his golf and, I noted as he sipped on a lager shandy, he had the air of a man who realizes his playing career is almost over.

Ricardo is also an Anglophile. He spoke perfect English, wished he had spent more than six months playing in England, and wanted to help England get over the penalty demons he has helped to create.

The 2006 defeat to Portugal was different from any of England's previous "deaths by twelve yards." For a start, England scored one penalty out of four, their lowest total in a shoot-out. They had at least managed three against West Germany in 1990 (World Cup semifinal) and Argentina in 1998 (World Cup first knockout round). Two of the players who missed against Portugal were regular penalty takers for their clubs: Frank Lampard and Steven Gerrard. Portugal even managed to miss two penalties themselves and still win. It was the nadir of all England penalty defeats.

Despite having a one-man advantage, after Wayne Rooney was sent off for stamping on Ricardo Carvalho, Portugal were in no great hurry to push for a winning goal. "Did we play for the draw?" Ricardo said. "Well, we didn't take any risks because we were confident about winning the shoot-out. That's purely because we won in 2004: they had extra pressure on them. I spoke with Sven before the game, and he told me: 'I don't want the game to go to penalties because I know my players don't want to face you.'" Already, the England coach was afraid of the inevitable.

As we sat overlooking the putting green, I showed Ricardo a video of the 2006 shoot-out on my phone. Reliving it with him was like watching a movie with the lead actor sitting next to you. He drew my attention to moments I had thought insignificant, and elements that seemed important to me had barely registered with him.

Portugal took the first penalty and, with a confident run-up, Simão Sabrosa scored past Paul Robinson. He pumped his fists at shoulder height as he returned to the center circle. Lampard was first up for England; he had scored past Ricardo in the shoot-out two years earlier. He grimaced as he walked to the area, then dribbled the ball to the spot. After spotting the ball, he turned his back on Ricardo, adjusted his collar, and waited for the whistle to blow.

"I knew Lampard would be coming first," said Ricardo. "This is a guy who had not missed for two years or something like that from penalties.* I said to the guys before we started, 'If I save their first kick, we've won.' Because I knew if they see Lampard miss a penalty, they will never recover."

Lampard shot to his natural side, to the right of the goalkeeper, and Ricardo dived to punch it away. The TV cameras focused on the England players, and you can see Gerrard looking up to the heavens, almost in tears. As Lampard trudged back to the halfway line, Ricardo saw the same reaction. "When I saved it, I saw Ferdinand and Gerrard, and they just went *pffffff*...

---

* This was wrong: in fact he had missed for England two months earlier in a friendly against Hungary.

Their heads went down, and I knew we had the advantage. I saw them deflate. The best guy they have has missed. '*Pssshhh*, what chance have we got now?'"

Whenever it was Portugal's turn to kick, Ricardo would look away from goal and directly at the crowd. It was not an act of nervousness, as I had thought, but of strength. "Looking at the crowd, I could see one or two Portuguese fans, but everywhere else was English, all in white shirts. The whole crowd were nervous. I could see they were thinking, 'Not again.' That was another advantage for me: it may be a little thing but everything counts. These little things can make a big difference."

Hugo Viana, up next for Portugal, hit the outside of the post; as he ran back to the center circle, Simão, Hélder Postiga and Maniche broke away from the group, moved forward and clapped. I felt that was a significant and supportive response; Ricardo did not register it.

Next for England, Owen Hargreaves: he carefully spotted the ball, adjusting it at least three times, then shot hard to his natural side. Ricardo got a finger to it but could not keep it out. "I was very close, but it was a great penalty by Hargreaves."

One-all, after two kicks each; and soon England had the advantage when Petit's penalty went wide of the post. England players pumped their fists in the center circle, Ferdinand and Hargreaves shouting "Come on!" as they grabbed each other round the neck.

Gerrard had the chance to put England ahead. As he took the ball from the referee, Gary Neville linked arms with Hargreaves in the center circle and smirked at him—a hint of confidence suggesting that England felt their hoodoo might be ending.

Ricardo had other ideas. "I'm behind my goal line, I'm not rushing. No time-wasting, no talking. I don't need to go to Gerrard and say, 'Hey, you're going to miss.' If I'm doing that, I wouldn't be focusing on what I need to do, on what I'm trying to do. I watch him, I study him, I read his behavior. But when I see him walk toward me, man, I could see his face. He didn't want to look at me! He never looked at me! I saw that face, all their faces, when they came toward me, they look at me like they're saying, 'Oh my God, oh my God!' I'm just cold, concentrated, and that kind of behavior passes to the other players. I think if you are confident, the spirit is different."

Gerrard struck his penalty hard, to Ricardo's left, but nowhere near enough to the post. "That one was my best save because when the ball came to me it veered up at the last moment," he said. "My right hand had to move up very quickly to grab the ball. I walked past Robinson to my position and he looked at me out of the corner of his eye and said, 'Fuck, fucking hell! Again!' And mentally I could see his confidence was going. He was thinking, 'If I don't save this, we will lose.'"

Postiga made it 2–1 to Portugal with a smart penalty. In 2004, he had chipped the ball down the middle, Panenka-style, and his straight and long run-up this time suggested a similar effort. Robinson stayed central but Postiga found the left corner.

Jamie Carragher was next for England. He had come on two minutes before the end of extra time, as a substitute for Aaron Lennon, specifically, it seemed, to take a penalty. He had scored from the spot five years earlier, the victorious penalty in Liverpool's Worthington Cup final win over Birmingham, but had not taken one since then.

He spotted the ball, turned away from Ricardo and without a break in motion started his run-up. The referee had not blown his whistle, and two steps before Carragher reached the ball Elizondo blew twice to signify the kick would not count. Could Carragher have stopped? There was time if he had wanted to, but he kept on going, and struck an excellent penalty which Ricardo watched go past him.

"Carragher turned away and before I knew it, he was running toward me. But I knew the referee hadn't blown so I just put my hands out and went, 'Wait, wait.' The referee smiled at him and said, 'Wait for my whistle.' I looked at him then and I thought,

'You're fucked, I'm going to save this.' This guy was screwed, his mind was fucked up, he was too nervous.'"

Would Carragher go the same way, or change his mind? "I felt he was going to change his mind," said Ricardo. "Second time, he ran almost straight and it's harder to open your body that way." Ricardo was right: Carragher switched sides and the goalkeeper pushed the ball on to the crossbar. Portugal were 2–1 up and only needed to score the next to win.

"When Cristiano Ronaldo walked up to take the last penalty, he looked at me. I put my hands out to make it look like it was over. 'It's finished,' I said. I knew he would score. England were already defeated."

Ronaldo took his time; he kissed the ball before spotting it and took a deep breath. He waited a while after the referee had blown his whistle. His penalty was perfect.

I asked Ricardo why England had lost, yet again. "These big players miss and that's not because they are the wrong players to take penalties. These players are at the best clubs in the world, but in these big games, I just don't know what happens to them. It's a mental thing. They need to do some mental work."

Ricardo felt he had another advantage during the two games against England: he was a former striker who was a penalty taker himself. At his first club, Montijo, he would play in attack but switch to goalkeeper when the opponent was a bigger team, like Sporting Lisbon or Benfica. He was excellent in the air, and when he joined Boavista at seventeen he played some youth matches at center forward before being persuaded to stay in goal if he wanted to make it as a professional.

He would always practice penalties, though, and often just on his own, with no goalkeeper to stop them. "I would try and hit the ball where I wanted to hit it. Simple and often. No problem." Before long, he was Boavista's penalty taker. He scored five from the spot, including in a shoot-out against Málaga in the 2004 UEFA Cup quarterfinal.

If Ricardo's best save was against Gerrard in 2006, his best penalty strike came two years earlier—against England at Euro 2004. He was actually down to take Portugal's penalty number six, but after Rui Costa missed the third kick he had lost count. He was concentrating on the score, not the numbers. The Lisbon crowd did not give Portugal as much of an advantage as you might have thought—Ricardo felt the support was about fifty-fifty—but instead he drew confidence from a surprising source.

"I noticed the linesman," he told me. "Every time I almost saved a penalty, he breathed out really heavily. I looked at him and thought, 'He wants us to win.' It was like he was relieved every time one of our penalties went in. I felt like he wanted us to win. I don't know if he did, but that's what it felt like. Probably I was just grabbing on to something to give me confidence, but it helped."

After six penalties each, the score was 5–5. Postiga had taken the sixth penalty, the one Ricardo was due to take, and scored. Ricardo then had a surprise. "We had practiced for penalties in training, and I had watched some DVDs looking at where England players had taken their penalties," he recalled. "But when I saw Darius Vassell coming toward me, I thought, 'Fucking hell, hang on! I have seen every player score a penalty on this DVD but not this guy. Nothing! Has he even taken one before?'

"I looked at my hands. Fuck, I have to do something. I ripped off my gloves, just took them off. Vassell looked at me, and he looked at the referee, who said, 'That's fine.' To this day I still don't know why I did that. I have never done it before, or since, but I felt I needed to do something. I was in that moment; and even now when I think back to it, the one thing I can't remember is the noise. I can't hear anything. It's all totally silent.

"I saw Vassell was very nervous and he did not want to be there. I knew I was next up to kick and said to myself, 'I will save this one and score the next.'"

Sure enough, Ricardo dived the right way and saved it. Then, when he saw Nuno Valente walking toward the ball—he was down to take one after Postiga—he shooed him away. "It was my turn as I missed my go. Nuno ran back so fast to the center circle. I had never seen him run so fast!

"David James was in goal, and when he spread his arms, he looked as big as a building. 'Where do I put the ball, man?' Just in the place where he can't reach, because he is a very big guy. The corner. I had a cold mind. It was a great moment for me."

Once the Portuguese celebrations had died down, Ricardo received a phone call from the company that makes his gloves. They were pleased he had contributed to the victory, but not so happy that the important penalty was saved gloveless. "They told me not to do it again, and I never did."

Seven years later, Ricardo joined Leicester City, playing in the Championship. The coach who signed him was Eriksson. On his first day at the club, Ricardo was sitting in the dressing room when he heard a roar from across the room. "Morning, morning, whaaaaaa— What are you doing here?!" It was Vassell. "He was a very nice guy, and we spoke about that moment a lot."

On that first day, his teammates made Vassell take another penalty against Ricardo. Again, Ricardo saved it. "We laughed, man, that was so funny! But then he told me that before the Portugal game he went to Eriksson and said, 'Coach, if it goes to penalties, I don't want to take one because I'm not prepared for it, I'm too young to do it.' The guy was just a kid." After his missed penalty against Portugal, Vassell never played for England again.

So what can England do to avoid future penalty angst? Ricardo gave me three solutions, because "I want to see England win and I want to give them confidence."

1. Only focus on the positive.

"This is an opportunity, not a problem. Lampard and Gerrard always score in the league, they score a lot. So how in big moments did they miss? It has to be mental. They must only prepare for good things, not for failure."

2. Block out the media.

"We do read the papers at these tournaments and every day you're speaking about penalties, praying for no penalties. 'We don't want penalties, we don't want penalties.' If you have bad memories of it, just don't talk about it. Get on with it."

3. Forget about the history.

"The players need to stay mentally strong, and learn what works for them. But when they lost to us, you could see them thinking, 'Oh, we lost again on penalties.' It was almost like it was fate. These guys suffer too much. We felt with the England team that it was like their world was falling apart. It's like a film going round in their head . . . and they know how it always ends."

Six months after our meeting in the Algarve, Ricardo had won his place back at Olhanense. In October 2013 he even scored with a free kick from outside the box. It's some consolation that England will never face him in a shoot-out again.

If Portugal had England's number when it came to penalty shoot-outs, then so did the Germans. Lothar Matthäus told me that confidence and consistency were the reasons why West Germany beat England in the 1990 World Cup semifinal in Turin. It was England's first shoot-out experience, while West Germany had beaten France 5–4 and Mexico 4–1 in the previous two World Cups.

Matthäus took West Germany's second kick that day. Captain of his country, he was one of four players who were regular takers for their club sides, and that was the major difference. "Look at us," he said. "Brehme-Matthäus-Riedle-Thon." He reeled them off as though they were one person, even twenty-three years after the event. "It's all about confidence and especially with penalties. We definitely had confidence. We didn't worry about it: we thought less and concentrated more, and focused on having specialists in the side."

Matthäus forgot to point out that Stuart Pearce, the player who missed England's fourth penalty in 1990—the first six in the shoot-out were all converted—was a regular penalty taker himself, for Nottingham Forest. It was only after his miss, and after Olaf Thon scored, that a nonregular taker, Chris Waddle, stepped up.

And this is where some of that "lottery" factor that the England coaches and players referred to may come into play. Waddle was not slated to be England's fifth taker; it should have been Paul Gascoigne, but the midfielder, the breakout star of the tournament, had been shown the yellow card that would rule him out of the final if England won and was too emotional and distressed to take one. England were also missing the injured pair of Bryan Robson, who had scored a penalty for England before, and John Barnes, scorer of five penalties for Liverpool that season. So it was Waddle, taking his first major penalty. And he missed.

England coach Bobby Robson was fuming after the game, but not at Pearce, or Waddle, nor at goalkeeper Peter Shilton, who seemed to wait too long before diving for every kick (he went the right way but never made up enough ground to save one): he was angry at the system. "There is a way," he said. "You have to beat them. You play on, to the first goal or another quarter of an hour, because eventually somebody will crack. Football's a game of stamina and temperament and fighting spirit and that will come out."

His opposite number, Franz Beckenbauer, seemed bemused by Robson's reaction. "It's the rules and that's how it is," he said. "It's slightly better than tossing a coin. There's no other alternative."

FIFA president João Havelange was asked at his prefinal press briefing whether it was appropriate for a World Cup semifinal to be decided on penalties. "How unsurprising I should be asked this in English," he sneered. "As I understand it, unlike the English, the Germans actually practice penalties." Robson, though, had set the tone: losing on penalties was not England's fault. This time, the first time, it was the format to blame.

It was a different story in 1996. For a start, England did actually win a shoot-out, beating Spain after Alan Shearer, David Platt, Stuart Pearce (with a vengeance) and Paul Gascoigne all scored. England coach Terry Venables had been in charge of Barcelona when they failed to score any penalties in the 1986 European Cup final defeat to Steaua Bucharest, and ten years later he made sure his players practiced their penalties.

In the semifinal against Germany, it turned out that the England team were more organized than their opponents. England's five kickers—Shearer, Platt, Pearce, Gascoigne and Teddy Sheringham—all scored. Germany, on the other hand, were in disarray. Dieter Eilts, who was named Man of the Match and subsequently made it into UEFA's Team of the Tournament, had asked to be substituted at the end of extra time so he wouldn't have to take a penalty. "I felt I was guaranteed not to score," he said. Coach Berti Vogts only had four players willing to take a penalty and he asked Thomas Helmer if he felt his Bayern teammate Thomas Strunz, on as a very late substitute for Steffen Freund, was up for the task. "Absolutely," came the reply, and Strunz grabbed the match ball from referee Sandor Puhl and did some keepy-uppies to get his eye in. Vogts then told Markus Babbel to sort out who would take penalties seven and eight with Marco Bode. "Marco, the boss said you are on penalty number seven," Babbel told him. "My legs were getting weaker and weaker," remembered Bode. Matthias Sammer, who would go on to win the Ballon D'Or for 1996 European Footballer of the Year, was desperate, along with Eilts, not to take a penalty. "There would probably have been a punch-up between us to avoid it," Sammer said.

None of Germany's players in 1996 had ever taken a penalty in a major tournament, but Thomas Hässler, Strunz, Stefan Reuter, Christian Ziege and Stefan Kuntz all scored. It was 5–5 after ten penalties.

England's remaining outfield players were Tony Adams, Darren Anderton, Paul Ince, Steve McManaman and Gareth Southgate. Even now it seems surprising that Southgate and not Anderton or McManaman took England's next kick. His effort against Germany was poor: struck to his natural side but nowhere near the corner, and with little pace. Andy Köpke went the right way, and saved it easily.

A few months after the game, German writer Ronald Reng spent an afternoon with Southgate in Birmingham, where the player opened up about the miss. "I think it was because I was a German, and he wanted to get things off his chest," said Reng. "It was that feeling of guilt that sometimes makes you do illogical things."

The interview ran in *Süddeutsche Zeitung* and in it Southgate told Reng that he knew the penalty would define his career. "Living with it is extremely difficult," he said. "It was my first major tournament for England and I played very well; but the only thing people remember is this small, silly mistake. The only opinion people have about Gareth Southgate is that he can't take penalties . . . For a lot of other people who have experienced pain, I've sort of become a source of help and encouragement. People are writing to me not only to cheer me up but expecting assurances for their own problems. I've become something of an agony aunt."

He admitted that it was a dreadful penalty. "But when the time came, how can I put it? I was surprised that the coach had picked me to take one. I had never practiced taking penalties and had only taken one in my life before that, which I'd missed. I can't take penalties well."

Southgate didn't remember much of what happened after the penalty. "I lay awake that night and thought, 'What will people think of me now?' and it was frightening. Stuart Pearce had said to me, 'Gareth, tomorrow I'm going home to feed my horses. I'll look at them and say, "We lost to Germany on penalties again." And they'll answer, "What do we care? Give us some carrots now."'"

Southgate later admitted that he knew things might not end well after Ziege had scored Germany's fourth penalty. He had already decided where he would place the ball, "But around the point where the score reached 4–4 and nobody had failed, my mind switched to the negative. 'What if I miss?' That simple thought, which with better mental awareness could have been dismissed, was now nudging its way into my subconscious and, with hindsight, I know that was the tipping-point of my failure."

Kuntz's mood had also changed as the shoot-out went on. He was a regular penalty taker in club soccer—in fact, his thirty penalties put him eighth in the Bundesliga's all-time list—but had asked Vogts to name him as the fifth kicker because he hoped the shoot-out would be over by then.

Vogts had proved himself a man of his word. Four months before Euro 96 began, he had promised Kuntz that because Jürgen Klinsmann was suspended he would start Germany's first game—and he did. That allowed Kuntz, then thirty-three, to do some extra training at Besiktas, and the striker worked superhard. "I won my first Germany cap at thirty and when you're older, these moments are more precious," he said. "I knew this would be my last tournament for Germany and wanted to make it special."

Kuntz, playing because Klinsmann was injured in a bad-tempered quarterfinal against Croatia, had scored Germany's equalizer and had an extra-time header ruled out for a foul.

"Never a foul," he told me.

As he watched England score penalty after penalty, he became angry. "It was terrible for me. I was fifth because I never wanted to take one, and when it came to it, my penalty was the most important of all. During that walk, you are so alone, so afraid. I had to find a way to conquer my nerves. So I made myself angry. That way, I forgot about the nerves." Kuntz thought about his children, who were then five and seven, and how their school-mates would tease them if he missed the penalty. "I got so angry at the thought of these clowns upsetting my kids. I thought,

'Don't do this to your family!'" Kuntz, left-footed, hit Germany's best penalty, high to his natural side. He was so wound up that afterward he forgot to smile. Just a deep breath as he returned to the center circle.

And next up was Southgate. "Of course I have sympathy with Southgate," said Kuntz. "It is traumatic to be the guy who misses. But remember he had the courage to take one, and half the team did not do that."

So why did England lose? "There was additional pressure because of the meaning of the game, the fact that it was against Germany. But also sometimes when you're at home, you can feel the doubt of your own fans. I wonder if Southgate thought, 'Even the fans don't think I will score this.' What is in your mind is often what will happen, and controlling your mentality is a huge part of the game."

Kuntz said that the game is still the highlight of his career, above the final against Czech Republic, which he started and Germany won. "It was my first game at Wembley, it was against England, I scored in the game and the shoot-out . . . It was everything to me." He is now focused on his job as chairman of FC Kaiserslautern, where he spent six years as a player. He doesn't like to talk too much about the old days; he's tried to steer away from it ever since he showed his grandma the blurb on his official sticker-card just before he retired. "It said '1990 Cup winner, 1991 Bundesliga winner, Euro 96 winner,' and all my goal records. And my grandma said, 'Very nice, but can you pay for groceries in the supermarket with it?' And then I realized you just have to move on with your life. Stop looking back. And maybe England should do the same with penalties."

After Kuntz's successful spot kick, the Germans had still not decided who would take their sixth penalty. That is, until Southgate missed. At that point Andreas Möller broke from the group and headed to the penalty spot. "He put himself forward and said, 'My turn now, hey?'" remembered Thomas Helmer. It was too late for anyone to object, and Möller scored. Game over.

Shearer had scored England's opener in the third minute, and netted the first penalty in the shoot-out, just as he had against Spain four days earlier. "It's all right people saying 'Practice, practice, practice," but you can never ever re-create the situation you will be in," he told me. Despite his personal success in shoot-outs—he scored against Argentina in 1998 as well, making him England's best shoot-out performer with three from three—his discourse was peppered with negative terms. "I wouldn't wish that pressure on my worst enemy," he continued. "The walk to the penalty spot feels like it's forty miles. And it's not so much the eighty thousand people watching in the stadium or the thirty million watching on TV that makes you nervous. It's the ten teammates behind you. The pressure to do it for them is greater than anything else."

Was that negativity still in place two years later, when England took on Argentina in Saint-Etienne? Certainly the trauma of England's defeat in 1996 had been far greater than in 1990. England were the home nation, it was Germany, and on penalties, again. The press had been full of military metaphors—the *Mirror*'s "Achtung Surrender!" headline before the game took it too far and as a result team sponsors Vauxhall pulled their advertising from the paper—but once again England had fallen short. "We knew that the media had turned this game into a war but for us it was never like that," Kuntz commented. "Look, even our parents were not involved in the war, it was two generations away from us, so we did not understand the headlines. It would have been more helpful for the England team if it was not about war or history, but if they just concentrated on football. I think the media built up this game too much and that added to the pressure for the players."

This was the moment when the psychological issue with shoot-outs took seed. It was England's great misfortune that they had to endure another one so soon after, against another nation with whom England have had a complicated sporting and political history: Argentina.

The soccer rivalry kicked off in 1966 when Antonio Rattin refused to leave the Wembley pitch for ten minutes after he was sent off against England. Alf Ramsey stopped George Cohen swapping his shirt with Roberto Perfumo, and declared the Argentine team "animals." In 1977, Argentine forward Daniel Bertoni punched out two of Trevor Cherry's teeth (his knuckle still has the scars to prove it), while in 1986, Argentina beat England with Maradona's "Hand of God" goal. "Winning the World Cup that year was secondary for us," Perfumo said. "Beating England was our real aim. Beating England is like schoolkids beating the teachers."

Glenn Hoddle did not make his players practice penalties in 1998, subscribing to the Shearer viewpoint that the real thing is never the same. Ironically, as the first-choice penalty taker Shearer was the only player who did practice. The night before every international match he would take five kicks to the same side of the goal, and in the game itself would always kick it to the other side. He was convinced that, even in closed training sessions, the opposition would have someone spying on him.

Against Argentina, it worked: three minutes after Gabriel Batistuta had opened the scoring, Roberto Ayala was penalized for bringing down Michael Owen (a generous decision), and Shearer scored. Minutes later, Owen broke from the center circle and ran at the heart of the Argentine defense. He skipped past Ayala and chipped the ball into Carlos Roa's far corner. Javier Zanetti equalized on the stroke of halftime, and after David Beckham was sent off, England were left defending stoutly in extra time to keep the score to 2–2.

Ayala, who was in Buenos Aires coaching Racing Club, was happy to discuss his memories of the game. "First of all, there was Owen," he said. "The penalty he won, and then what a goal he scored. But I have to tell you: [José] Chamot and I, we made a lot of mistakes for that. We were too far apart, I was in the wrong position, but also, we didn't know anything about this kid. Shearer, we knew all about, but Owen: nothing."

England had a brief advantage in the shoot-out at 1–1 when David Seaman saved from Hernán Crespo, taking Argentina's second kick. Paul Ince, next for England, failed to take advantage. Juan Verón and Paul Merson scored; Marcelo Gallardo and Owen scored; then it was Ayala's turn.

"I was no specialist penalty taker and we had not practiced penalties in training," he said. "The first four guys, they were all regular takers, but I wasn't. I would never say no, though I never asked the coach [Daniel Passarella] why he picked me to take number five. I decided straight away where I was going to kick it. I figured that Seaman would think I was a lumbering defender, that I would kick it to my natural side, so I would go the other way."

Ayala also had none of the fear factor that Shearer spoke about. "I felt no pressure walking to the spot. In fact, it was exciting. There are so many dreams behind a team and I thought about all the people supporting us, and me. Missing it never crossed my mind. I knew I was going to score. I didn't even look at Seaman. I just spotted the ball, and kicked it. And I scored. That was it."

Roa shouted out to Ayala after his penalty: "Hey! What happens if I save this one?"

"We win!" replied Ayala.

Roa had a habit of forgetting teammates' names. Ayala thinks this forgetfulness helped him in the shoot-out.

David Batty stepped up for England. He had replaced Anderton to shore up the midfield after Beckham's dismissal. He had never taken a penalty, and before leaving the center circle had asked Shearer where he should kick it. "I told him to blast it down the middle, but by the time he got to the spot he had changed his mind," said Shearer.

Batty struck it to Roa's left, and the goalkeeper dived the correct way to win the shoot-out for Argentina.

"Roa did great," said Ayala. "But I still can't say for sure why England lost this shoot-out. We were disappointed not to win the game in normal time, but we didn't practice penalties either. I think Roa was quicker to move than Seaman, and we were just able to do better from the penalties. Sometimes, that's how it happens."

For Gianluigi Buffon, penalties will always remain a mystery. The Italy goalkeeper won the 2006 World Cup final against France after a shoot-out, and was in goal when England lost on penalties in the Euro 2012 quarterfinal. "I'd rather lose a match in normal time than on penalties," he said. "But for me it comes down to which of the players are least exhausted, and those who can focus a little better."

Buffon is an intuitive goalkeeper: the day before the game, while Joe Hart was talking about analyzing the patterns of the Italian players, he joked that he had been watching adult videos instead.

When it came to the Euro 2012 shoot-out, Hart saved no penalties and Buffon saved one, from Ashley Cole. [Riccardo Montolivo, for Italy, and Ashley Young, for England, both missed the target.] "I could see he was waiting for me to dive but I stood tall for as long as I could. Then, when I went the right way, I was able to save it." By then Italy already had the momentum, as Andrea Pirlo, with his side 2–1 down, shifted the mood of the shoot-out with his perfectly chipped "Panenka" penalty down the middle of the goal. "That gave us huge belief to go on and finish it off," Buffon confirmed. "Pirlo turned the shoot-out into our favor; after his penalty, the England players looked frustrated, like they had lost some determination."

Despite that 2006 World Cup final shoot-out win, Buffon still is not sure that there is a winning strategy for spot kicks. "I don't think you can give anyone advice for penalty shoot-outs," he said. "If you tell the keeper to wait until the last minute to dive, even if he goes the right way, he will not get there if the kick is well taken. Some players prefer to kick to a certain side, but everyone knows that. There is luck involved in a shoot-out, but history also plays a part, because that affects your confidence. Italy overcame that: we lost so many shoot-outs in the 1990s [four, in 1990, 1994, 1996, 1998], but then won the World Cup on penalties in 2006. So I guess you just never really know."

Pirlo himself didn't even know he was going to attempt that outrageous effort when he started his run-up to the ball. He only decided at the last second, because, as he put it, "Joe Hart was doing all his dramatics on the line." As soon as Hart moved, Pirlo made his decision. "I had to find the best solution in order to reduce the margin of error to the minimum," he said. "It was improvised and not predetermined. I felt it was the only way I could get closer to that 100% margin of success. I wasn't showing off. It's just not part of myself. Before that game, we didn't even have time to train properly because of all the trips between Poland and Ukraine, so how could I have tried that trick again and again? I did it because of pure calculation—in that moment it was the least dangerous thing I could do. It was the safest and most productive one at the same time. After the game, team-mates asked me, 'Andrea, are you a fool?' They were astonished. But I wasn't. I knew why I did it."

I asked England's two scorers against Argentina, Alan Shearer and Michael Owen, why the shoot-out had now become such a problem for England.

Shearer told me that we need some luck. "We need five guys to hold their nerve at the right time and we need luck and we need courage. That should get us over the line." I pointed out that we had five such guys against Germany in 1996, and that wasn't enough. "Yes, but not many shoot-outs go beyond five kicks. If we could just get that first important win under our belt, then mentally we will be over it."

Owen was convinced that previous experiences of penalty shoot-outs played on players' minds. "Confidence is a huge factor in taking penalties and as I had scored during the ninety minutes against Argentina I had a strong belief I would score when I took

PENALTY ICON —
MATT LE TISSIER

Matt Le Tissier watched the 1998 World Cup defeat to Argentina at the house of his friend and Southampton teammate Francis Benali, tearing his hair out as the shoot-out approached. Le Tissier had not missed a penalty for over five years and his omission from Hoddle's squad was surprising (not least because he scored a hat-trick for England B the week before it was named). "I did think it was odd that my penalty record did not help me get a call," Le Tissier told me. "In a squad of twenty-three players, you always get four or five who come back without playing a single minute, so why not take a specialist penalty taker, just in case you need one? My record from the spot was good."

It was more than good: in his entire professional career Le Tissier missed only one penalty, against Nottingham Forest in 1993, and scored his other forty-seven. He practiced more when he hadn't taken one for a while, and would incentivize youth-team goalkeepers, then earning £40 a week, by paying them £10 for every penalty they saved. "There were a few occasions when I paid out," he remembered. "But only a few."

The key, according to Le Tissier, is that the players must look forward to taking their penalty. "I wanted the whole stadium to watch me, it appealed to my ego. I also liked scoring goals and this was the easiest way to do it, especially as I didn't have to run!" He would wait to see where the goalkeeper was going to dive, but always targeted his nonnatural side first, as it was easier to make a late change to his body shape and kick to the other side if required. "If you try that the other way round, it's virtually impossible, unless you're prepared to rip your knee ligaments."

Le Tissier was involved in only one shoot-out in his career. It was at the end of an FA Cup tie against Manchester United in February 1991, and his Southampton coach Ian Branfoot asked him to take the first penalty. Le Tissier said no, and asked to take the fifth. After four penalties each, Southampton had won 4–2, so Le Tissier was not even required. "I wanted to be the hero and that served me right."

So how can England get over their problem? "A lot of it is down to perception: if people tell you that you're rubbish then you turn up expecting to lose," said Le Tissier. "I can look at the players' eyes and they look like they don't want to be there. But there is enough pressure around Premier League games for them to be able to manage expectations. There are lots of complex issues at play here."

I wonder if England's penalty trauma would have been so acute had Le Tissier been part of that shoot-out against Argentina.

CHAPTER 2

THE OSLO SOLUTION?

The answer to England's problems may be found in a wooded northern suburb of Oslo, in an unprepossessing office in Sognsvann located next to Norway's swanky Olympiatoppen training center. Taking the city train out north, you pass the Ullevaal, Norway's national stadium, where, in the 2012 Norwegian Cup final, second division side Hødd caused a sensation by beating top-flight Tromsø 4–2 on penalties.

In his office, former soccer player Dr. Geir Jordet clicks up penalty after penalty on his computer screen. Jordet used to play for second division side Strømmen, but his career took an altogether different course after Ricardo saved David Beckham's penalty at Euro 2004. At the time, Jordet was studying sports psychology at the Norwegian School of Sports Sciences. He had just written his dissertation, about the peripheral vision of elite midfielders, and was invited on to a Norwegian radio station, P3, to talk about England's defeat.

Jordet criticized Beckham for not checking the penalty spot properly before his kick; fellow guest Henning Berg, a former teammate of Beckham's at Manchester United, insisted that Beckham was as mentally tough as they come, and laid into Jordet. Jordet took it badly—"I felt like crap"—and when he moved to Holland for a job at the University of Groningen one month later, he changed the focus of his research to examine the psychology of penalties. He is obviously more sensitive than he looks.

The university had good access to contacts at the Dutch FA and it happened that Jordet, through his work back home, knew a few Swedish national team players who had played in Norway. He pooled these contacts and suggested a unique study into what players thought about during a shoot-out. He interviewed, at length and in one-on-ones, ten of the fourteen players who took penalties for either Holland or Sweden in their Euro 2004 quarterfinal shoot-out. The game had finished 0–0 after extra time. With the score 2–2 on penalties, Zlatan Ibrahimovic missed for Sweden; two penalties later, Phillip Cocu's miss leveled the scores. After five penalties each it went to sudden death and Sweden captain Olof Mellberg, then a high-profile player at Juventus, had his shot saved by Edwin van der Sar. Arjen Robben scored the winning Dutch penalty for their first ever shoot-out success.

Jordet came up with the most honest depiction of players' stresses and anxieties throughout the process and divided up his findings into three academic studies, one of which, "Stress, coping and emotions on the world stage: the experience of participating in a major soccer penalty shoot-out," is particularly fascinating. For the purpose of his interviews, Jordet broke up the shoot-out into four phases:

1. The Break after Extra Time
2. The Midcircle
3. The Walk
4. At the Penalty Mark

Figure 3: Moments of highest anxiety in a penalty shoot-out

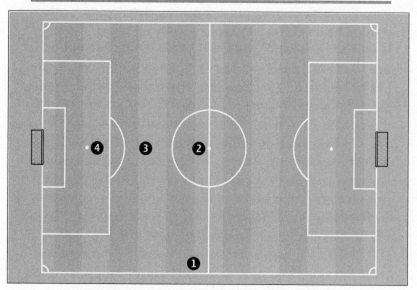

He then assessed each player's reaction at each phase. Six interviewees knew before Phase 1 that they would be taking a penalty; two specifically did not want to take one—one even said, "In advance, I had personally said that I did not want to take one"—and another was annoyed that three other teammates had, during Phase 1, expressly ruled themselves out of taking a penalty. Four players felt more stressed when they were told what number they would be shooting, as they didn't know and therefore couldn't prepare for what the game situation would then be; another four were calm or relaxed.

Surprisingly, it was Phase 2 that was the most stressful for the players, particularly those on the losing side (Sweden), who were not standing as a group nor talking to or encouraging each other. "We hardly talked about anything during the shoot-out," one player said. "Nothing. I didn't say anything and nobody said anything to me." This was the phase when Gareth Southgate admitted that negative thoughts affected his performance. Only three players used the Midcircle phase to focus on their own penalty; for the others, tension grew as they waited for their shots. "I became incredibly nervous," said one player. "I thought it showed on television that my legs were shaking, that's how nervous I was." Another became less nervous after a teammate had missed. "First, I felt bitter and angry, but then the nervousness went away. I became much calmer."

The Walk, Phase 3, was far less stressful for these players than you might expect, though the loneliness of it, for three players, was the toughest part of the shoot-out process to deal with. One was comforted as soon as he got to the ball: "Is it not so that things get less stressful if you have something in your hands? I swirled it around a little bit. I think it was very important." Three players also noticed their anxiety decrease during the walk.

By Phase 4 only two players were expressing anxiety. One broke from his normal routine to turn away from the goalkeeper, which Jordet interpreted as a classic avoidance strategy.

His conclusion was that coaches could learn something about every phase of the shoot-out: from Phase 1, that players like to know the order in which they'll be kicking as early as possible, and don't like surprises (or teammates bailing on them); from Phase 2, that passively waiting for your turn throws up negative emotions; from Phase 3, that the solitariness of the walk requires a coping mechanism; and from Phase 4, how best to face the goalkeeper in a confrontation.

The three papers launched Jordet as a rising star in the field of sports psychology, and today he is Director of Psychology at the Norwegian Centre of Football Excellence. "I look at how you can most effectively think and feel to get the best performance, and also how to deal with failure," he said. One of the teams he now works with would collapse whenever they conceded the first goal, so he was brought in to stop the rot.

Because of his academic background, Jordet has a more data-driven approach to sports psychology. When I asked him why

England so often lose on penalties, he came up with several possible explanations.

"I spent three years searching for the perfect penalty," he told me. "I looked at the ideal number of steps you can take in a run-up, whether you should kick the ball high or low, strike it with power or go for accuracy, and there are no real significant effects. The big effects were all about pressure and how you deal with stress. It was not about football, but psychology."

One of these psychological factors was, as we have seen, the weight of history. Jordet did a study on the effect losing one or two shoot-outs had on the next shoot-out.* For example, would England be more likely to lose a shoot-out in its next major tournament simply because it had lost its last two shoot-outs? The answer is yes.

Figure 4: Preceding team outcome and individual shot performance

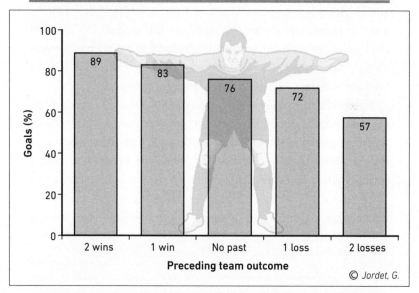

---

* Jordet, Hartman & Vuljk, "Team history and choking under pressure in major soccer penalty shootouts" (*British Journal of Psychology*). This 2012 study used 309 penalty shoot-out kicks from European Championships and World Cups to study the effect of previous team outcomes on individual current performance.

As you can see from Figure 4, a player's likelihood of converting a penalty for a team whose last two shoot-outs ended in defeat drop considerably, to 57%, even if that player was not part of the team at the time of those defeats. The winning habit is also contagious: the chances of scoring for a side that has won its last two shoot-outs rises to 89%. The cycle of defeat, though, is a vicious one. The figures are even lower for a player who took a penalty in the last shoot-out defeat—even if that player scored the last time. His likelihood of scoring drops to 45%. I asked Jordet if England's regular failures and Germany's successes skewed the numbers, and they did not.

You can see why. Imagine a nine-year-old boy, let's call him Ashley, whose first experience of watching England at a major tournament ends in a shoot-out defeat. That leaves its own scar. As Ashley grows up and becomes a professional, he sees England lose two more shoot-outs. By now he is playing for his country, and England lose another two shoot-outs. Ashley then becomes a senior player and scores in shoot-outs for his club; but the idea that winning a shoot-out with England is much harder has already taken root. He is thirty-one and experienced when it's his turn to take a penalty for England. He misses.

This backs up studies in social psychology that reveal that the negative effects of bad things affect us much more dramatically than the positive effects of good things.* Penalties distil this effect: rather than one team doing well, the other team doing badly is what makes the difference in most shoot-outs. England's

---

* In "Bad is stronger than good" (*Review of General Psychology*, 2001), Dr. Roy Baumeister writes: "Perhaps the broadest manifestation of the great power of bad events than good to elicit lasting reactions is contained in the psychology of trauma . . . Many kinds of traumas produce severe and lasting effects on behavior, but there is no corresponding concept of a positive event that can have similarly strong and lasting effects. In a sense, trauma has no true opposite concept . . . It is possible that such events have simply eluded psychological study, but it seems more likely that the lack of an opposite concept for trauma indicates the greater power of bad than good single events to affect people."

failures lead to more failures. But why are they failing in the first place?

As a psychologist, Jordet has pinpointed two penalty strategies that players use when they are extranervous—avoidance strategies. For regular penalty takers their impact is less significant, as they might be part of a well-rehearsed routine, but for the infrequent kickers in the shoot-out—"they are the more interesting ones for me, because for them it comes down to pure psychology," said Jordet—these correlate to performance.*

One is when a player turns his back on the goalkeeper after spotting the ball to start his run-up. "You can't turn your back forever, at some point you have to turn around and face the stress full on," Jordet said. He clicks up picture after picture of players in the center circle facing away from the goal where the shoot-out is taking place: Paul Ince at Euro 96, two years before he missed one at the 1998 World Cup; Ricardo Carvalho at Chelsea's 2008 Champions League final loss in Moscow (in which Roman Abramovich also has his hands clamped on the back of his head, looking down at his feet); Ukraine coach Oleg Blokhin watched his side beat Switzerland in the 2006 World Cup from the dressing room, as he couldn't bear it.

Jordet then clicked on to the statistical breakdown of players who turn their backs on the goalkeeper after spotting the ball.

---

* The key phrase here is "correlate to performance," as opposed to cause the performance. All of Jordet's findings are correlations, the big difference (at least for economists) being that causations are what explain the reasons behind something. The most famous example is Franz H. Messerli's graph which shows "Correlation Between Countries' Annual Per Capita Chocolate Consumption and the Number of Nobel Laureates per 10 million Population," in "Chocolate consumption, cognitive function and Nobel laureates" (*New England Journal of Medicine*). The graph depicts almost a straight line from bottom left to top right, despite the x and y axes having no obvious causal link. It is in fact another variable (maybe income) which causes both. In the same way, Jordet's figures do not in isolation, or even together, provide certain or causal reasons for England's failure, but they do provide correlations that are relevant and worthy of further investigation.

Figure 5: Country and avoidance looking

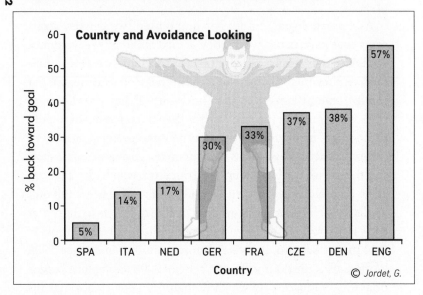

Country and Avoidance Looking

% back toward goal

SPA	ITA	NED	GER	FRA	CZE	DEN	ENG
5%	14%	17%	30%	33%	37%	38%	57%

Country

© Jordet, G.

As Figure 5 shows, England players did this a whopping 57% of the time, compared to 17% for Holland and a minuscule 5% for Spain. These figures are particularly dramatic, not because England are out in first, but because no other country comes close to their avoidance looking strategy. On its own this is not a clear indicator of performance, but when allied to another avoidance strategy, that of rushing to take a penalty kick, there is a clearer correlation. This can be seen in a table of reaction times after the referee blows his whistle to signify that the penalty taker can start his run-up.

There may not seem that much difference between these numbers—they are fractions of a second—but there is one (by way of comparison, Usain Bolt's average reaction time is around 0.17 second). No nation is faster at taking penalties than England, whose average reaction time is just 0.28 second. The reason Jamie Carragher was made to take a second penalty against Portugal was because he rushed his first one (he rushed the second as well). Back in 1996, Gareth Southgate still seems to be walking back to his mark when the referee blows, and he uses that as a signal abruptly to stop walking and instead start his run-up. As he said in his book *Woody and Nord*, "All I wanted was the ball: put it on the spot, get it over and done with." Chris Waddle, referring to his penalty miss in 1990, said something similar: "I just wanted it to be over."

Figure 6: Country and response speed

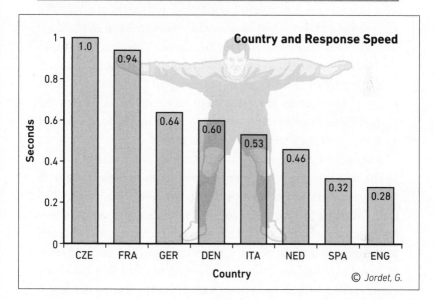

Steven Gerrard felt even more rushed before his penalty against Ricardo in the 2006 World Cup. As he wrote in *Gerrard: My Autobiography*, "I was ready. Elizondo wasn't. Blow the whistle! Fucking get a move on, ref! Why the wait? I'd put the ball on the spot, Ricardo was on his line. Why do I have to wait for the bloody whistle? Those extra couple of seconds seemed like an eternity and they definitely put me off. Doesn't he know I'm on edge? Jesus Christ! I was screaming inside. In training, it seemed so easy: ball down, step back, run in, goal. No wait, no tension. Not here. Not with Elizondo delaying everything. At last he blew, but my focus had gone. The moment I made contact with the ball I knew it wasn't going where I'd planned. It was 18 inches from my chosen spot, making it easier for Ricardo. Saved. Nightmare."

Jordet told me that players prepare their shots twice as fast when they are under extreme pressure, and that a relatively large proportion of the players who prepare their penalties quickly—and that includes taking the ball and putting it on the spot—fail to score. He showed me a video of Marco van Basten, who scored over a hundred penalties in his career and was the world's best player when he stepped up for Holland in the Euro 92 semifinal shoot-out against Denmark. Van Basten spotted the ball far quicker than he normally did, and his shot was saved.

A team that reached a recent Norwegian Cup final was made aware of this factor. The game went to a shoot-out. Two of the players were almost yellow-carded for waiting too long—eleven seconds—to take their penalty. Both scored.

Jordet acknowledges this may be taking the findings too far, as the data suggests that many players miss because they rush their preparation, not that players score more the longer they wait. "Waiting for five to ten seconds can bring on a series of new psychological challenges that the player needs to cope with, such as thinking too much about the mechanics of the performance. My advice would be to make sure that players don't rush by simply asking them to take an extra breath, lasting for half a second or a second, and not necessarily more."

As the average penalty success record is around 78%, failure from one penalty in a five-kick shoot-out should be expected. That figure drops to 71% in World Cup shoot-outs—a reflection, Jordet believes, of how increased pressure affects players.

For teams facing England, though, the figure rises. Let's go back to those first penalty shoot-out tables (see pages 11–12). In England's seven European Championship or World Cup matches that have gone to a shoot-out, their opponents have scored 83% (29/35) of their penalties. England themselves have scored 66%

of penalties in shoot-outs (23/35), and Jordet thinks he knows why they are so far below the average.

"The causes of England's problems with penalties are multi-fold," he said, suggesting there are higher expectations on players in England than in other countries, and those players struggle to respond to that. "The pressure also mounts from history, as the more you lose, the more you lose. The effects of those expectations and history become multiplied as England is one of the most individualistic countries in the world and has a media that focuses on scapegoats."*

He conducted a study looking at the top eight European nations in shoot-outs. He then calculated how many times goalkeepers dived the right way. If a goalkeeper dives the right way, his chances of saving a penalty increase by around 30%.

Figure 7: Goalkeepers who dive the right way†

Against Holland—63%
Against England—58%
Against Italy—46%
Against Germany—46%
Against France—45%
Against Czech Republic—37%
Against Spain—35%

Average—47%

So goalkeepers get it right more often than not against Holland and England than against other teams. How could this

---

* In "Why do English players fail in soccer penalty shoot-outs? A study of team status, self-regulation, and choking under pressure" (*Journal of Sports Sciences,* 2009), Jordet writes: "English players fit the model of choking under pressure well, with high egotism, escapist and misguided self-regulation, and poor performance."
† Data from ibid.

be? Are Dutch and English players easier to read? What might they have in common that the Czechs and the Spanish don't have? It's not turning their backs (only 17% of Dutch players do that) and it's not rushing, because while England are the quickest, Spain are also pretty fast. "This is the table where there is some element of chance involved," Jordet explained, "and I suspect England has been unlucky in history." Ah, so it is luck! All those managers who derided the shoot-out as a lottery after losing were right all along!

Not quite.

"You can't rule out the role of luck in these things, like who wins the toss, which teams have all their best kickers available, that kind of thing," Jordet added. "And I accept that you can't control everything, and even great players can miss. In part it is a lottery, but you can do many things to make it a lot less of a lottery."

The only time Jordet clammed up in our two meetings was when I asked him who he has worked for. Discretion is such an important part of his job, he replied, that he would never reveal any of the teams he works for (although he did have an AC Milan pendant hanging on his office wall).

"But you've worked for Holland's youth teams," I persisted.

"That's right, but I never mentioned that until the coach, Foppe de Haan, went public with it. With everyone else, I have a vow of silence."

So maybe Jordet was already working with the England team. He has a good poker (or penalty taking) face, so it was hard to know.

Jordet first started working with the Dutch youngsters after moving to Groningen and was part of the backroom team for the Under-20 World Cup, held in Holland in 2005. "I tried to create a positive aspect around penalties. I told them this was their moment to shine, but it didn't really work." Holland lost a shoot-out 10–9 to Nigeria in the quarterfinals. "As I watched, I thought, 'I'll never work with the Dutch again, they'll never let me in the country again.'" They did, and in 2007 de Haan called on Jordet to help with the preparations for the Under-21 European Championship. By then Jordet had developed a new program. "I worked out which behaviors would increase the probability of doing well, because that's all it is, helping them have a bigger chance to succeed."

There were two strategies that Jordet focused on with his players.

1. Take an extra second.

Jordet showed the team van Basten's quick penalty in the Euro 92 semifinal—the players were toddlers when that happened—and explained the table which showed England's players are almost as fast as Bolt when it came to reacting to the referee's whistle. He told the players how important it was to take their time.

"When I took a penalty, I rested a second and took a breath and I knew exactly where to shoot the ball," said Gianni Zuiverloon, whose job it was to take the thirty-second and final penalty in a dramatic semifinal shoot-out against England in that 2007 tournament. The game had finished 1–1, the first five penalties had finished 4–4, and Holland had already missed two chances, via Arnold Kruiswijk and Daniel de Ridder, to win the game. Zuiverloon had already scored with penalty number seven and his second strike won the game 13–12.

"Taking time is not a guarantee that you will score, but at least you will not miss like so many other players from my studies have done, by carelessly and sloppily rushing through their movements before their shots," Jordet reiterated. "By focusing on a strategy grounded in data you will immediately feel more in control of yourself and the situation and therefore it's more likely you will do well. Taking an extra second to breathe can often have a relaxing and centering effect, and though it will hardly bring players into a meditative state, it may provide some buffer to the negative effects of stress."

After the game, Jordet analyzed the gaze behavior and response times of both teams during the shoot-out. He was pleased to note that the Dutch players had taken his advice on board.

Every single Dutch player looked at the goalkeeper while walking to his mark after spotting the ball; nearly 40% of English players opted for the avoidance strategy and looked away. The Dutch players also took more time before kicking the ball: their average response time after the referee's whistle was one second, compared to England's 0.51 second, which in itself is almost twice as slow as the senior national team's average.

Figure 8: Intervention effects

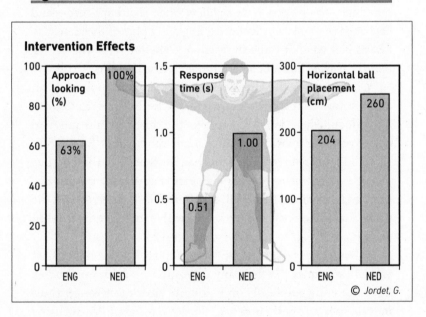

Intervention Effects

Approach looking (%): ENG 63%, NED 100%
Response time (s): ENG 0.51, NED 1.00
Horizontal ball placement (cm): ENG 204, NED 260

© Jordet, G.

2. Have a failure strategy in place.

The worst presentation he ever gave, Jordet told me with a cringe, was to the University Hospital in Groningen about performing under pressure. He had spent a week inside the hospital learning about the pressures surgeons face, what happens if and when they make errors, and how they communicate about failure and overcome it. Jordet wanted to tell them what surgeons could learn from soccer players, but when it came to delivering his findings he realized it was the other way around: soccer players had more to learn from surgeons. He choked. His presentation sucked. It can happen to anyone, even the experts.

Jordet learned from the experience and realized that soccer players, at least those he had worked with, had never been told how to behave when they make errors. The example he gave came from the Sweden–Holland shoot-out in Euro 2004. There is a picture of Mellberg after his miss, walking back to his teammates. Nine of them stand on the center line, arms linked, like a powerful yellow wall. Mellberg approaches, looking down, upset. The wall does not move. The wall is not a welcoming place.

Jordet's "Error Management" paradigm, learned from his hospital case study, was a simple one:

1. Embrace your errors
2. Success leads to complacency
3. Anticipate small errors before they happen

"There was no social support, no plan for defeat, so before the 2007 tournament with the Holland Under-21s, I made a plan," he said.

Jordet spotted that most teams stand on the center line or behind it while the shoot-out is in progress. He told the Dutch to stand at the front of the center circle and link arms. When a teammate scored, he urged them to celebrate with gusto, to build the confidence in the group; but his most significant directive was what to do when a player missed. He told the players to move forward and welcome the player back into the group. The regulations state that players must stay in the circle and Jordet warned them to "respect the referee," but the key was the forward movement so that the player was immediately reintegrated into the group. The plan was not just to make the player who missed feel better but for the next player in line to see that there was a strategy in place if he missed too, to decrease his anxiety levels.

On penalty nine, when Kruiswijk missed Holland's first chance to win the shoot-out, the players jumped away in anger before quickly remembering Jordet's instructions. They then poured forward to usher Kruiswijk back into the group.

Holland went on to win the tournament, and after their celebrations, Jordet employed a student to speak to each player. He showed me a selection of their comments.

"In almost every penalty shoot-out there is always going to be a miss."

"It's normal to miss a penalty once in a while."

"Nobody misses a penalty on purpose."

But the most helpful lesson Jordet had given them, many of them agreed, was this: "We had a plan in place for what to do when we missed."

So, I pushed him again. Regardless of whether you have worked for England or not, what would you do to solve England's problems?

"In the way that I think is the opposite to what is being done," he replied. "Like any team, they are trying to push it away when in fact they need to treat it head on. The coaches are big avoiders of the subject: they don't want to talk about it, they don't want to practice properly, and then it only becomes an issue or important when it's in the present.

"I would give the players known success factors to hold on to, to give them a higher chance of scoring. Also, I would prepare for failure, so they know what to do if one player misses. They need to not rush their penalties. And they need to know the difference between practicing penalties and preparing for penalties."

He showed me a picture taken during an England training session at the 2006 World Cup. Steven Gerrard is taking a penalty, and all the players are standing on the edge of the box, waiting for their turn. "Practicing penalties is mindless if it's not planned or deliberate," Jordet commented. "That picture looks wrong. That's not a shoot-out. You don't take penalties with the players around you. It's bad practice to rehearse a way of doing things that is much easier than it will be. Of course the players will be intimidated when they have to do the walk to the spot, if they have not done it before in practice."

Before Euro 2012, every England player took part in a penalty competition after training. Six players against each of the three goalkeepers, three kicks each, after every session. Their records were assessed. But did they re-create any match conditions? Did they play fans' noise through loudspeakers as the Czech Republic did in 1976? Did they make the players walk from one penalty spot to the other before the kick, as Guus Hiddink did to prepare his South Korean players the day before they beat Spain on penalties in the 2002 World Cup?

Was Jordet right? It all made sense to me, but then I'd never played for England nor, aside from my Packie Bonner "moment," taken an important penalty. So I sought answers from the player with the best penalty record in Europe's biggest five leagues: Rickie Lambert. When we spoke, the Liverpool and England forward was on a run of thirty-three consecutive successful spot kicks.

Lambert knows his penalties. He peppered our conversation with examples from the past: Dida stopping John Arne Riise's effort in the 2005 Champions League final, Pepe Reina becoming the first goalkeeper to stop Mario Balotelli scoring from the spot. He remembered watching England lose to West Germany in 1990, when he was just eight, and said the 1996 defeat "was a hard one for me to take." Understandably he did not want to divulge the secrets behind his own penalty success, but he was keen to look at Jordet's findings. These are his responses:

1. Weight of history: the more shoot-outs you lose, the more likely you are to miss a penalty.

I'm not going to argue with the numbers, but from the type of person I am, I wouldn't say it's true. If you go into a tournament with new players, what happened in the past shouldn't mean anything. I can understand why it might happen to some players, but that's not how I would feel about it.

2. Turning your back on the goalkeeper as an avoidance strategy.

When I put the ball down, I walk backward and take a set number of strides to get to my mark. I think if you turn around after spotting the ball, it does show some nerves. Maybe it means the taker doesn't want eye contact with the goalkeeper in case he plays mind games. I can see why that might be the case.

3. Reaction times after the referee blows his whistle to take a penalty.

I can definitely see how that is related to nerves. Sometimes I have been nervous before a penalty and rushed it. There are always some nerves before you kick, it depends how confident you feel at the time. I see a penalty as a free shot from twelve yards, and a professional should score from that distance ten times out of ten, so if you hit it well, you'll be all right. The minute you start thinking about where the goalkeeper might dive, or if you think he might reach it, then you are giving him an advantage. But I would agree that the more nervous you are, the more you would rush the penalty.

4. England goalkeepers have a poor success rate.

I don't think there's anything in this. I actually think these figures are down to luck because English goalkeepers have been confronted with good penalties. Think of the quality of the penalties that West Germany took in 1990, or Portugal in 2004. I don't remember watching and being frustrated, thinking the goalkeeper could have done better. For the goalkeeper, there is luck involved; it's about gambling and going to the right side. OK, they may have seen the video analysis, but they still have to judge where to go and make the save. As a taker, you just don't want to make it easy for them, but if they dive for a shot that's going to hit the inside of the side-netting, you have to hold your hands up and say, "Quality save." The problem with not saving so many is that it then puts more pressure on your takers. For me, I try and hit the penalty as if I know the goalkeeper is going that way as well; and that if he does, he still won't be able to save it.

5. Opposition goalkeepers dive the right way 58% of the time against England, 46% against Germany and 35% against Spain.

Again, I think this is down to luck. I don't think there are many goalkeepers capable of waiting until the ball has been struck, then diving the right way. The goalkeeper normally decides before or at point of impact, so that's why I say those numbers are down to luck.

Lambert was also unconvinced by the idea of implementing a failure strategy. "Missing for your club is very different to missing for your country, as with your club you can probably rectify the mistake very quickly. With your country, you might not get another chance, and there is no manual about how you will feel if you miss. I can imagine that would affect you much more emotionally."

So what about discussing that with a psychologist beforehand, maybe get some coping mechanisms if required?

"Are you joking? If I was a manager and I heard someone talking about how you might cope if you miss, I would get him out of the building. It should be all about 'when you score' and 'how you will feel when you score.' Nothing else."

Lambert has won all four shoot-outs in which he has taken part: two for Bristol Rovers, when he kicked (and scored) third, and two for Southampton, when he was successful first up. I mentioned Le Tissier's frustration at not getting an opportunity in 1998 and floated the idea of a specialist player coming off the bench in extra time specifically to take a penalty. "If he was a specialist he would still be confident but it would be a better situation if he had been involved in the game beforehand," Lambert said. "You need touches of the ball to get confident, to control the ball, and to get to know the feeling of the turf. Having confidence in the turf sounds silly but it's very important. All those things mean it would be a hard task for a new player coming on—they would prefer to be on the pitch."

Lambert did agree with Jordet, and Michael Owen, that the media plays a part, even if it is unknowingly, in increasing the penalty pressure. "Good news is good but negative news is better," he remarked. "The players know that if they miss they will get slaughtered by the papers—but in other countries, I doubt that is going through their players' minds."

"You will never be able to replicate the occasion 100%, we know that, but you can try for 70% or 80%," Jordet told me. "It's all about the performance mindset and for regular penalty takers, they already have it. That's why for me, the others, those who have not done it much or before, are more interesting."

A look at the players who have missed the final penalties for England in shoot-outs—Waddle, Southgate, Batty, Vassell, Carragher, Ashley Cole—suggests that Jordet's work with non-frequent penalty takers would be beneficial to the team.

"For these guys, it comes down to pure psychology. The fascination of the shoot-out is that it puts psychology in pole position."

PENALTY ICON—
ANTONIN PANENKA

I was sitting with Antonin Panenka outside his local pub in a village near Prague, trying to think of players who have had soccer moves named after them.

"There's the Cruyff turn," I said.

"Yes, and the Zidane roulette," he replied.

And we went quiet. Looked into the middle distance. Were we missing something here? Surely Pelé, Maradona or Puskas trademarked a move, made it their own? What about today's PlayStation generation—Lionel Messi, Cristiano Ronaldo, Neymar? It would seem not. So that leaves three players, I said. Cruyff, Zidane and Panenka.

"Not bad players!" he laughed. "Not bad at all!"

Panenka, of course, invented a new type of penalty—nowadays everyone calls it "the Panenka." Cruyff's turn and Zidane's roulette don't score goals. They don't win matches. They don't secure trophies. I believe that the impact of a Panenka in a shoot-out now has more value to the scoring team than a single goal because of its psychological advantage.

You have to go back to 1974 for when the idea first took seed.

Panenka was playing for Bohemians in a league game against Plzen. He was the playmaker, the team's most creative and skillful player, but not blessed with much pace. He didn't enjoy tracking back, and tended to neglect his defensive duties. "I hated tackling," he confirmed to me. But he had an eye for a pass, and his teammates forgave his occasional slackness because he would always set up goals. He also took excellent corners, free kicks and penalties. Not against Plzen, though. He missed a penalty. The referee ordered a retake. He missed it again. Later in the match, a third penalty. This time he scored, but Panenka was so annoyed at missing the previous two that he resolved to practice harder.

For the next two years, after every training session Panenka stayed behind with Bohemians' goalkeeper Zdenek Hruska and took penalties. His normal method was to wait for the goalkeeper to move and then place the ball to the other side. They would bet on the outcome of the penalties, sometimes with money but more often with chocolate and beer. "To start with he saved a lot because he was a good goalkeeper," Panenka said. "But then I started thinking of new ways to succeed. I lay awake at night and thought about this. I knew that goalkeepers usually choose one side, but if you kick the ball too hard, he can save it with his leg. However, if the contact with the ball is lighter, he can't dive back to the center if he has already picked one side."

Panenka's new penalty was all about chipping the ball slowly down the middle of the goal. But he would only do it once he felt the goalkeeper was committed to diving to one side. "I tried it against Hruska and started to win our duels. The more chocolate I won, the fatter I got!"

Johan Neeskens had scored a similar penalty for Holland in the 1974 World Cup final, a scuffed second-minute effort that went down the middle of the goal as the West German goalkeeper Sepp Maier dived to the right. Academics Wolfgang Leininger and Axel Ockenfels credited Neeskens with a penalty innovation: making the middle an option for the penalty taker.

"It gradually changed the perception of the essence of the penalty game by kicker and goalkeeper from a 2x2 [left or right] game to a 3x3 [left, middle or right] game."*

The Neeskens penalty had no influence on Panenka. He had seen the game but never felt inspired by the Dutchman. Neeskens mishit his penalty, he reminded me; Panenka's was all about striking it perfectly. Any mishit would end in humiliation.

Panenka started trying out the penalty in friendly matches, then league games. One of the first times he attempted it, he missed. It was against Vodnany, a village side in south Bohemia, and it was pouring with rain. "The goalmouth was really muddy and I'm convinced the goalkeeper saved the penalty because he didn't want to dive and get dirty."

Mostly, though, he scored, even when facing goalkeepers who knew him well. In May 1976, Bohemians played Dukla Prague whose goalkeeper Ivo Viktor was his friend and roommate with the Czechoslovakia national team. Viktor knew about the Panenka but still failed to save it. "He didn't stay on his feet. If you stay still and concede the goal, people will ask why you didn't try to save it. That's why it's important to get the goalkeeper to the position where you want him to be. You have to persuade him with your eyes, with your run-up, with your angle, with your body, that you are aiming for a corner."

Fast-forward six weeks to June 20, 1976. Czechoslovakia were the surprise European Championship finalists having beaten Holland 3–1 after extra time in the semifinal. In the past, the Czechoslovakia team had been divided: as well as eating separately, the Czechs and the Slovaks used to train apart too, making any coherent tactical preparation impossible. The 1976 side was different, united by coach Václav Ježek, a Slovak, and captain Anton "Tonda" Ondrus, a Czech. The team had pace, leadership,

---

* Leininger, W. & Ockenfels, A. (2008), "The penalty duel and institutional design: is there a Neeskens effect?" in Andersson, Ayton & Schmidt (eds), *Myths and Facts about Football*, p. 73.

technique, goals—and confidence. "We had some good results going into the tournament and because we were from Eastern Europe, no one took us seriously," Panenka said. They were unbeaten for twenty matches before the tournament began.

They were up against West Germany, the reigning European and world champions. They too had had a tough semifinal, needing extra time to beat Yugoslavia 4–2, and had had one day less preparation time before the final.

The Czechs raced into a 2–0 lead but West Germany fought back, Dieter Müller reducing the deficit before Bernd Hölzenbein leveled the scores in the 89th minute. The players looked shattered during extra time, and for the first time a major tournament would be decided by penalties—although this had only been confirmed a few hours earlier.

On the way to the final on that Sunday night, German FA president Hermann Neuberger had consulted coach Helmut Schön and team doctor Erich Deuser and decided that he would ask UEFA to drop plans for a replay, scheduled for the following Tuesday, if the scores were level. Neuberger felt the players were burned out. "The decision was absolutely correct. The players' health is the first priority," said Deuser. UEFA and the Czech FA agreed, but the German players were only told of the plan when they returned to the dressing room after the warm-up. "Even Franz Beckenbauer was surprised; why wouldn't the team captain be asked of his and the team's opinion on such a change of course?" wrote newspaper *Munich Merkur*.

It was not the only communication issue between the German players and their federation during the tournament. On the Saturday before the game, the German FA had agreed to raise the win bonus for each player from DM5,000 to DM10,000 for reaching the final, and to DM15,000 if they won it. Two years earlier there had been a row over World Cup bonuses and West Germany had almost refused to play. The German FA was keen to avoid a repeat—except they forgot to tell the players about the new figures until after the final.

The German players, then, had not practiced penalties and had only one player, Rainer Bonhof, who assumed the spot-kicking duty for his club. Czechoslovakia, and not just Panenka, had been practicing. After one pretournament friendly, coach Ježek had organized a shoot-out in match conditions. There were 10,000 fans watching and Ježek spoke to them with a megaphone. "We want you to whistle, shout and do anything you can to try and put our players off. That's what it will be like for us in Yugoslavia at the Euros."

It took the German coaches ten minutes to work out the order for the takers. Goalkeeper Maier put himself forward for the fifth penalty because no one else fancied it. Beckenbauer eventually said he would take it. "They trudged over to the center circle like a troop of losers," wrote *Merkur* the next day. "They already looked a beaten team."

Czechoslovakia kicked first in the shoot-out, striker Marián Masný making no mistake. Bonhof scored. The next five all went in and the Czechs led 4–3. Up stepped Uli Hoeness. His shot flew over the bar. "I was exhausted and my whole body was limp and lifeless," he said. "I wasn't able to take a penalty, but because nobody put themselves forward, I said yes."

It was now the turn of Panenka. Two years of practice distilled into one kick; all those efforts against Hruska (and all that chocolate), the hours spent honing the chip, perfecting the approach, convincing the goalkeeper. Viktor begged Panenka not to try it, but this was his moment. "I saw myself as an entertainer and I saw this penalty as a reflection of my personality," Panenka said. "I wanted to give the fans something new to see, to create something that would get them talking. To come up with something at a moment when no one expects it. I wanted football to be more than just kicking a ball."

Before the penalty, Panenka experienced the same feeling he got before some of his free kicks for Bohemians. He loved the duel with the opposition goalkeeper, and would get a sixth sense—"it was like goose bumps, really"—about when he might score. Even if a goalkeeper moved the wall across so he could have a better view of the ball, Panenka would put some of his own teammates in to make it harder for the keeper.

And so, as we watched the video of the decisive penalty together, I noted how long his run-up was—from behind the D outside the box. "I used the long run as it gave me time to see what the goalkeeper was going to do and how he was going to react," he explained. "I also ran fast, because then it's harder for the goalkeeper to read your body language. You can see that even when I'm a yard away from the ball, Maier is already moving to his left. Even if I wasn't using the chip, I would have put the ball in the opposite direction."

Before there was even a name for it, he hit the perfect Panenka. The ball sailed slowly, impudently, over Maier, who dived early and wafted his right arm in vain, as if letting the ball through. He knew he was beaten. There have been some fantastic Panenkas taken since—Zinedine Zidane, Francesco Totti and Andrea Pirlo have all scored dramatic and important ones—but this remains the pick of them, the original and the best.

After the game, politicians told Panenka that had he missed he would have been punished, as his penalty could have been interpreted as disrespecting the Communist system. What sort of punishment? I wondered. "Thirty years working down the mines," he replied.

"That makes his achievement all the more remarkable," said Spanish soccer writer César Sanchez Lozano. "His penalty is fascinating from a visual point of view: it's beautiful, like a piece of art. But then add the pressure, the shoot-out, the last kick, and that he is from a Communist country, and still comes up with something so spontaneous, well, it's astonishing."

Lozano was so taken by the moment that when he wanted to launch a new soccer magazine that focused on untold stories, unexpected characters, and embraced the romantic side of the game, there could be only one title: *Panenka*. "History is not only written with victories," he said. "Sometimes it's more important *how* people do what they do. No one remembers any other player from that team. Panenka did something unique, and his impact goes beyond that one kick."

Panenka is proud his name has global recognition but modestly claims it's only because it's easy to say. "Panenka—it sounds the same in any language."

The pub we were sitting outside, Staha Hospada (which translates, imaginatively, to "Old Pub"), was getting busy. The locals of Nespeky were flocking to watch the Czech Republic play a crucial World Cup ice hockey game against Norway.

I explained my theory that a successful Panenka in a shoot-out can be worth more than a single goal. Look at Spain and Italy at Euro 2012. In the Donetsk quarterfinal against Portugal, at 2–2 after three kicks each Spanish defender Sergio Ramos scored with a Panenka to make it 3–2. Portugal's next kicker was Bruno Alves: he hit the crossbar. Spain won 4–2. One night later in Kiev, Italy were 2–1 down after two kicks each in the shoot-out against England, whose goalkeeper Joe Hart was looking confident, making windmills with his arms and pulling faces at the opposition takers. Up stepped Pirlo, who coolly took a Panenka as Hart dived to his right. Almost straight away the momentum shifted: Italy's players laughed and clapped and England's looked nervous. The next taker was Ashley Young, who couldn't even look at Gigi Buffon. Just like Alves the night before, he hit the crossbar. Two Panenkas, followed by two misses: coincidence, or not?

"It shouldn't make a significant difference but it's possible that it can play tricks in the mind of the guy who has to take the next kick," Panenka said. "It could distract their concentration. He might think 'What did he just do?' and then lose focus on his own kick. It's all in the mind."

Lozano was unequivocal on this point: "I agree 100 percent that it has a greater value [than a normal penalty]. The Panenka gives confidence to the whole team, and will upset the goalkeeper for all the other penalties."

There was something else unique about Panenka's penalty. No one has beaten Germany in a shoot-out since. Five shoot-outs, five wins. As for the Czech national team, they can top even that: three shoot-outs in all, three wins, and not a single missed penalty among them. Twenty penalties, twenty goals. Impressive. "I think there is something in the Czech character that makes us good at penalties," Panenka said. "We don't take ourselves too seriously, like the Good Soldier Svejk. It's all a bit of a laugh. We also have a good ability to improvise, to react in a different way to how people expect. That was our biggest weapon."

These days, Panenka is honorary president of Bohemians, a yo-yo club which every other season seems to be fighting relegation or promotion; when I met him he wore a green rubber Bohemians bracelet on his left wrist. He was recovering from hip surgery that has left him with a slight limp—he walked as if he had just stepped off a long-haul flight—but he was confident of a full recovery and couldn't wait to get back on the tennis court. The golf course, not so much.

Before he joined his friends watching the ice hockey, I asked him about something he'd told *Panenka* (yes, Panenka did talk to *Panenka* about the Panenka). "I am a prisoner of this penalty," he had remarked. Is that how he really feels?

"Well, on one hand I am very proud of it, and feel lucky that I scored it," he replied. "But then again, that one penalty has overshadowed my whole career: all my performances, my passes, my other goals. So it's a bit of both."

CHAPTER 3

THE DNA OF PENALTIES

Antonin Panenka found the right club to play for: he was a bohemian as a player, and remains one. He liked players who were different, who challenged and excited, and who subverted expectations. That's why he mentioned the Good Soldier Svejk, the eponymous hero of Czech literature's most famous book, written in 1923 by another bohemian, Jaroslav Hašek.

Svejk was the archetypal "wise fool," a satirical character who bumbled through a series of misadventures as a soldier of the Austro-Hungarian empire, always upsetting the authorities yet coming out on top. When he was told news about the assassination of Archduke Franz Ferdinand and his wife in 1914, Svejk claimed to know only two Ferdinands: a messenger at the chemist and a dog-poo collector. "Neither of them would be any loss," he quipped, oblivious to the seriousness of the situation. During his medical examination for conscription, Svejk was asked a series of questions to determine his ability to think on the spot. "Do you believe in the end of the world?" "How do you work out the diameter of the globe?" He responded with his own riddle. "Take a three-storied house, with eight windows on each floor. On the roof there are two dormer windows and two chimneys. On every floor there are two tenants. And now, gentlemen, tell me, in what year did the housekeeper's grandma die?" Svejk, despite showing up the system for all its faults, was passed fit to serve.

"*The Good Soldier Svejk* should be read by anyone who truly wants to understand the Czech psyche," said Jan Velinger, a self-confessed "Svejkologist." Panenka was not quite at that level of buffoonery but he made his point quite clearly. Because the Czechs don't like to take a serious situation seriously, he said, it helps them cope with it. Surely a fictional character created ninety years ago can't be credited for Czech players' 100 percent shoot-out record? "No," he admitted, "but there is something in our character which makes us not worry about serious things. It might be a reason why."

What about the country with the second-best winning record from shoot-outs, Germany? I was pretty sure their success wasn't down to taking it all easy. I assumed it was because, traditionally, German players excelled in three areas of the game: technique, practice and mental toughness. The first two are embedded in the history of German soccer, the third a by-product of the type of players German coaches liked to pick.

I got different answers to this question depending on whom I asked. Jens Lehmann, the Germany goalkeeper in the 2006 World Cup, insisted it was because the country had so many great keepers. "Our strikers are under less pressure than other teams because they know that we will always save at least one penalty, so they don't have to worry as much," he said. Then again, he would.

When he was at Arsenal, Lehmann had shoot-out competitions with his teammates, and whoever scored the fewest penalties would have to take the goalkeeper out for dinner (the first time it happened, Patrick Vieira was his date). With the German national team, the forfeit was slightly different: whoever missed would have to serve dinner to their teammates that night.

A similar spirit was evident in club games. When a penalty was awarded in a match between Stuttgart and Bayern Munich, it pitted against each other two national goalkeepers, Jens Lehmann (in goal) and Hans-Jörg Butt (Bayern's penalty taker). Before the spot kick, Lehmann approached Butt and said, "Let's have a bet. If you score, I will give you twenty euros, and if you don't, you give me two hundred euros." Butt agreed, and scored. Lehmann paid up—but only after going to the bank and getting all the money in one-cent coins.

Butt laughed as he recounted that story. He agreed with his former Germany teammate's views on robust keepers, and explained why he felt the tradition was a strong one. "In other countries, fans like to see the spectacular, but in Germany, fans like goals but they also understand the importance of the defense. People in Germany are not so emotional and see the value of keeping clean sheets; a goalkeeper is a respected position here, I would say more so than in other countries. For us, it's enough to win 1–0. The role of the goalkeeper is a more valued one in Germany than elsewhere."

Lothar Matuschak also backed up this view. Matuschak is barely known outside German goalkeeping circles, and certainly not for his spell between the sticks at Bundesliga 2 side Westfalia Herne in the late 1970s. But since 1995 he has been Schalke's goalkeeping coach; he is the man who persuaded the club not to reject Germany's current number one, Manuel Neuer, despite his (lack of) size. "They wanted to get rid of him as he was very small but I fought them and told them he had to stay," he said. "He grew and became Schalke's greatest ever goalkeeper." (He also remembers Neuer's grandfather appearing behind the goal at youth matches and slipping him a ten-Deutschmark note that the youngster would put into his sock. "He did it to motivate him, and I now do the same for my grandson.") In October 2012, Matuschak set a unique record when five starting goalkeepers on one Bundesliga weekend were trained by him: Mohamed Amsif (Augsburg), Christian Wetklo (Mainz), Patrik Ravkovsky

(Nuremberg), Lars Unnerstall (Schalke) and Neuer (Bayern)—and they only let in three goals between them. Neuer's goalkeeping coach at Bayern is Toni Tapalovic, another graduate of the Matuschak school.

"It's true that German football gives more respect to the position of goalkeeper, we've always thought it a very important position," Matuschak said. "Germany produces players who want to become goalkeepers because they feel that goalkeepers are important for the team." That used not to be the case in South America and—he hesitated before saying the word—England. "English goalkeepers are really devalued nowadays," he continued. "I watch a lot of English football and I can see that when an English keeper makes a mistake, all eyes are on him, and that creates a lack of assurance. If you're strong in your head, you can get through it—but maybe the problem is that people convinced English goalkeepers that they are no good. So English clubs decided to buy foreign goalkeepers from countries with good goalkeeping traditions. They missed the opportunity to develop their own goalkeepers."

For Matuschak, confidence is the key when it comes to penalty success. "The goalkeeper has to be convinced that he can manipulate or irritate the opposing striker, and when it comes to penalties, a little bit of 'the circus' is no bad thing. Draw attention to yourself, distract the kicker, say to yourself, 'This guy's a bastard, he's not going to get past me.' In penalties, goalkeepers have a head start. No team said they lost because of the goalkeeper. But you can win because of the goalkeeper. We Germans have always taken the position seriously, and that's why we have produced so many great goalkeepers."

Then there is the trauma of that first defeat . . . did losing in 1976 really spur on the team to ensure it would never happen again? "For a collective of people you identify a group with trauma or big success but the opposite way is what this German national team did," explained Dr. Michael Froese, a psychoanalyst based in Potsdam. "They developed an absolute conviction of success, as opposed to this unconscious identification with failure—which is actually the definition of a complex. On the surface, you can say that in penalties, Germany is identified with success, and England with defeat. But if you look deeper, you will find from the German side a strong conscious identification with the unconditional, the defiant, a desire to succeed and a rebelling against the fear of failure. This naturally leads to implications for training penalty situations: namely, an active, systematic practice rather than the 'magical rationalized avoidance,' which derives from a subconscious fear of failure."*

The 1976 defeat marked the end of the best ever West Germany side. It had won Euro 1972 and the 1974 World Cup, but this time was without Paul Breitner, and Gerd Müller was on the decline. That shoot-out has a unique status in history, as it was won by Panenka rather than lost by Uli Hoeness. Not that that helped Hoeness much: the Bayern winger had given away a second-minute penalty in the 1974 World Cup final, and after his miss in Belgrade he never played for his country again (though that was because of injury). Fifteen years later, Hoeness returned to Belgrade as general manager of Bayern Munich for the 1991 European Cup semifinal. The night before the game, he returned to the empty stadium and stood on the penalty spot where his soccer playing fortunes had reached their nadir. It was his time to get closure.

West Germany went on to win Euro 80, so how much of a "losers" mark can the previous championship have left on their collective psyche? More significant still, they won their next shoot-out, against France in 1982. In that game they were 3–1 down in both the game and the shoot-out, but went on to win 4–3. That leaves us with a tantalizing question: if West Germany had lost to France in 1982, would they have ever recovered?

---

* Froese's suggestion that the English are "magical rationalized avoiders" makes you wonder if the English approach to the unavoidable reality of a shoot-out reflects their deeper nature, with its supposed instinct to avoid embarrassing social situations and not say what is really being thought. Does the default English response to social situations kick in during a shoot-out?

Maybe the German team, not England, would now be the lame ducks of penalty shoot-outs.

"Most of the guys in the current Germany squad weren't even born in 1976 so they only know about winning on penalties, they don't even know another option exists," said Shad Forsythe, an American fitness coach who understands the German psyche better than most. Forsythe works for Athletes Performance, an American fitness company that has been helping the Germany national team since Jürgen Klinsmann brought them in before the 2006 World Cup. Forsythe was with the team for eight years. He was Performance Director for *Die Nationalmannschaft* for Germany's successful World Cup campaign in Brazil, and was so trusted by coach Joachim Löw that at the 2010 World Cup it was he who delivered the final words in the dressing room before the players took the field.

His job was to ensure the players are in peak condition for every game, specifically at major tournaments. This was made easier by the fact that the German players bought into his methods—"It helps to be successful as they now have confidence in our systems," he said—and that his evaluations could take place throughout the season. "We monitor them through regular communication with their clubs, so we know exactly what situation they are in when they join up with us." Not quite the same situation as with the England national team, then.

Forsythe also had to keep the players happy while they were cooped up for up to six weeks at a time, so it was his job to introduce new cross-training disciplines for the players to enjoy themselves. In 2006, the German squad spent a day doing archery to improve their composure and hand-to-eye coordination. "Archery is just like a penalty—one shot is all you've got," Forsythe said. They also spent an afternoon dismantling and then rebuilding classic watches: "That was to work on their fine motor skills and magnifying skills for visual perception." In 2010, former New Zealand rugby great Jonah Lomu spent two days teaching the squad to play rugby union. They learned to scrum and throw line-out balls, and ended with games of touch rugby. "It was another team-building exercise but the players loved it, and of course they all have to work as a unit in rugby so there are plenty of overlapping skills." Ahead of the 2014 World Cup in Brazil, Forsythe was planning some lessons in jujitsu and samba-dancing.

Penalty practice takes place in the Germany camp throughout the qualifying phase, but stops once the tournament begins. It only restarts once the team reaches the knockout stages. In 2006, after training every player took a penalty; before doing so he had to nominate into a camera where he would kick the ball—bottom right, top left, that sort of thing. Anyone who missed would be eliminated, and the competition would continue until only one player was left. It normally took four or five penalties to find a winner. The process helped Klinsmann select penalty takers. When midfielder Tim Borowski, for example, nominated his spot—"Bottom left," he said—the goalkeeper overheard him and stood next to the post where Borowski had said he would aim. Borowski did not flinch and powered his shot toward the same spot. He scored. Germany's quarterfinal against Argentina went to penalties, and who did Klinsmann bring off the bench, and who scored a penalty? Borowski. "You can't say he came on just for the penalty but it's definitely a positive to know that he is confident from the spot," said Forsythe.

Forsythe would know everything about a player before he took a penalty, from his mineral deficiencies and VO2 max (a measure of the body's ability to transport oxygen during exercise) to his napping patterns and how much sleep he got the previous night. "Sleep is very important, and if a player has one night of bad sleep, they need to tell us, not wait for three or four bad nights." The most important time to be asleep, he explained, is between midnight and six in the morning. All individuals differ in their sleep requirements, but those hours are vital. "We also want the players to nap on game day for half an hour after lunch. That's built into our planned perfect day. Some guys are good at napping, others not. But we want to know their routines so we can find a solution if it's broken. We can't afford to wait until it affects performance."

Given that preparation and recovery are such key parts of Forsythe's methodology, I wondered if standing upright for ten minutes after playing for 120 minutes was the ideal preparation for a penalty. Shouldn't the players be stretching, running on the spot, anything rather than just standing there? "From a physiological point of view," he replied, "the most important thing is that they are calm, and part of that is cooling—so you always see them drinking cool fluid. Usually the adrenalin will keep them going but if they have to wait longer than fifteen minutes then they will stiffen up and that could be a problem."

Forsythe agreed with the theory that German goalkeepers have a history of excellence.* In fact, he thinks the current crop of keepers has the potential to be better than Oliver Kahn and Jens Lehmann. "The paradigm has shifted and as well as great goalkeepers, these guys are better athletes. Add that athleticism to a great goalkeeper and he will save even more penalties."

To Forsythe, the penalty is 90% psychological and 10% physical. His job was making that 10% work to ensure the 90% works too. "Confidence comes from knowing that physically they are ready for this, so from that point of view I am their secret weapon. They know they will be ready for any scenario."

He made it sound like none of the German players suffered from self-doubt. Surely that wasn't right? "If they don't want to take penalties, it will be because of physical reasons: they have a weak shot, they don't score many goals—those physical issues will limit their confidence," he said. "But remember that the strongest shooters do not necessarily make the best penalty takers—you need to factor personality in too—and that penalty failure is just not on the German horizon."

---

* There is still a belief in Germany that you only become a great goalkeeper after succeeding in a shoot-out. Oliver Kahn's finest hour was saving three Valencia penalties in the 2001 Champions League final, while Neuer's breakout performance was saving two Porto penalties for Schalke in their 2008 Champions League Round of 16 victory.

So is there an ideal personality type to take a high-pressure penalty?

"If I said there was, I reckon that type is pretty German!"

The cultural difference was all too clear to Forsythe, who when watching a shoot-out changed his routine. He now stands on the touchline and watches the crowd—a true avoidance strategy. "I have a hundred percent record with that method so I will stick with it," he laughed. Forsythe left the Germany team after the World Cup and joined Arsenal as the Head of Athletic Performance Enhancement. Germany did not need a penalty shoot-out to win the World Cup, though it was close: Mario Götze's winner came seven minutes before the end of extra-time. Would Germany have won if that final had gone to penalties? Probably . . .

The Czechs and the Germans had differing mindsets but both produced winning records at shoot-outs. Maybe the one thing they did share was luck, that crucial ingredient which England coaches past and present seem to agree has been denied them. If you get fifty people in a room and ask them all to toss a coin ten times, there may well be one person whose coin comes up heads ten times and another whose coin falls tails-up ten times. That's natural randomization. Maybe England is heads and Germany is tails and that's just life. I wasn't so sure.

I wanted to know if it was possible for national teams to have a penalty DNA, so I took some data from the original All-time Shoot-out table and added it to data from over four thousand penalties* to see if English players struggled from the spot as a general rule or if it was only while wearing an England shirt. See Figure 9.

---

* This data was taken from every World Cup (1930–2010) and European Championship (1962–2012), every penalty taken in the top league in England, Italy, Germany, Spain, France and Holland from 2007/08 to 2012/13, and Champions League penalties from 2002/03 to 2012/13. The data was supplied by Infostrada Sports and analyzed by James W. Grayson, a long-suffering Lincoln City fan and a PhD candidate at the University of British Columbia. The sample was 3,646 open-play penalties and 551 shoot-out penalties.

The results are clear. English players, in open play for their club teams, have an above-average conversion rate of 82% from the penalty spot. Get them in an international tournament shoot-out, though, and that rate plummets to 66%. The opposite is true of German players: they have a 93% record playing for the national team, but in club action that drops to 76%. Dutch players rise from 67% to 79% without de Oranje on their backs.

Figure 9: Open play conversion for club teams v. shoot-out conversion for national team

Nationality	OP Pens	SO Pens	OP Conversion	SO Conversion
England	237	35	82%	66%
Italy	398	41	81%	71%
Argentina	208	43	80%	77%
Holland	285	24	79%	67%
Brazil	264	47	79%	76%
Spain	360	31	78%	76%
Germany	163	28	76%	93%
France	244	31	75%	81%

Infostrada sports

Of course the sample set is small with the national team. If the coin tossers flicked a hundred coins and not ten, there would be regression to the mean. But Geir Jordet had already explained to me how a cycle of defeat, or winning, can continue. He specifically connected England's failure to high expectations and the scapegoat culture of the media. Other countries have neither of those burdens yet still struggle. Why is that? So I posed another question: do different countries have different reasons for penalty failure?

"Prick! You unbelievable prick!" Frank de Boer was yelling at himself in his car. He thumped the wheel. It was July 2000, weeks after Holland lost the Euro 2000 semifinal to Italy. It was the third straight European Championship that Holland had lost in a shoot-out and, including a loss to Brazil in the 1998 World Cup, a third elimination at the penalties stage in four years.

The circumstances of this one were particularly tough to bear. The game was in the Amsterdam Arena and the final was set for Rotterdam. Holland, the tournament cohosts, dominated the match. Italy had Gianluca Zambrotta sent off in the first half. And Holland missed two penalties in normal time. De Boer, the Holland captain, was the main culprit. He missed the first of the two penalties, after 36 minutes, and Holland's first in the shoot-out.

De Boer thought his first attempt was a decent one, but the Italy goalkeeper Francesco Toldo, who was booked for protesting the award of the penalty, had psyched him out. At least de Boer thought he had. A few days earlier de Boer had scored a penalty against the Czech Republic, kicking to his nonnatural side. At the 1998 World Cup, against Brazil, he had done the same. "That's how I should have shot against Italy, but I decided at the last minute to do something else," he said. On the day before the game he had overpracticed penalties, taking forty after training, even shooting with his eyes closed. "Scoring in both corners the previous day did not help. I thought that Toldo had seen my penalties and that put doubt in my mind." On reflection, de Boer wished he had practiced by hitting four penalties, and no more, into his favorite corner.

"What did de Boer do wrong?" Dutch TV's touchline reporter asked Johan Cruyff at halftime.

"He didn't score," Cruyff replied, "but at least he picked his corner. That's one way of doing it. Look, you can't prepare for these situations."

Fifteen minutes into the second half, referee Marcus Merk awarded Holland another penalty. De Boer didn't fancy it and offered it to Patrick Kluivert, Holland's in-form center forward. "I had a feeling we were in trouble when Frank missed the first penalty, as that was normally a guaranteed goal," said Kluivert, who at least managed to send Toldo the wrong way with his effort. It hit the right-hand post, and Italy scrambled away the rebound. "It was then I thought that we might be cursed in this game."

Italy had their own nightmares to erase. They had lost on shoot-outs in 1990 (World Cup semifinal), 1994 (World Cup final) and 1998 (Round of 16). When the game went to penalties, both teams expected to lose.

Dutch coach Frank Rijkaard had already subbed off Dennis Bergkamp and Boudewijn Zenden. Peter van Vossen had come on, and he was slated to take the fifth penalty. Embarrassingly, it never reached that stage.

Italy scored first, Luigi di Biagio redeeming himself for missing the crucial penalty in the 1998 loss to France. De Boer was up next. Dutch commentator Theo Reitsma wondered, "Who will keep Holland happy for the next few days by helping us win this? Frank de Boer? Yes, he would never miss twice, so he will step up." De Boer's twin brother Ronald told him to go hard down the middle, and that was the plan. "I was not even that nervous," Frank said. "Toldo made it into a game. He winked at me. But this time I had no doubts. I wanted to tell him: 'So you know where I'm going to shoot, good for you.'" De Boer winked back; but he hit a weak shot, right of center, which Toldo stopped with his feet. "It was only because I was tired that I hit it badly. We were mentally drained by this time, and our previous record at penalties was not giving us any hope."

Then Gianluca Pessotto scored and Jaap Stam blasted over the bar. "I took it just as I always did in training, because I never take penalties; but the tension changed everything," Stam said. The big defender had taken one before, for FC Zwolle in a Dutch Cup tie. "I missed that one too."

It was 2–0 to Italy, and Francesco Totti was next. The previous day, Totti had beaten Alessandro Nesta at PlayStation soccer after training and scored one of his goals with a penalty *cucchiaio*, or "spoon"—Italian for the Panenka. "One of these days I will do it in a game," he told him.

When di Biagio returned from his kick, Totti said to him, "*Mo je faccio er cucchiaio*"—"Now I will do the spoon." Paolo Maldini overheard him. "Is he crazy?" said the captain. "There's a final on the line." Totti did not change his mind. Van der Sar dived right and Totti's chip flew perfectly down the center of the goal. "To take a penalty like that you must be crazy or very good," Totti later said, "and I don't think I'm crazy."

Italy were 3–0 up, but Holland had a glimmer of hope when Kluivert scored and van der Sar saved Maldini's effort. Paul Bosvelt now needed to score to keep Holland alive. He hit a weak shot and Toldo saved easily. Both Bosvelt and de Boer had had excellent tournaments, but that was soon forgotten.

Bosvelt was called for a doping test after the game. He stayed behind in the stadium, without knowing that Rijkaard had resigned in a radio interview and his teammates were long gone. "I know that some players said no when asked to take a penalty," he reflected. "Otherwise the coaches wouldn't have come to me."

Before the tournament, Rijkaard had promised that he would make eight players practice penalties after every training session. "If your run-up is good and you hit the ball midheight, in the corner, with the right speed, a goalkeeper has no chance. That is trainable," he insisted. "I don't want to be eliminated because penalties are being missed." After his team was eliminated, he spoke like a true Cruyff protégé: "We practiced almost every day, but it's something unique to the game and we showed once again we're no good at it."

Rijkaard's predecessor Guus Hiddink said something similar following Holland's quarterfinal exit from Euro 96 after losing on penalties to France. "A penalty is always a lottery," Hiddink remarked. "You can't blame anyone if they miss a penalty." In fact Hiddink himself was getting the blame, mainly for picking Kluivert and Clarence Seedorf, both just twenty years old, to take penalties in place of the substituted Richard Witschge and Bergkamp.

Seedorf's case best sums up Holland's penalty failings. The young midfielder played the full ninety minutes of Holland's opening goalless draw against Scotland but was taken off against Switzerland after only 26 minutes. He started the next game against England as a defensive midfielder and played "like a headless chicken,"* criticizing his teammates after the 4–1 defeat for not sticking to their tasks. He started the quarterfinal against France at Anfield on the bench, coming on after an hour. Holland might have had a penalty with five minutes left—Marcel Desailly handballed in the area but referee Antonio López Nieto ignored the appeals—and Seedorf missed a late chance from close range to win the game.

It finished goalless and went to penalties. Hiddink did not ask, he told the players who would be taking them and in what order; Seedorf was number four. The score was 3–3 when he stepped up. His teammates, watching on, were a divided group:† some players had their arms around each other, others did not. Away from the main group stood Danny Blind and Frank de Boer, out on their own.

Two months earlier, Ajax had lost the Champions League final to Juventus on penalties. The two players who missed in that game, Sonny Silooy and Davids, had kicked to their nonnatural side. The Dutch press had warned the players not to make the same mistake. Seedorf paid no notice: he kicked to his right, too

---

* As described by Matty Verkamman's match report in *Trouw*, June 24, 1996.
† Seedorf had been a central figure in that tournament, but not in a good way. He was the loudest member of the *kabel* (cabal) of four black players—with Edgar Davids, Michael Reiziger and Kluivert—that divided the squad that summer. Davids was annoyed that Hiddink's preferred confidants in the squad were Ronald de Boer and Danny Blind, though the row was more about lack of respect for youth than race (though *Voetbal International* did not help matters by reporting the Ajax players' wages, which had the de Boer twins each making £200,000 per year compared to Davids's £40,000). Davids had been dropped for the second game against Switzerland and was then sent home after telling the press, "Hiddink should stop sticking his head up other players' arses."

near the middle, and France's goalkeeper Bernard Lama easily saved it.

As he walked back to the center circle, Seedorf had tears in his eyes. His black teammates consoled him, as did France's Christian Karembeu, his Sampdoria teammate, who later compared the shoot-out to Russian roulette: "It is loading the bullet into the chamber of the gun and asking everyone to pull the trigger. Someone will get the bullet; you know that. And it will reduce them to nothing." De Boer actively ignored Seedorf. Vincent Guérin and Laurent Blanc scored for France, who won.

The next day, Seedorf said he was over the disappointment and that it was only a bad penalty because Lama dived the right way. "In training before the match, Clarence took fifteen corners and he rarely got the ball in the air," wrote Matty Verkamman in *Trouw*. "He was as weak at corners in the game; the same from free kicks. And Hiddink let this man take a penalty?"

Seedorf was unbowed. In his eyes, he deserved the status of a senior player and he would do anything to achieve that. The following April, a few weeks after he had turned twenty-one, he took another penalty. Except this time no one had told him to.

Holland were trailing 1–0 in a World Cup qualifier in Turkey. With five minutes left, Alpay Ozalan fouled Pierre van Hooijdonk and there was a chance to equalize. Wim Jonk was the nominated penalty taker but he'd had a poor game and gestured to Frank de Boer, back in his own half, to take it. Before de Boer had crossed the halfway line, Seedorf had picked up the ball and put it on the spot.

Less than one minute elapsed between the award of the penalty and Seedorf striking the ball. Striking the ball over the crossbar. Holland lost, and for a while qualification hopes were in the balance (they did eventually go to the 1998 World Cup— where, it barely needs stating, they lost on penalties in the semifinal). "Seedorf's ego is bigger than his experience and he finds it hard to accept that he is the youngest player in the Dutch team," wrote Robert Misset in *Het Parool*. The same paper's editorial called him "a douchebag." Johan Cruyff, commentating for Dutch national broadcaster NOS, was furious that a young player had been allowed to take the responsibility. If he was playing, he stormed, he would have kicked Seedorf off the pitch and made an experienced player take the kick.

Hiddink said it was his fault, de Boer said it was his fault. The only person who didn't say it was his fault was Seedorf, who just said he felt confident. That was his biggest problem, wrote Pieter van Os in *De Groene Amsterdammer*. "The miracle of Seedorf is that he has no fear of penalties—yet he always misses. To ignore this penalty fear is disastrous. Clarence, let your fear take over!"

By the time the 1998 World Cup came around, the Dutch camp had wised up. Seedorf did not take a penalty in the shoot-out against Brazil, despite coming on as a late substitute. When Ronald de Boer, his nemesis in 1996, missed the decisive penalty, Seedorf was the first player to console him.

Seedorf's fear never did materialize, and you can guess what happened when he volunteered himself for a penalty in the 2003 Champions League final at Old Trafford. His team, AC Milan, were 1–0 up in the shoot-out and Seedorf, kicking second, went to his natural side this time; Juventus goalkeeper Gigi Buffon dived the right way and saved it. But Juventus missed their next two kicks so Seedorf did at least end up on the winning side.

As European champions, Milan traveled to Yokohama in December to face Boca Juniors in the Intercontinental Cup. The game ended 1–1 and went to penalties. Guess what? Seedorf, second up for Milan, missed again, hitting it over the bar. "I went to the right of the keeper, high, but a bit too high," he said. "Again, that wasn't a matter of technique. With penalties it's about psychology, the last few seconds before you kick. I'm still practicing that."

"If you did not know his history as a penalty taker, you would pick him as he has an excellent kicking technique," said van Hooijdonk, a penalty specialist himself. "It was very strange that Clarence missed so much. It was probably psychological and in that sense the goal becomes twice as small from the spot."

Seedorf continued to practice. Anyone can miss a penalty, as Hiddink put it, but it takes a special type of confidence to keep on coming back for more. And he did: in 2007, against PSV in a preseason friendly tournament in Russia, Seedorf hit his penalty against the crossbar, knocking Milan out. In May 2013, playing for Botafogo, Seedorf's spot kick hit the crossbar again in a 1–0 win over Fluminense (the result secured the team's Carioca championship). Seedorf was thirty-seven, he had the status he'd always craved, he was the experienced player that Cruyff would now want to take a penalty. But it was the same outcome as seventeen years earlier.

Holland's Euro 2000 defeat to Italy was the nadir of their penalty crisis. Five kilometers from the Amsterdam Arena, almost in a straight line away from the stadium, a soccer-obsessed management consultant had been taking notes. A few months earlier Gyuri Vergouw had published a book, *De Strafschop*—The Penalty. After Brazil had beaten Holland on penalties in the 1998 World Cup semifinal, Vergouw decided he was fed up with the same old excuse, that penalties are a lottery. He had been collecting data on penalties for over twenty years and was convinced that proper practice would improve Dutch chances of success. "There's practicing and then there's Practicing," he said. "And they are two very different things."

The book came out shortly before Euro 2000. Vergouw sent a copy to all the players in the Dutch squad and was a guest on the soccer chat show *Villa Barend and Van Dorp*. The other guest was the Dutch secretary of state at the time, Dirk Bensdorp. Vergouw showed him how to take a penalty, turning him from a flop into a scorer in the space of two kicks.

Vergouw asked the live studio audience to visit his Web site and vote for which players should take the Dutch penalties in the upcoming tournament. Frank de Boer and Patrick Kluivert were the overwhelming winners. Vergouw disagreed. In his book, he had listed the top five players who must "absolutely not take a penalty." Number one was Kluivert and number two was de Boer (the others were Marc Overmars, Phillip Cocu and Roy Makaay). "When De Boer and Kluivert guys missed against Italy, the book became legendary," Vergouw said.

But there was one thing Vergouw had not predicted: the Dutch players were furious with him. They saw him as an outsider and the book as overly critical. "I wrote it for the Dutch players, but the opposite happened." Whenever he met them, they would refuse to shake his hand. One was a fellow guest on another radio show. Just before going on air, the player hissed, "If I had known you were coming, I would not have agreed to appear."

Vergouw was shaken by the response. "I felt like a loner. To five percent of Dutch people, I'm a hero, but to the rest, I'm a nuisance. The negative response I have had from the football world is astonishing, but I just keep on repeating it. We still don't know how to take penalties."

Part of the reason for Vergouw's struggle came from the Dutch attitude that penalties can't be practiced. Here are some reactions to the Italy defeat:

Leo Beenhakker: "Penalties are about what's in between the ears, but in a nerve-racking shoot-out everything is different."

Willem van Hanegem: "I hope people now don't tell us all to start practicing penalties. It's bullshit. They are simply not trainable."

Johan Cruyff: "The pressure, the excitement and the fatigue all make a difference. Honestly you can't prepare; taking penalties in training is useless. The penalty is a unique skill outside of football."

Dennis Bergkamp had watched the shoot-out from the touchline; it was the fourth time he was part of a losing Holland team after penalties. The defeats clearly still rankle: his autobiography, *Stillness & Speed*, features a heated conversation with coauthor David Winner in which Bergkamp, a deep thinker about the game, repeats the usual excuses for penalty failure. "Penalties are never in your hands . . . You can never simulate the same pressure. You can practice and practice but it's still different when you get to a real shoot-out . . . There's an element of chance as well . . . you can't criticize people by saying: 'You took a bad penalty, you should have done better' . . . With all due respect, you've never been in that situation. And still you're judging someone who has been there?" The conversation comes to an abrupt end when Winner draws a distinction between a penalty missed because of a great save and one skied almost out of the stadium. Bergkamp's response is out of character for a man who played the game with a different view of things. He said: "I don't see that [distinction]."

It is the opinion of Cruyff, a national icon, which has more than anything else dictated this national attitude. The more Cruyff said that penalties couldn't be trained for, the tougher it was for Gyuri Vergouw to be taken seriously. In *Brilliant Orange*, Winner compared Vergouw to Cassandra, the prophet who was never believed even though her predictions came true. Vergouw sees himself more as Galileo: "Everyone is telling me the sun is going round the Earth, but I'm saying it's the other way around." Dutch broadsheet *NRC* ran the headline "Johan Cruyff has no idea about penalties," based on its interview with Vergouw.

The theory, according to Vergouw, is that Cruyff is assumed to be a spot-kick expert because on December 5, 1982, against relegation-threatened Helmond Sport, he scored a famous penalty after exchanging passes from the spot with teammate Jesper Olsen. Never mind that Cruyff was not the first to succeed with this type of penalty—that was Rik Coppens, in 1957 (see page 192 for his story); more significantly, this was the first and indeed only official penalty he took for Ajax, after ten years and over 250 appearances for the team. If he took them in training, reserve goalkeeper Ron Boomgard recalled, it was only "to try crazy things and humiliate his opponent." Henk Groot, Gerrie Mühren and Johan Neeskens were ahead of Cruyff in the penalty list for Ajax, and for Holland, Neeskens and Rob Rensenbrink had the responsibility.

At the start of his final season as a professional, at Feyenoord, Cruyff played a friendly tournament against Roma. The game went to penalties, and Cruyff, hoping to impress his new team, stepped up. "I'd played two games in two days plus extra time, and was living on my nerves," he said on *Villa Barend and Van Dorp*. "You do your little walk back to run up at the ball. You close your eyes and you see where it will end up. That one, it ended up in the second-tier seats. The goal was small before the penalties began. The higher the tension, the smaller the goal gets."

There are two theories about why Cruyff did not fancy penalties. One is that the essence of Cruyff the soccer player was all about movement and intuition and that the idea of standing still and waiting for a referee's whistle before he could kick the ball was anathema to him. The other comes from Bert Hiddema, author of *Cruijff! Van Jopie tot Johan*. "Good penalty takers have a hard shot," he said. "And that was exactly what he lacked. At a young age he didn't have the strength [for it] and would instead use a curved kicking style, which was much more suitable for creative passing than penalties."

"Johan didn't do it himself," Rob Rensenbrink told me. "I think maybe he was frightened of missing." Rensenbrink was one of Holland's most reliable penalty takers. He scored four out of four at the 1978 World Cup and was assiduous at practice. He would take between ten and twenty spot kicks after every training session, sometimes telling the goalkeeper where he would aim before kicking, other times sticking poles half a meter inside each goalpost and striking the ball in between the pole and the post every time. "It's like free kicks: the more you take, the better you get. Saying you can't practice is bullshit. Just do it every day."

De Strafschop was the first of Vergouw's tetralogy of books written for the Dutch soccer fan, who repeats the same questions every time Holland reaches a major tournament: "Why can't Holland take penalties? Why can't Holland beat Germany? Why haven't Holland ever become world champions? And couldn't I do a better job as national coach?" His prescience shines through in each of them. In *De Laatste Minuut* (The Last Minute), he asks why Germany scores so many late goals and concludes that the team learns from its mistakes—in a way that the likes of England and Holland don't—as has been proved by the development of talent it has produced since their Euro 2000 failure. His next instalment, *Oranje wereldkampioen* (The Dutch as World Champions), explains why the Dutch have never won a World Cup. It came out just before the 2010 tournament, and in it Vergouw bemoans Holland's reluctance to pick a true number 9—"We think Huntelaar is lousy because all he does is score goals but if he was German, he'd have statues in his honor"—and to take extra time seriously. In the final against Spain, Holland lost in extra time.

His final book, *Bondscoach: Coaching handboek voor 16 miljoen Nederlanders*, breaks down the qualities needed for a top national team coach and cites those who only make value-driven decisions, with no personal attachment at all, as best at the job. It sounds obvious, but Vergouw says it's not. He was surprised at how many boxes Louis van Gaal, Holland coach when he was writing, ticked.*

Would Holland have won the 2010 final on penalties? "I don't think so," said Vergouw. "Even though they had the penalty analysis from Ignacio Palacios-Huerta, the coach van Marwijk did not believe in practicing, and we know where he got that from."

---

* Vergouw noted that Van Gaal made one obvious personal decision during Holland's knockout matches at the 2014 World Cup: to keep captain Robin van Persie on the pitch for as long as he did. "If Van Gaal was not about to coach Manchester United, where Van Persie was playing, I don't believe he would have kept him on for 96 minutes in the semifinal against Argentina. That felt like a personal decision to me."

Vergouw has been nicknamed Professor Penalty in Holland and organizes penalty-based "bonding sessions" for businesses, in which they hire out a big stadium, take penalties at their boss and listen to Vergouw link business practice to spot kicks. After one such talk at Amsterdam's Olympic Stadium, two youngsters in the audience, students at the nearby Johan Cruyff Academy, thought they had misheard. "Did you really say that you can practice penalties?" they asked him. "Because Mr. Cruyff always told us you can't."

Johan is a Dutch soccer magazine named after Cruyff, but that did not stop one of its writers calling him out on his penalty blind spot. "Maybe it's time to switch off when Cruyff talks about penalties," wrote Auke Kok. "Not because it's terrible that he rarely took them but because, even if the truth bears little resemblance to what he says, everyone blindly accepts it. The only question is: who would dare do such a thing?"

Louis van Gaal would. No one quite knows the exact reasons behind the feud between Van Gaal and Cruyff. Some suggest it began in 1972 when Van Gaal joined Ajax as a player (he never made the first team) and lectured his teammates, Cruyff among them, about tactics. Van Gaal has claimed it began in December 1989 when he was an assistant coach at Ajax. Van Gaal was having dinner at Cruyff's house with the Koeman brothers when he took a phone call telling him that his sister had died. He rushed out of the house. "Later I heard that Johan was angry I didn't thank him for the meal," he wrote in his autobiography. Cruyff denies it.* Both men, though, wanted to be seen as the king of Ajax and the king of Barcelona.

---

* Others have suggested that Cruyff was jealous that Van Gaal coached Ajax to Champions League victory in 1995, something he never managed to accomplish. Van Gaal blamed his short spell as Barcelona coach (2002–2003) on the fact that Cruyff continually criticized him in the Catalan press. "I will never forgive what he did," wrote Van Gaal. "I tried to do a good job despite his attempts to frustrate." In 2011, Cruyff took Ajax to court after four supervisory board members appointed Van Gaal as technical director without the support of the fifth member: Cruyff himself. The appointment was blocked.

There is also a philosophical difference: Cruyff believes in the quality of the individual, Van Gaal in the *collectief*. And so even after Van Gaal's Holland side beat reigning world champions Spain 5–1 in their opening match in the 2014 World Cup—playing not with the Dutch 4–3–3 model but with a 5–3–2 formation, with three goals coming from diagonal long balls—Cruyff was reticent in his praise. "The conversation about formations is ridiculous!" he wrote in his *De Telegraaf* newspaper column. "We are doing this to reach the next round, and that's why we made the change, but it's clear that it will not last."

Cruyff may have felt that Van Gaal's pragmatic tactics, forced upon him by the absence of injured midfielder Kevin Strootman, were against Dutch principles. He said after the Round of 16 win over Mexico that he only enjoyed the last thirty minutes, which was when Holland switched to 4–3–3. But Cruyff was being harsh. Van Gaal's side switched systems midgame, used space and movement cleverly, and had players like Daley Blind and Dirk Kuyt constantly dropping into different positions. "The fluidity and shape-shifting of the side, as well as the sophisticated and game-affecting changes from the sidelines, meant this was a side in keeping with Dutch traditions," Winner confirmed.

There was one tradition, though, that Van Gaal was happy to end. It came at the end of Holland's goalless quarterfinal against Costa Rica. Holland had dominated for 120 minutes: Wesley Sneijder twice hit the post, while Costa Rican goalkeeper Keylor Navas was having one of those "nothing can get past me" games. Costa Rica had beaten Greece in the previous round on penalties, scoring five out of five, and, as the shoot-out approached, had the momentum.

Until, that is, Van Gaal sent out reserve goalkeeper Tim Krul to get warmed up. "When I started my warm-up the whole Costa Rican bench was confused about what was going on," Krul said. "Their manager's face when he saw me was priceless. He was looking over to see what our manager was doing." With one minute left to play, Van Gaal took off his first-choice goalkeeper Jasper

Cillessen and brought on Krul, specifically for the shoot-out. In a soccer industry dominated by conservatism, Van Gaal had dared to do something different.

In the past, this move has had mixed success. Greuther Furth coach Mike Büskens swapped Max Grun for Jasmin Fezjic two minutes before the end of the 2012 German Cup semifinal against Borussia Dortmund. But two minutes was long enough for Dortmund to get a winner: Ilkay Gundogan shooting from the edge of the area on 119.56 with a shot that hit the post, struck Fezjic on the shoulder and cannoned into the net. In 1996, Leicester City coach Martin O'Neill took off goalkeeper Kevin Poole and brought on Zeljko Kalac after 119 minutes of the first division promotion play-off against Crystal Palace. Before full time, Steve Claridge scored a winner for Leicester, and Kalac did not touch the ball.

On the other hand, in the 2004 African Champions League—in the semifinals and the final—Felix Omordi, coach of Nigerian side Enyimba, subbed off Vincent Enyeama and brought on Dele Aiyenugba for the shoot-out. It worked against Esperance in the semis and in the final against another Tunisian side, Etoile de Sahel, when Aiyenugba saved Sabeur Ben Frej's kick to help Enyimba win the shoot-out 5–3.

Ciaran Kelly was even more successful for Sligo Rovers, coming off the bench to save four penalties out of four in the 2010 Irish Cup final against Shamrock Rovers; he saved another two a year later in the Cup final against Shelbourne.

While Cillessen had not saved any of his previous sixteen penalties, Krul had saved only two of his previous twenty, which meant that third choice Michel Vorm, with three saves from eleven penalties, was in fact the team's penalty specialist. But that was not the point. Krul's presence had planted a seed of doubt in the Costa Rican minds. They were left thinking: "This guy must be good if he's coming on just to save penalties."

Krul was brash and aggressive, taking any possible advantage he could to destabilize the Costa Rican shooters. He is also left-handed, and perhaps that came into play given that three kickers were left-footed. Before every kick, he walked up to each kicker as they were spotting the ball and spoke to them. To some he said, *"Vamos!,"* Spanish for "Come on!" To others he told them where they were going to shoot. "I don't think I did anything wrong," he said. "I didn't shout in an aggressive manner. I did nothing crazy. I told them I knew the way they were going with their penalties because I had analyzed it. I was trying to get in their heads, and it worked. It is a way of trying to psyche them out. They were under massive pressure. I was under massive pressure. So I did everything in my power. [Van Gaal's decision] definitely had an impact. It was a fantastic move."

Holland had scored their first two penalties when Bryan Ruiz stepped up. Krul had walked over to the right of the goal while Ruiz was approaching. The Costa Rica captain struck his penalty left-footed to his natural side and Krul saved it. "I have no problem with Krul's actions," said Ruiz after the game. Michael Umana, fifth up, had scored Costa Rica's winning penalty against Greece; this time, though, he was kicking to avoid defeat, and his effort was saved, again to Krul's natural side.

Holland had won their first World Cup shoot-out—and "won" is the key word. This was one of those rare shoot-outs where the focus was not on Ruiz or Umana. They had not lost it for their team, but Van Gaal, and Krul, had won it. Not since Antonin Panenka's penalty in 1976 has an international tournament shoot-out focused so much on the "winning move" rather than the losing one.

"He has a golden cock," said Arjen Robben, referring to Van Gaal's Midas touch. "I don't know, [wife] Truus had never told me that," Van Gaal countered. "We thought it through. Every player has certain skills and qualities and they don't always coincide. We felt Tim would be the most appropriate keeper to save penalties. We're a tiny bit proud this trick has helped us through."

It was significant that the first person Van Gaal turned to as he celebrated was Frans Hoek, his goalkeeping coach. Aside from a spell as Poland goalkeeping coach under Leo Beenhakker (2005–2009), Hoek has worked with Van Gaal at Ajax, Barcelona, and Bayern Munich. Van Gaal may have taken credit for the decision, but it was based on Hoek's know-how. He divides his goalkeepers into two categories: A-type and R-type. *A* is for "Anticipation" and refers to ball-playing goalkeepers who are happy to participate in possession, not scared of a back pass, and quick to move if their defense plays a high line. "Anticipation goalkeepers could be easily used as field players, as they are able to function as the eleventh player," Hoek explained.

R is for "Reaction." "This type of goalkeeper is an absolute winner. He will go to any extreme in order to win, is physically strong and has a high muscle tone. He is very strong and has quick reactions . . . a lot of muscle strength and great charisma," Hoek said. The R-type is a great shot-stopper but less good at one-on-ones and, personified by Krul's physique and charisma, is preferable for a penalty shoot-out.

"Louis van Genius" reveled in the praise coming his way, and while he might not have seen it as the opportunity to stick up two fingers at Cruyff, it was another example of the differences between the two men. Despite that, Cruyff was impressed with the switch: "I wondered if he would do it and enjoyed it when he did. These are the things that I love." For someone who sees penalties as "outside of football" and claims you cannot practice for them, I found it hard to believe that Cruyff saw the Krul move coming. Perhaps assistant coach Danny Blind came closest to the truth when he admitted to Fabio Cannavaro: "We have a terrible record from penalties, and so we thought we just had to try something different."

Holland had reached the semifinal and Van Gaal was two games from greatness. One by one, he was ridding the Dutch of their World Cup complexes: already he had avenged the 2010 World Cup final loss to Spain, ended the long-running issues of squad disunity, and overturned Holland's penalty hoodoo. With the two teams that beat Holland in the 1978 and 1974 World Cup finals— Argentina and Germany—potential opponents in the semifinal and final, Van Gaal was closing in on history. He could have over-taken Rinus Michels and Cruyff in the pantheon of great Dutch coaches. Winning the World Cup would have sealed his legend.

It didn't quite work out like that. The semifinal against Argentina was a tight affair: Van Gaal wanted to stop Lionel Messi, and Argentina's job was to keep Arjen Robben quiet. Both succeeded. All eyes were on Van Gaal and his substitutions. He took off Bruno Martins Indi at halftime, because the full back had been booked and risked a red card up against Messi. Nigel de Jong and Robin van Persie had been pregame injury doubts but played, though neither could last the full match. Jordy Clasie replaced De Jong and Klaas-Jan Huntelaar came on for Van Persie, who had scored the first penalty against Costa Rica.

The game went to a shoot-out, but this time there was no Krul for Holland. That had to have handed Argentina a psychological boost. Robben won the toss and kicked first, but Van Gaal strug-gled to find a replacement for Van Persie as the first shooter. Huntelaar was down to kick fifth in both matches. The coach asked two players and they refused before Ron Vlaar, outstand-ing in the match, stepped up. Vlaar had never taken a penalty before and it showed. His reaction time after the referee's whistle was very quick, and goalkeeper Sergio Romero saved his effort, which was aimed to the nonnatural side but too central. For Vlaar in 2014, you could read Bosvelt in 2000.*

Messi took first for Argentina and, despite Cillessen's un-convincing efforts to ape Krul, consolidated the advantage by scoring. After Robben had scored, Wesley Sneijder was third up.

---

* Vlaar was almost very lucky: after Romero saved his shot, the goalkeeper ran off to celebrate and the ball rebounded toward Vlaar. It may have lightly brushed his shoulder before spinning back and settling on the goal line. It did not cross the line, but for a tantalizing moment, Vlaar looked at the ball and wondered. It's a lot of ifs, but: if he had not touched the ball before it spun back, and if it had crossed the line, then the goal would have stood. A FIFA spokesman confirmed that referees kept their Goal Line Technology watches activated for the shoot-out; he added that Vlaar had told Cuneyt Cakir, the referee, that his shoulder had touched the ball.

Despite his reputation as a dead-ball specialist, he had never scored a penalty in open play, and like most nonregular kickers, he aimed for his natural side (as he had against Costa Rica). Romero saved again.

It was a strange move for Van Gaal to publicly admit that two of his players had refused to take a penalty. Maybe he had meant to shift blame onto the two players—they remain unknown, though rumor has settled on two of the younger squad members—but the only person who looked bad was the coach himself. He knew that Van Persie was unlikely to finish the game, so it was his responsibility to organize a kicker for the number one position in the event his captain was off the pitch.

Vergouw wrote in *Bondscoach* that the coach should always take responsibility for the shoot-out, whatever the result. So if Van Gaal was responsible for the game-changing Krul switch, the same has to be true for the Argentina shoot-out. "Van Gaal's weakness is that he takes all the credit when things go well, but when it goes wrong, it's never his fault," said Vergouw. "There is always someone else to blame."

In the end, Van Gaal was not able to exorcise all the Dutch ghosts. The penalty success was fun while it lasted, but fleeting. So did anything change for the Dutch and penalties in 2014? Not really, no. There was no anger, sadness or confusion after the latest penalty loss—just acceptance. "It was just another day in the office for Dutch fans," said Vergouw. "Go to a game, lose on penalties. Even I am learning to accept it now."

"It's the most terrible scenario, to lose on penalties," Van Gaal said, and as though the Costa Rica moment was a mirage, he added: "We didn't lose against Argentina, but penalties are down to luck." That, at least, is something Cruyff would agree with.

Ghana, Vergouw told me, was an African version of the Dutch. "Ghana are all about creativity, inspiration and feeling," he said. "Penalties are the opposite of that. Ghana are exactly the same as Holland. If anything they are too skillful, don't believe in practice, and have the impression that penalties don't matter because having the skills is more important."

Ghana won the African Nations Cup final in 1982 by beating Libya 7–6 on penalties but have lost every shoot-out since: the 1992 African Nations final, the 2010 World Cup semifinal and the 2013 African Nations semifinal.* One man present for all three defeats was Kwesi Appiah, a quiet left-back who made his debut for Ghana in a crucial African Nations Cup qualifier against Zaire in 1981. He marked danger-man Ayel Mayele out of the game so comprehensively that he was instantly nicknamed "Mayele." It was also the match in which Abedi Ayew "Pelé," then just fifteen, made his Ghana debut.

Appiah was part of the squad in 1992 that was inspired by Abedi, who scored a Maradona-esque solo goal to win the quarterfinal against Congo. Abedi scored again in the semifinal win over Nigeria but picked up a yellow card that ruled him out of the final against Ivory Coast. His suspension was compounded as Abedi had been named captain—in fact, he had replaced Appiah just before the tournament began. Before the final there was a row over who should wear the armband. Tony Yeboah was next in line but he was overlooked in favor of Tony Baffoe, who grew up in Germany (he was the first Ghanaian player to be nationalized) and was one of the least experienced players in the squad. "The team went on to the field deflated and disaffected," said one player, who wanted to remain anonymous even twenty years after the event.

The Ivorians had not conceded a goal throughout the tournament and a myth had built that spirits were helping them keep clean sheets. Goalkeeper Alain Gouaméné had saved three penalties in a semifinal shoot-out win over Cameroon.

---

* Libya gained revenge for that loss by beating Ghana on penalties in the 2014 African Nations Championship final, a version of the African Nations Cup that features only local-based players. Ghana missed their first two penalties and the score was 3–3 after five kicks each. Ghana ended up losing 4–3 and Libya won their first ever African title.

Unsurprisingly, with no Abedi for Ghana the final ended goalless and so began one of the longest and most dramatic shoot-outs in history. After five penalties each the score was 4–4, Isaac Asare (Ghana) and Joel Tiehi (Ivory Coast) having missed. It was sudden death. The players kept scoring: 5–5 . . . 6–6 . . . 7–7 . . . 8–8 . . . 9–9. All ten outfield players had taken penalties and next it was the goalkeepers' turn. Gouaméné scored for Ivory Coast. Ansah scored for Ghana. 10–10. And back to the start it went. Aka Kouamé for Ivory Coast—goal. Next up, Baffoe, who had taken the first penalty for Ghana and scored. The captain of the side. Born in Germany. He missed.

Three mystics from the Ivorian village of Akradio claimed the credit for the win, but as no one acknowledged their input, they were said to have jinxed the Elephants' subsequent campaigns: Ivory Coast failed to reach the quarterfinal in three of the next four tournaments. A government minister was dispatched to Akradio to apologize and ask for help. Did it work? Ivory Coast has lost four shoot-outs since, including two in African finals. As for Gouaméné, he was unmoved by the mystics. "I didn't believe any of that stuff," he told Ian Hawkey in *Feet of the Chameleon*. "I am a Christian, I trusted in God. In fact I used to have my bible in the back of my goal with me."

For Ghana, too, a penalty nightmare had begun. Their next shoot-out was in 2010, when they were a penalty kick away from becoming the first African side to reach a World Cup semifinal (and by which time Appiah was assistant manager). Ghana were drawing 1–1 with Uruguay when Dominic Adiyah's last-minute header flew past goalkeeper Fernando Muslera. Infamously, Luis Suárez popped up on the line to punch it away; he was sent off and a penalty was awarded. Asamoah Gyan was one of Ghana's star players at the tournament but he had a mixed penalty record for the Black Stars. He had scored from the spot in the 2008 African Nations win over Guinea, but missed in his first World Cup game, a 2–0 win over the Czech Republic in 2006. In South Africa he had already scored two penalties in the group stage: the only goal of the game against Serbia and the equalizer in the 1–1 draw against Australia. In the Round of 16, it was his goal that eliminated USA.

Against Uruguay, Gyan stepped up and struck his penalty against the top of the crossbar. Minutes after this miss he was standing over the ball again, ready to take the first kick for Ghana in another shoot-out. His was a stunning response: composed, he scored a fantastic penalty. The same cannot be said for John Mensah, whose weak shot was saved.

Later it emerged that the Black Stars had not practiced penalties before the game, and that the decision about who would take them, and in what order, had been left up to the players. When Adiyah missed Ghana's fourth kick—an excellent save by Muslera—he was seen to mutter the words *"Ewurade me wu"* (meaning "God, I am dead") in his Twi dialect. He was already afraid of the response back home, but he need not have worried. Adiyah was not the villain of this piece, Gyan was. And so, infinitely more so, was Suárez.

The day after the game, there was a somber mood in the Protea Hotel in Bramfontein in downtown Johannesburg. But while most of the Ghana squad mooched around wearing flip-flops and a frown, Gyan cut a calm and sensible figure. He was smiling and providing comfort to his teammates. "I scored from the spot in the last two games so I was the right man for that penalty," he told BBC reporter Michael Oti Adjei. "Missed penalties are normal in football and I will bounce back. I will come back stronger for this experience."

At his next tournament, Gyan's penalty jitters struck again: he missed against Zambia in the 2012 African Nations Cup semifinal, a game Ghana would go on to lose 1–0. This time the abuse got to him and he quit international soccer. When he returned a year later, he was off penalty duty.

One year on, Appiah was in sole charge of the Ghana team. He is an unassuming man and it was widely thought when he took the job that his quiet demeanor would be a weakness. In fact he proved to be robust and swift in his decision making, which included exiling the Ayew brothers, sons of Abedi Pelé, from the squad for the 2013 Nations Cup.

Without the pair, Ghana progressed to the semifinals and were huge favorites to beat Burkina Faso. This time Appiah made his players practice penalties and he was as surprised as anyone when Isaac Vorsah missed Ghana's first kick in the shoot-out. "He never missed in training and we were convinced he would score," said Appiah. The coach had subbed off Ghana's first-choice penalty taker, Wakaso Mubarak (who had scored from the spot in the first half), and could only watch as Emmanuel Clottey and Emmanuel Agyemang-Badu missed to allow the Burkinabe to win 3–2.

"Maybe we haven't got the right players for penalties any-more," shrugged Ben Koufie, who played for Ghana in the 1950s, coached the team in the 1970s, and was Ghana FA president in the 2000s. "I think some of the modern players lack concentration because they are thinking of so many things, and some of them have difficulty in focusing when it comes to penalties."

This comment relates to an interesting remark Jens Lehmann made about his brief spell with Arsenal's reserve side as a forty-year-old. On the team coach on the way to a game he was surprised that everyone was silent. "No one was talking," he said. "I thought, 'Has everyone gone to sleep?' But then I looked around. Everyone was on their phones, typing away on Twitter or Facebook. They were all hanging on their devices and I think this has a major impact on communication. These kids are not used to quick language commands and all their time on the phone makes them incapable of quick commands on the pitch. They text instead of talk and that means they are not quick thinkers anymore. I really do think this is influencing the games now: we have to teach them how to communicate on the pitch. I know of some players who have been told to get off Twitter as they are addicted."

Koufie is a bright-eyed eighty-one-year-old and was not so

sure that Twitter was to blame for Ghana's penalty woes. But he did advocate more purposeful practice for coaches to assess their players under pressure. "That's the only way they will find out which players have the ability to cope. Not all players have the right temperament, and any of them can become agitated and nervous. We have to recognize this as a problem and then work toward improving it."

Another former Ghana great, Osei Kofi, thought that Adiyah's initial reaction to his miss was telling. "When you have twenty-four million coaches in the country who can take players to the cleaner's if they miss a spot kick, it affects some players too much. That's all they think about before they take the kick."

One thing they won't be able to manage is the trick Osei pulled off at the 1968 African Nations Cup in a tense match against Zaire. With the score at 1–1, Ghana had a penalty and Addo Odamtten hit the crossbar. The referee ordered a retake, claiming the goalkeeper had moved too early. Without the referee noticing, Osei stepped in to take the penalty instead, and scored. The game had restarted before the Zaire players were alerted to the switch, and despite their complaints, the goal stood. Ghana won 2–1.

In a national team jersey, then, it would seem that the Czechs and Germans have innate penalty prowess while the English, Dutch and Ghanaians have major flaws. But a losing tendency can be overcome. Italy lost four shoot-outs in a row in the 1990s, a run that ended when they had the fortune to face Holland in 2000. Totti's *cucchiaio* may not have sealed the victory but its impact on the squad would have far-reaching consequences. It was the equivalent of calling heads four times in a row and then tails three in a row.

Spain needed only to get past their bogey side; once they did that they broke a psychological barrier that allowed them to become the first team in history to win three consecutive major tournaments. In fact, if a twenty-one-year-old taking his first penalty as a professional had not scored, Spain's era of dominance may never have happened.

Certainly when Spain's Euro 2008 quarterfinal against Italy went to penalties, the nation feared the worst. Spain had never beaten Italy in a competitive match, a run going back nearly ninety years to a 2–0 loss in the 1920 Olympics. They were still moaning about the unfair win in the 1934 World Cup, when Italy had nationalized five South American players and kicked goalkeeper Ricardo Zamora, who had two ribs broken, out of the game. That finished 1–1, and the subsequent play-off was a similar story: Spain had three players go off injured and two goals disallowed, and when Giuseppe Meazza scored for Italy, Zamora's replacement Nogues was fouled.

A draw and an Italy win followed at Euro 80 and Euro 88 respectively, but the spirit of '34 returned in the 1994 World Cup when Mauro Tassotti elbowed Luis Enrique and left his nose broken and bloodied. No penalty, no foul even, no red card; instead they played on, and Roberto Baggio scored a late winner to win that quarterfinal 2–1. The amount of coverage given to the Tassotti elbow embarrassed even Enrique. "It's starting to get a bit tiresome, seeing that photo all the time," he said. But it showed how deep-seated the psychological wounds were of always losing to the "dastardly Italians."

That 1994 defeat also started Spain's quarterfinal jinx. They fell at the same stage at Euro 96, Euro 2000, and at the 2002 World Cup. After a goalless draw in Vienna in 2008 it was penalties again. All three of their previous shoot-out defeats—to Belgium in 1986, England in 1996 and South Korea in 2002—had come at the quarterfinal stage. And all of them had come on June 22—the date of this Italy game. No Spanish goalkeeper had even stopped a penalty in a shoot-out before (although Luis Arconada did save a twenty-year-old Michael Laudrup effort in the Euro 84 semifinal before the referee, George Courtney, ordered a retake and he scored). "We looked over at them and we could see they were so confident—they felt they had won," remembered Xavi Hernández.

Spain coach Luis Aragonés told his players in what order they would be shooting. He picked Dani Guiza at four, and straight away intuited his error. This was Guiza's first tournament, he was not a regular in the side, and at twenty-eight he had enough experience to realize the enormity of his task. Guiza looked nervous, and after Iker Casillas had saved from Daniele de Rossi, he threw away Spain's advantage with a penalty that Gigi Buffon stopped. By this stage Casillas's mother Dolores had fainted in the stands.

Casillas consoled Guiza on his way back to the center circle, and then saved Antonio di Natale's penalty. Cesc Fabregas stepped up to take the fifth kick for Spain. Fabregas had last taken a penalty at the age of fifteen for Barcelona's youth team, as usually Lionel Messi and Víctor Vázquez would not let him near them. In his five years at Arsenal, Thierry Henry and occasionally Robert Pires had been the penalty takers. It was a Sunday night, 11:20 p.m., and 16.2 million Spaniards were watching the game on TV station Cuatro: it was the most-watched TV moment in Spanish history up to that date (though it was pushed close that year by the 14.3 million watching Rodolfo Chikilicuatre in the Eurovision Song Contest).

Fabregas had been the subject of some debate during the tournament: was he or Xavi Spain's best creator in midfield? Fabregas was not assured of his place in the team—he came on for Xavi after an hour against Italy—and as he walked to the spot he started talking to himself. "The coach came, he gave the names, and I was fifth. Perfect. I wanted to return the confidence that I had been given," he explained. "That is why I was talking as I went up to take the penalty. I was making myself aware of that. There had been a lot of talk of me being a substitute, my performance . . . I said to myself, 'I must score.'" And he did.

With that kick, Fabregas killed all the bogeymen in one go: the Italians, the quarterfinals, the date—all conquered. "That game changed the history of Spanish football," wrote *Marca*. "Italy was everything that Spain wanted to be but could not, a team capable of competing always, even in the worst circumstances . . . Spain was the eternal aspirant, Italy the eternal winner . . . But in the shoot-out, the loop stopped repeating itself . . . Cesc put an end to so many years of anguish and frustration, reflected in his face as he stepped up to take the decisive kick. He put it away and made a miracle."

Carlos Marchena, who played center back in that side, later wrote in his column for *El País*, "Cesc's penalty was the biggest of liberations, because it meant a break with all the myths and legends. The feeling, and the voice, of the group was expressed in two words: *Ahora, sí* [Now, yes]." "It would have been very tough for us to fail at this point again, and to recover from that," admitted Casillas, who claimed he was lucky with his penalty saves. "Winning that match mentally unblocked the whole generation of players," said Juan Mata, who was not in the squad, but would be in 2012. "We'd spent years living in a negative spiral, and all of a sudden that shoot-out acted like some kind of light at the end of the tunnel."

Two years later, Fabregas was crucial to Spanish success. In the 2010 World Cup final again he came off the bench and proved decisive, making the pass for Andrés Iniesta to score the winning goal. Spain now had the psychological advantage that had been lacking in previous tournaments, so when the Euro 2012 semifinal against Portugal went to penalties, there was only one favorite.

Xabi Alonso kicked first and his shot was saved. His Real Madrid teammate Cristiano Ronaldo had spoken to Portugal goalkeeper Rui Patricio before the kick. Had that played on Xabi's mind? Casillas then saved from João Moutinho. When Sergio Ramos stepped up fourth for Spain, the score was 2–2.

Ramos's last penalty, less than two months earlier, when Real Madrid lost on penalties to Bayern Munich in the Champions League semifinal, had flown high over the crossbar. The miss generated a popular app in Spain called "Angry Ramos," which involved guiding Ramos's skied penalty as it traveled the world, past Pep Guardiola riding a rocket and José Mourinho appearing from behind clouds. Ramos was particularly upset that people called him a bottler; he insisted the ball had lifted when he planted his left foot down, so his point of contact was higher than it should have been. That night he spoke to his father and his brother Rene. "The next penalty, Panenka. You'll see. They'll soon shut up."

Ramos had been practicing, though not at the team's training camp in Gniewino. There were too many cameras around. Instead, he would practice just the moment of contact, the little dink away from the penalty spot. He told some of his teammates about his plan. "He'd been talking about it for a long time but I didn't believe him," said Alvaro Arbeloa.

"The moment's come," Ramos told Jesus Navas and Raúl Albiol when the shoot-out began. He knew exactly what he was going to do, even then.

"When I did it, everyone said 'What bollocks!' or 'Are you mad?'" he told the *Guardian*. "But if you think coldly, it's logical. The goalkeeper doesn't expect it after what I'd been through. I had heard a lot of things: it's a lot of pressure, that you're not equipped to take on that kind of responsibility and all that . . . In fact it's the complete opposite: I like to take on the responsibility. I never doubted that I had *huevos* [balls]!"

Rui Patricio watched Ramos's brilliant Panenka sail over him, and next up was Bruno Alves, who thought he was taking Portugal's third kick but had been recalled so Nani could take it. Was it that or the Panenka that put him off? He hit the bar and, just like four years earlier, Fabregas stepped up for the fifth penalty. "I had a premonition on the morning of the game that if I took the fifth penalty, we would win," he said. Assistant coach Toni Grande had asked Fabregas to be number two on the list, but he said no, five. They didn't argue, and as Fabregas spotted the ball, he said to it, "Don't let me down—we have to make history." He scored again. "It was like déjà vu from 2008, the sensation of what was going to happen. And it worked out perfectly."

"The guy has a psychological power with penalties," Casillas laughed. Spain went on to win a third straight tournament, beating Italy, once their bête noire, 4–0 in the final.

It was the same story in the 2013 Confederations Cup semifinal between the sides. The game ended goalless, and Italy kicked first in the shoot-out. Despite Antonio Candreva opening the scoring with a glorious Panenka, Spain responded to going behind every time with a goal of their own. Six times they were behind, and six times the Spanish players—now confident and no longer burdened by the weight of history or the significance of their opponents—kept on scoring. Eventually Leonardo Bonucci fired over for Italy and Jesus Navas, who earlier in his career was too anxious to leave his home town of Seville to play for the national team, scored for a 7–6 win.

Although it was only a friendly tournament, it was described as one of the best penalty shoot-outs ever. It was also incontrovertible proof, if any were needed, that Spain's penalty hoodoo was broken, as were any hang-ups over their fierce rivals. Maybe this is what England need to do: face up to Germany in a semifinal shoot-out and give the match-deciding penalty to a rookie. That might just do it.

PENALTY ICON—
HARALD SCHUMACHER

There is no doubt who was both the hero and the villain of the first penalty shoot-out in a World Cup finals match. The name Harald "Toni" Schumacher is enough to send most French soccer fans into a state of apoplexy. His performance in the 1982 World Cup semifinal between France and West Germany earned him a place in soccer folklore.

Both sides had topped their Phase Two groups to reach the semifinal, played in Seville on July 8. Given that West Germany, whose team was rugged and not very popular, had beaten hosts Spain (and England) to get there, they were marginal favorites. But they felt France had the better chance to win. On the day of the game the players were stuck in their hotels, battling their nerves and biding their time, waiting for the evening kick-off, the French in the Parador Hotel, the Germans in Los Lebreros. This is their view of the game, from the key players involved.*

*

---

*I am indebted to Rémy Lacombe, *France Football* editor-in-chief, who gave permission for background information and interviews from *France Football* magazine (edition number 3,456) to be used here.

Alain Giresse (France midfielder): It was such a hot day! When I woke up, I looked out of my hotel room and saw a poor donkey tied to a tree, looking for some shade, while the heat of the sun made your eyes go fuzzy.

Klaus Fischer (West Germany forward): We had a normal program set out for the day: breakfast at 7:30 a.m., then a walk, lunch, a nap, a snack and then we go to the stadium.

Harald Schumacher (West Germany goalkeeper): Goalkeepers are all similar. They want to stay in their corner, be on their own and work harder than others. I had my body-building equipment with me. I was a workaholic. I always tried to have a perfect mental approach. I would picture images from the game, but seeing only the ball, never the opponents. The goal was never to lose sight of the ball, like a tiger should never lose sight of its prey. I kept telling myself that I was the strongest, the fittest, and I could control my nerves. I've never been part of the team, I'd isolate myself as soon as I had the chance. If you wanted me, you would know where to find me: I was always in my room.

There was some tension in the France camp. The players had been together for seven weeks and cliques had developed. Michel Platini celebrated his birthday on June 21 and was presented with a cake. Two days later it was Jean Tigana's birthday, and no one mentioned it. Tigana went to the hotel kitchen, came back with an apple into which he stuck a candle and said, "Happy birthday, Jean." It was also hard for the players who were not in the starting eleven.

Patrick Battiston (France midfielder): I didn't play against England because Manu [Amoros] was picked. I wanted to go home but [France assistant coach] Marc Bourrier told me that I would get my chance.

The Germany squad also had their issues. Outspoken midfielder Paul Breitner was a conflicting presence and coach Jupp Derwall was too permissive, allowing clans to develop and not punishing players, even when they criticized him. *They also had injuries, including Karl-Heinz Rummenigge, who started on the bench because of a thigh strain.*

Late on the afternoon of the game, both teams left their hotels for Estadio Ramón Sánchez Pizjuán. But there was a delay before the Germans' bus could leave.

Fischer: Schumacher, [Pierre] Littbarski and me, we were stuck in the lift. There were quite a few of us in there, including some women who began to panic. After a few minutes, Schumacher opened the doors with all his strength, between two floors. He was mad with rage, boiling mad.

The German trio was stuck for fifteen minutes, according to Littbarski. Once they got out, another piece of bad fortune struck Schumacher before the game. When he was already inside the stadium, he realized he had left his blue shirt on the bus.

Schumacher: It was my lucky shirt and I always wore it. The bus had gone. I needed a few minutes to recover, as I was upset and tense. I had to wear a red shirt, the same as [French goalkeeper Jean-Luc] Ettori. But with my blue shorts, I did not match at all.

Alain Giresse: We started badly. The Germans imposed their game on us because they thought that with the stakes so high, we would be nervous.

It worked: Germany took an early lead. Breitner's through-ball was met by Fischer, whose shot was blocked by Ettori. The rebound fell to Littbarski, who drilled the ball in from the edge of the area. By then, Amoros had already had his nose bloodied in a challenge with Schumacher and Battiston had told his teammates on the bench that the German goalkeeper was "mad" and "aggressive."

Within ten minutes, France were level. Karlheinz Förster was adjudged to have pushed over Dominique Rocheteau in the area. The

*referee for the game was Charles Corver, but only after the first
choice, José Antonio Garrido, had been vetoed by French FA
delegate Roger Machin. Garrido had officiated France's opening
game in the tournament, a 3–1 loss to England, and the French
camp felt that was a bad omen. Corver awarded the penalty, and
Platini sent Schumacher the wrong way.*

*At halftime, France midfielder Bernard Genghini was struggling
with a calf injury after a late challenge by Manfred Kaltz. He lasted
only five minutes of the second half. Battiston came on to replace
him.*

Battiston: I started to warm up. The atmosphere in the ground
was exceptional. I warm up, I don't hear anything. It was like I was
on my own. [France coach] Michel Hidalgo called me and I start to
take my kit off and pull up my socks. But I don't remember anything. I know I went on to the pitch but I don't know how I did it.
It was like I was in a cloud. I was floating. I didn't have the feeling
that I was playing in the semifinal of a World Cup.

*Within five minutes of Battiston's arrival, Maxime Bossis won
the ball, passed to Platini, and he chipped an exquisite pass over the
German defense for Battiston to run clear on goal.*

Battiston: When Platini passed the ball, I thought, "This one is
for me." My impression, although it's difficult to believe, is that
the pitch was like a corridor and there was nobody in it, like the
Champs-Elysées at five o'clock in the morning. All of a sudden I
see something black coming closer to me. But I didn't have time
to get out of the way and I collided, and from then on I don't
remember anything.

Schumacher: So the pass comes, I think it was from Platini.
Battiston is running directly toward my goal. And I think the ball
arrived as I was running for it. Patrick arrives one or two seconds
before. And I think it's going to go above my head so I jump
without knowing where the ball is. I go with my knees out in

front but twist at the final moment because I see that it could be bad if I hit him with my knees . . . and I hit him with my hip. I was always on the edge of my box, always anticipating long balls, I was never back on my goal line. When I look back on it thirty years later, I would do exactly the same again. Because I was 100 percent convinced that I would get the ball.

Battiston reached the ball first, and his effort went wide of the post. Schumacher made contact with the forward's jaw, and Battiston lay unconscious on the pitch for seven minutes. Schumacher returned to his goalmouth and bounced the ball while the stricken Frenchman received medical help.

Maurice Vrillac (France team doctor): Not only did I see what happened, I heard it too. I ran on to the pitch before the referee gave permission and as soon as I saw Patrick, I was very worried. He had fallen badly and I was worried about his neck. He had small shakes as well.

Giresse: The first thing we thought about was the seriousness. What's happening to him? He was flat, he had lost consciousness. Also we had to put up with the attitude of Schumacher, and the referee who didn't blow for anything, not a red card, not a penalty.

Bruno Bellone (France forward): When you saw Schumacher just walking around his own goalmouth, as if he had no worries in the world, it was disgusting!

Schumacher: The only thing I would change is what I did while Patrick was lying immobile on the pitch. Then I thought, "Uh oh, something bad has happened." I returned to the goal and played with the ball because I was afraid; because nobody came to talk to me, because all of the crowd were against me. And next to Battiston were Tigana, Amoros, all of their strongest guys, and if I go close to there and something's said, then a fight breaks out. So I just thought, "Stay out of the way," and I messed around with the ball because I didn't know what to do. I'd already had to keep myself away from three potential arguments with [Didier]

Six, Amoros and Rocheteau. I was a coward not to go to Battiston, I should have gone to lend a hand while he was lying down there.

Charles Corver (referee): It was absolutely impossible to see the collision, because I was watching the path of the ball that Battiston had hit just wide of the post. My linesman, Bob Valentine, was in exactly the same situation as me. I ran to him and said, "Did you see something that I didn't see?" He said it was not intentional and so I gave nothing.

Giresse: It was an injustice. We had to put up with the injustice, the drama of Patrick Battiston. And despite all that, we had to keep on playing the match. I spoke to Michel Hidalgo who had gone mad and was saying, "It's not possible. This is a scandal!" And I say, "Michel, Michel, we have to keep on playing." What I'm saying is cruel because they were taking a teammate off the pitch on a stretcher. We didn't know what was happening to him, if he was seriously injured or not. The match hadn't finished and we had to keep on playing.

Corver: I refereed in five important UEFA competition finals and this is the only decision people remember me for. I can now say it was a wrong decision, but it was hard for me to admit that in the beginning. After the game I was given a rating of 9.5 from the referee's observer for the game, Mr. Latychev [who refereed the 1962 World Cup final]. But it's true, Schumacher should have had a red card.

Platini shared a room with Battiston and held his hand as he was carried off the pitch. Substitute Philippe Mahut jumped off the bench and accompanied Battiston into the dressing room. Battiston had lost two teeth, cracked three ribs and damaged vertebrae but had regained consciousness. He was about to get married and Mahut phoned his fiancée to say he was all right—or at least he would be.

The game continued, and France came closest to winning it with a last-minute long-range shot from Manuel Amoros that thumped the crossbar. Two minutes into extra time, Marius Trésor volleyed

France ahead from ten yards out; the lead became 3–1 when Six squared the ball to Giresse, who struck from the edge of the area and it flew in off the post. His celebration, arms waving as he ran to the bench, was similar to Marco Tardelli's in the final—and might have been as iconic had West Germany not made two crucial substitutions, Horst Hrubesch and Rummenigge coming off the bench. Rummenigge needed only five minutes to reduce the deficit to 3–2, diving in to flick Littbarski's near-post cross beyond Ettori. Three minutes into the second period of extra time, Hrubesch headed a deep center back across goal and Fischer volleyed home from close range. It was 3–3, and the stage was set for the first ever World Cup penalty shoot-out.

Horst Hrubesch (West Germany forward): Before the shoot-out, I could see that we would win it, just by looking at their eyes. For us, it was an opportunity; for them, a challenge.

Schumacher: I had done my research before. My friends and family helped me by watching matches and taking notes. I kept all the information in a book: player name, club, right- or left-footed, does he shoot low or high. Coaches helped me, Stuttgart players told me how Six hit. The only problem was Platini, because he relied on his instinct. I sat down on the bench to prepare myself mentally. I just said to myself, forget the crowd is even there. When I opened my eyes, Jupp Derwall was standing in front of me. In that moment he seemed like a boxing referee, and he just said, "Stay calm." I told him, "You look after the kickers, I will stop two shots anyway." I had great confidence in myself. I really enjoyed penalties because I always thought that when they arrive, you can become a hero.

Alain Giresse kicked first for France.

Giresse: The distance between the center circle and the penalty spot, it's miles. It is endless. I decided in the build-up that I would not look at Schumacher. And so I turn my back on him.

This is obviously related to what he did in the game. I don't want to look at him. My back is turned and I wait, I wait. And it's a long wait! The problem is you have to keep your concentration, you hope no grain of sand disturbs your concentration. Considering his behavior during the game, his manner, his look, his eyes . . . in his eyes there was a kind of dynamite that I did not want to see. He may make me unsettled. Nothing was bothering him; what he did physically to my mate, I did not want him to do psychologically to me. So I turned away.

Giresse scored. The next four penalties were also put away. So France were 3–2 ahead when Uli Stielike stepped up.

Uli Stielike (West Germany libero): When I had the ball in my hand I had the idea of putting it to the left hand of the keeper. And when I put the ball on the spot I took five or six steps back. I said to myself, "The goalkeeper has already got the idea and knows you are going to go to his left." And when I took my second step I changed my mind. I didn't take five or six steps but instead seven or eight smaller ones. When I missed it, I didn't just think I had missed out on the final but also wasted six or seven weeks of hard work being together as a squad. We had won and lost together and then it was my fault that six or seven weeks' work hadn't been for anything. And Toni picked me up and said, "Don't worry about it, I'm going to stop the next one."

Stielike's reaction was one of devastation: he fell to the ground as if he had been shot, and stayed there, on his knees with his head in his hands. He needed Schumacher to lift him out of the area. Could France make the advantage count?

Didier Six (France forward): Hidalgo came to see me. I was injured: I had a swollen calf. And he asked me to take the penalty and I said, "No, I won't shoot." He went round everyone and there was no one else who wanted to. He came back to me. And like the idiot that I am, there's no other word for it, I decided to play the hero and said, "'OK, make me number five." So when the German guy misses penalty number three, I don't move, I sit in the center circle. I just stay where I am. One of the referees comes up and says, "This one is yours." And I say, "No, no, I'm number five." And that's when I found out that Michel [Platini] had changed the order. Looking back, why did I not hit the ball harder? Why? It was not my style to stroke it in softly . . .

Marius Trésor (France defender): Six told Platoche [Platini], "I want to take the last penalty." But Platoche said no. And so he got up and walked to the spot, very angry, definitely not focused. He saw himself scoring the last kick and the headlines: "Six sends France to the final."

Michel Platini (France midfielder): I don't think Didier wanted to shoot last.

Six's penalty was weak, at an easy height just a step to Schumacher's right. Stielike didn't even see it. He was in tears, being consoled by Littbarski, who released his teammate and punched the air in delight after Six's miss. Littbarski scored next, to make it 3–3, and then it was Bossis for France.

Maxime Bossis (France defender): I'm in the middle of the pitch surrounded by teammates who don't really want to take one, especially Jean Tigana and Christian Lopez. They said, "Not me, not me." That's the memory that stays with me. I had to take responsibility and go. It's a little silly to say but maybe I would have felt a coward if I hadn't taken my responsibility at that moment. I had a moment of hesitation as I thought to myself, "Where shall I aim to put the damn ball? Shall I hit it hard, or soft?" I had to make up my mind before the whistle.

Schumacher: Bossis, he was not confident. He knew that I had already saved one and that his shot was the most important.

Bossis: When the ball left my foot, I knew Schumacher had gone the right way. And before the ball reached him, I knew he'd stop it. After, I crouched down for a few seconds saying, "It's over." And then I really thought the sky would fall on my head. You know players miss penalties all the time but you still feel guilty. It is a failure; even I know immediately that it was not a personal failure, but a collective one. I would rather we lost in extra time. I've never taken another penalty since then.

Hrubesch, the substitute nicknamed "Das Kopfball-Ungeheuer" (the Heading Beast), then showed considerable composure on the ground, slotting the ball to his nonnatural side to complete a dramatic win for West Germany.

Jean-François Larios (France midfielder): We forgave Bossis because he was a defender. Six was a striker and a striker, he has to score a penalty. But both guys have to live with the memory.

Six: Ah yes, I suffered because I'm pissed off with it, I was pissed off with it all my life. At a certain point, it gets too much. You are forty-five but people still see you as missing the penalty. The toughest to deal with. It's not evil, it's what happens when you try and live your life in your own industry, by that I mean football, and avoid any obstacles in your way. Because I missed a penalty, we can say this world is ungrateful, perhaps it's even wrong too. I struggled to get my coaching qualifications, I had difficulty finding a job, because they said, "That one is unstable." And all of that has come from this missed penalty kick.

Schumacher: I made three mistakes. I was a coward not to go to Battiston; I should have gone to lend a hand while he was lying down there. After the game, a French journalist told me Patrick had lost two teeth; I replied that to apologize I would pay for his crowns. There was no mockery or arrogance intended. But in hindsight, that was a silly reaction. In fact I was relieved, because I feared he could have been in a coma. And one more: not going to see Battiston at the hospital. We were under police escort with the team and were taken straight to the airport to go to Madrid.

Corver: It was claimed that after the game I was in the airport with the German players and we were drinking beer together. Not true! That's a joke—it's the last thing I would have done! I actually wanted France to win because of my relationship with the federation. They had recommended that I get the game, and after it, I got a nice gift from them. And from the Germans, nothing.

Corver had intended to retire after the World Cup, but he did not want to leave on a low point, so he refereed for one more season. He is proud that UEFA gave him some big games to officiate that season.

Corver: In my final year as a referee, UEFA gave me the European Cup semifinal between Juventus and Widzew Łódź and the UEFA Cup final between Benfica and Anderlecht. I don't think they would have done that if they considered me a bad referee.

Bossis: Many think this is a nightmare, an awful memory. Even though it ended in a very painful way, it's still, collectively and individually, a great, great memory.

Six: I quickly became old in the eyes of the French, while I still had a lot to give. What remained was this image of me as a loser, which made me miss Euro 84 and the 1986 World Cup. I only realized some years later that I was the scapegoat. I had so many things stopping me working in this industry, but I fought through them.

Platini: The legend of this game comes from the fact that we lost it. In losing it, we became a great team. It was the end, but also the beginning of something. In the history of French football, the two turning-points were Sevilla 82 and the 1998 World Cup final. Sevilla marked a generation of football fans, gave them a collective state of mind: it's why books and plays have been written about the game. No movie in the world could have provided as much conflicting emotion as Sevilla 82. It's certainly a beautiful moment in my career. It's the moment that makes you say afterward, "I'm glad I was there!" Even if you lose.

*

The game had finished at 11:41 p.m. local time, which goes some way to explaining why the Schumacher incident barely registered in the next day's analysis. "*Fabuleux!*" ran *L'Equipe*'s headline, praising the France team for its attacking verve and coach Hidalgo for fielding three playmakers in Giresse, Platini and Genghini. "*Si près du paradis*" ("So close to heaven") ran the inside headline: "It's hard, so hard to take, more than we can say. Germany will play in the final but France, we can say without bitterness or patriotism, deserved it more. This was a great day for French football."

One day later, the mood changed as the severity of Schumacher's challenge took top billing. "Red-handed!" was *L'Equipe*'s front page, with an image of Schumacher's hip making contact with Battiston's jaw. "A story of unpunished violence . . . Schumacher was a brute. It's a morality tale which we will tell our children." Hidalgo changed his tone from valiant loser to angry victim: "You say Corver is an international referee? I have my doubts, if he risks the safety of the players like that."

The hostility between the countries continued: *L'Equipe*'s switchboard was jammed with anti-German calls; cars with German number-plates parked in French campsites had their tires slashed and windows broken. To improve relations, Chancellor Helmut Schmidt sent an open letter of condolence to President François Mitterrand. "Our hearts go out to the French, who deserved to go through just as much as the Germans."

After Italy had beaten West Germany in the final—"Justice!" crowed *L'Equipe*—someone had the bright idea to send Schumacher on a diplomatic mission to France to say sorry in person. Schumacher traveled to Metz the day before Battiston's wedding and presented him with an FC Cologne pennant and an apology. But the trip was not a success. "Schumacher forgets himself," said German magazine *Kicker*. "It was a gesture of reconciliation with unpleasant consequences." The pair were photographed sitting next to each other at a hastily arranged press conference, looking in opposite directions. Schumacher, objecting to questions from the French press, cut the conference short. "This is something that concerns only Battiston and me," he said. "If I had known, I would have brought my own German journalists with me." The peace offering had turned ugly. "The bad guy just wanted to poke fun at the good guy," wrote *Le Figaro*.

One day after the failed reconciliation, Mitterrand considered asking Hidalgo to get his players to state publicly that they had no problem with Schumacher. Hidalgo had his response ready: "What, shall I ask them to take the Germans on holiday with them?" That gave *France Football* magazine an idea: it asked the France team where they would take Schumacher on holiday. Here are the answers:

Giresse: To visit the Padirac Cave.

Platini: To climb the Grandes Jorasses mountains.

Bossis: To scale the heights of the Vallée Blanche.

Rocheteau: To watch a sunset from the cliffs of Étretat.

Trésor: To do a parachute jump with a delayed opening.

Battiston: To help me pick mushrooms in the forest as I still can't bend down.

It does not take a mastermind of psychology to spot the common theme.

But, as Platini commented, that heroic failure inspired creativity. France's 1982 defeat spawned books, documentaries, plays and music, all created by a generation for whom the game was a defining moment. In 2006, scenic-representation artist Massimo Furlan pretended to be Platini in his performance *Number 10*, in which he mimed the France midfielder's pass to Battiston, reaction to his injury, and his penalty kick, in an empty stadium save for one observer: Hidalgo, watching from the sideline. Red, a French musician, played a concert he called *Sevilla 82* against a visual backdrop of the game. *France-Allemagne* was a play examining the relationship between the two countries, set in a Frenchman's living-room as he entertains a German guest with the game on in the background. French choreographer Pierre Rigal, who was nine in 1982, produced a dance piece,

Injury Time, which he took to Potsdam in Germany. "I remember it as a great injustice and frustration, an event that went beyond sport," he said, "and my piece was a way of looking at how we treat childhood memories."

The memory of what happened to Six also never left Bruno Bellone, who was a substitute watching from the bench in Seville in 1982. Four years later, the winger, then at Monaco, was in the France side (crowned European champions in 1984) that drew 1–1 with Brazil in the 1986 World Cup quarterfinal in Guadalajara. Bellone knew that four kickers were certain—Yannick Stopyra, Luis Fernandez, Manuel Amoros and Michel Platini—but the fifth was unknown. He watched as coach Henri Michel went round the players, and kept his head down. "I'm far away, I'm quiet, he's not going to come to me," Bellone remembered thinking. "Then I see him coming and think, 'This can't be possible!' The coach, he said, 'Listen, you have no choice, you need to take one.'" Bellone wanted to say no but he couldn't bring himself to do it. Without thinking, he said OK.

Bellone's mind turned to his parents watching on television, the fans at home, and then his teammates who were spread out among the Brazil players in the center circle. "I thought to myself, 'What the hell am I doing here?'" He remembered the fates of Bossis and Six after their missed penalties. "That one kick, it can kill a career. It feels like there are snipers in the crowd with guns trained on you, ready to shoot if you miss. I said to myself, 'If I miss, they will lynch me. Fine, I will come back to France in a canoe!'"

Socrates kicked first for Brazil, and off a short, insouciant run-up had his high shot punched away by Joel Bats. Then four goals—by Stopyra, Alemão, Amoros and Zico—made it 2–2 and Bellone made his way to the spot. "When I put the ball down, the goalkeeper stepped off his line and spat in my direction." Bellone respotted the ball, and then made the mistake of changing his mind about where he wanted to kick the ball. "I was full of hate toward the goalkeeper, so then I wanted to hit the ball as hard as

I can, at his head, so the ball and the goalkeeper ended up in the goal. I was angry!"

Bellone hit the ball hard—so hard that on his follow-through both his feet were in the air. The ball struck the foot of the post. It bounced against the back of Brazil goalkeeper Carlos's head and went into the goal. "The ball did hit his head and go in, so I wasn't far from what I wanted to do," joked Bellone.

Bellone was lucky, and he knew it. When he returned to the center circle he barely cared about the result. "It was over for me and I would not have nightmares about this moment. You need luck in life. Luck is between 40 percent and 60 percent of football anyway. But I was rewarded for not saying no when I was asked."

Platini missed France's next kick, hitting his shot high and wide. Brazil's Julio César hit the post, smashing it Bellone-style, but without the lucky rebound. Then, to win the game, Fernandez scored. In the dressing room, Bellone began to realize the impact of his good fortune. Platini embraced him and thanked him for scoring: "You saved me, I was dead!"

"If I had missed, I would have been in bad shape," said Bellone. "It's indelible, you can't take it back. I could not have lived with that burden for the rest of my life." Even now, people talk to Bellone all the time about his penalty. "It's unbelievable: I know Didier Six had a nightmare, and it's still ongoing, as a result of Sevilla 82. He was bothered by it all the time. All the time."

Twenty-seven years after the Seville game, totally out of the blue, Patrick Battiston received a package from his old teammate Platini. It was his full uniform from the game—blue shirt, white shorts with the distinctive circled number three, and red socks—which had been left in the dressing room, kept in a Seville museum, and then presented to Platini on one of his UEFA presidential trips. Battiston was emotional when he opened it; the uniform now hangs in his son's bedroom. Schumacher also gave Battiston his goalkeeping jersey before a friendly between the two sides in Strasbourg in April 1984. Battiston has no idea where it is now, or even if he still has it.

CHAPTER 4

ALL THE WORLD'S A STAGE

The eyes. It's all in the eyes. As the men walk backward to their marks, always looking at each other, you can tell so much by their eyes. The camera closes in. They look nervous. Focused. It will be all over within seconds. Sweat dripping from their foreheads. Tension rising. They adjust their uniforms, make sure they're comfortable. Never take their eyes off their opponent. The camera pans out; the wide-view is majestic, beautiful. Silence. So much at stake. Deep breath. Camera pans in again. Back to the eyes. Those eyes. Fear, or confidence? This is the shoot-out as the denouement. Look at the eyes. And then: BANG!

This is not a description of another England defeat on penalties. It's actually the end of *The Good, the Bad and the Ugly*—the same as *A Fistful of Dollars* and *Once Upon a Time in the West*. All are spaghetti westerns directed by an Italian, Sergio Leone, where the key part of the narrative is the shoot-out as denouement. Two hours of back-and-forth tension is ended. It's the battle between good (your team) and evil (the opponents). Death or glory. No middle ground. The drama even has the same name:

the shoot-out. You don't nearly survive a shoot-out, just as you can't narrowly lose at penalties.

In the mid-1960s, Leone took the traditional Hollywood western and gave it a twist. He shaped his hero into a more morally ambiguous figure, an antihero with little going for him but his rebellious style and gunslinging ability. Clint Eastwood was his leading man, and he personified this new cool, standing in contrast to director John Ford's wholesome, all-American family man as often portrayed by John Wayne.

The spaghetti westerns, so-called because Italian studios made the films (even if some were shot at the Tabernas Desert in Almeria, south-east Spain), built up the tension of the shoot-out to an almost ludicrous degree. Leone would use Ennio Morricone's haunting musical scores, close-ups of his actors' eyes and shots of their fingers twitching next to holsters to delay the inevitable violence. In the last scene of *The Good, the Bad and the Ugly*, the main protagonists, Blondie, Angel Eyes and Tuco Ramirez, wait in position for over four minutes before the shoot-out begins.

Aside from the terminology and how film and television directors presented the build-up to the moment of reckoning, I wondered if there was anything else linking the narrative drama in the two different shoot-outs, cinematic and sporting. There's the landscape that never changes—the pitch for penalties, bleak land for westerns; the glare of the sun set against the glare of the floodlights; the lack of dialogue. Both western heroes and soccer players let their actions speak louder than words. "There's something in the visual language of the western that carries into many areas of popular culture and the perception of narrative that we see," explained Dr. Austin Fisher, author of *Radical Frontiers in the Spaghetti Western*. "These character archetypes carry over into the narrative that we try to attach to our daily lives."

This happens in soccer, where the media presents a narrative around each player, and, regardless of the reality, it sticks—take the recent example of Luis Suárez as an antihero. Similarly, Leone and Ford set up character types and situations for their leading men—witness the rivalry between Eastwood, with his swagger, playing to a different set of rules, and Wayne, who was forced to express disdain for the amorality he was portraying. "Eastwood would shoot people in the back. I would never do that," he once said. In soccer parlance, Eastwood may be like Suárez, and Wayne, the boy next door representing the virtues of American society, Gary Lineker. Film-goers wanted to believe that the romanticized movie version of "the West" was actually similar to historical reality. As newspaper reporter Maxwell Scott tells US Senator Ransom Stoddard in *The Man Who Shot Liberty Valance*, after learning that Stoddard had not shot the eponymous outlaw, "This is the West, sir. When the legend becomes fact, print the legend."

In the case of Brazilian goalkeeper Marcos, the legend became fact. Marcos saved a penalty in his first start for Palmeiras, in May 1996 from Botafogo's Paulo César, but it was a full three years into his Palmeiras career that one save earned him a reputation as a penalty specialist, an appearance for the national team (and an eventual World Cup winner's medal) and a new nickname.*

Palmeiras had drawn the 1999 Copa Libertadores quarterfinal against Corinthians 2–2 on aggregate. Palmeiras took an early lead in the shoot-out when Dinei hit the post for Corinthians. Already 2–1 up, Marcos then stopped Vampeta's penalty. After the save, he fell to his knees and crossed himself. Palmeiras won 4–2, their fans christened Marcos as São Marcos (Saint Marcos), and later that year he won his first cap for Brazil. "I owe it all to Vampeta," he later said.†

The following season, Marcos again faced Corinthians in the

---

*That 1996 Palmeiras team in which Marcos made his debut contained four other players who would help Brazil win the 2002 World Cup: Cafu, Junior, Rivaldo and Luizão (as well as internationals Djalminha, Flávio Conceição and Muller).

†Vampeta and Marcos became close friends, and the story goes that when Marcos thought about retiring after making an error in the FIFA Club World Cup against Manchester United, it was Vampeta who talked him out of it.

Copa Libertadores, this time in the semifinal, and again it was penalties. The tie had finished 6–6 on aggregate and Marcos was convinced the Corinthians penalty takers knew that he knew where to dive; so he decided to go the opposite way. Ricardinho, Fabio Luciano and Edu all scored, aiming just where Marcos's goalkeeper coach Carlos Pracidelli had told him to go. "Tell that motherfucker to start diving the right way otherwise I will kill him," Pracidelli told the team's masseur, Biro. Palmeiras were 5–4 up when Marcelinho Carioca, Corinthians' star player, stepped up. Marcelinho, known as Pédeanjo (Angel-Foot), rarely missed, and his preference was to kick to the goalkeeper's left. He kicked right, and Marcos, still choosing "the other way," this time saved it. He had won the game again for Palmeiras (though they lost the final to Boca Juniors).

São Marcos was the penalty king, and so it continued: in 2001, Palmeiras beat São Caetano in the Libertadores Round of 16, after penalties; Palmeiras then beat Cruzeiro in the quarterfinal, with Marcos stopping three of the seven penalties he faced. Cruzeiro's players seemed affected by Marcos's reputation. Before the seventh (and final) kick of the shoot-out, Cruzeiro forward Oséas could be seen wagging his index finger as if saying, "No, I will not take one." Marcos Paulo was virtually pushed by his teammates into taking the penalty. He missed the target. "It's good to know that I have respect from penalty takers," Marcos wrote in his autobiography *São Marcos de Palestra Itália*. "I'm big, so perhaps the goal looks smaller to them. My reputation as a penalty saver probably helps. But I want to stop this reference to me being a saint, a hero, that kind of stuff. Because it obliges me to make Palmeiras win all our penalty shoot-outs, and that's not possible."

He stopped another three—"making three miracles," as they say in Brazil—in the 2009 Copa Libertadores Round of 16 against Sport Recife; and three more in 2010, in the Brazilian Cup against Atlético Goianense (though that wasn't enough, as Palmeiras missed four in that shoot-out).

Marcos never claimed to be a penalty expert; it's just as possible that the myth surrounding his heroics against Corinthians grew and forced takers to adjust their tactics and aim for the furthest corners in order to succeed. "I am not a saint," wrote Marcos. "I am tired of this penalty save. It seems that's all I did in my career, but a whole career is much more than a lucky stop or a mistake. I don't want my football life to be reduced to one penalty against Corinthians."

It was not quite as bad as he made out: Marcos was Brazil's starting goalkeeper throughout the victorious 2002 World Cup, and with Palmeiras he won two Brazilian leagues, one Brazilian Cup, four state championships, and the 1999 Copa Libertadores. He ended his career second on the appearance list for Palmeiras goalkeepers with 532 (behind Emerson Leão on 617) and is credited with the most penalty stops for one Brazilian club: forty-five, of which thirty-three were saves. It started out that Marcos's penalty legend became fact, but by the end of his career the fact was self-fulfilling. It became legend.

In the classical western genre, the hero's virtue is most often shown by his restraint. *Shane*, a 1953 film, tells the story of a stranger who tries to save a farming community in Wyoming from a ruthless cattle baron. Despite serious provocation, he does not resort to violence until the final scene. He tries to find other ways to succeed, but cannot.

As I watched the film, I couldn't stop thinking about Andrea Pirlo at Euro 2012 (this was before Pirlo grew the beard that could have earned him a lead in a Leone film). In that quarterfinal against England, he poked and prodded, he passed and shot, but could not find a way past Joe Hart in open play. In the shoot-out, though, he was like Shane: decisive and heroic. He found the way to win and did so in the true style of a spaghetti western gunslinger.*

---

*The obvious difference between the two scenarios is that in westerns, the "bad" guys rarely win. Sergio Corbucci's *The Great Silence* (1968) is an almost unique example of such an ending, as the bounty-hunters win the shoot-out. It's a bleak and nihilistic conclusion (Corbucci had to reshoot it for the Asian market), which in soccer happens all too often.

The drama of the shoot-out was perceived to be essential for modern American sporting audiences when soccer started to establish itself across the Atlantic. In fact, in some ways the North American Soccer League (NASL) was ahead of its time. The two men who set it up in 1968 were both British: Phil Woosnam, a former winger for West Ham, Aston Villa and Wales, and Clive Toye, an ex-reporter for the *Daily Express*. To sell the game, they came up with several ideas to try to make it more exciting, including a clock that counted down as opposed to up; a thirty-five-yard line rather than a halfway line, for offside; players' names on shirts; three substitutes in a game; a points-scoring system similar to fantasy soccer (two for a goal, one for an assist) to value players' offensive contributions; and, in 1974, a penalty shoot-out to decide league matches that ended in a draw.

"There were so few of us that when things like that were discussed, I'm not even sure we had an NASL board, we basically just did things," Toye, now in his eighties, told me from his New York home. He remembers rejecting the suggestion to have wider goals or thicker posts so there was more chance of the ball coming back into play. "We said no and no to those."

By the time Woosnam adapted the shoot-out in 1977, Toye had become general manager of the New York Cosmos, for whom he'd persuaded Pelé to come and play in 1975.* The new shoot-out rule was that each player could start anywhere he wanted along the thirty-five-yard line and had five seconds in which to score. No rebounds were allowed, so if the goalkeeper kept out the first attempt, that was it. Watching clips from the period, it was a surprise there were so few injuries: as soon as the whistle went,

---

*Much of the glamour surrounding the Cosmos was down to Toye. He said that in 1971, when tasked with naming the New York club, he was so committed to calling it the Cosmos that he rigged a competition inviting fans to name the club, promising a trip for two to Switzerland for the winners. Other entries included New York Lovers, New York Blues and Gotham Soccer Club. Toye even designed the Cosmos uniform to reflect Brazil's yellow, green and blue colors. He went on to be general manager of Chicago Sting and Minnesota Blizzard and was commissioner of the NASL.

the player usually kicked the ball straight ahead of him, and the goalkeeper rushed out to block. A collision was inevitable. The scoring rate was low, with two goals out of five usually enough to win.

In 1981, FIFA told the NASL to ditch the thirty-five-yard line and the extra substitution, or it would expel the US soccer federation. The NASL capitulated, but two weeks later received a letter from FIFA president João Havelange claiming it could keep the rules for one more season. That was the season the Soccer Bowl—the final played between the teams with the two best league records—went to a penalty shoot-out for the first time.

Chicago Sting played New York Cosmos on a Saturday night in Toronto. Because the TV contract had only specified Sunday kick-offs, it wasn't broadcast live; fans tuning in to ABC TV had to watch *The Love Boat* instead. The league games between the teams had ended drawn, and the Sting had won both shoot-outs. In fact, the Sting had won three out of three shoot-outs during the season, while the Cosmos had won one out of four.

The Soccer Bowl finished goalless, and once again goalkeepers had the upper hand in the shoot-out. The first five efforts were all missed—Sting missing their first three—then Vladislav Bogicevic scored for Cosmos. Up next was Karl-Heinz Granzita, Sting's top scorer that season in terms of both goals (seventeen) and offensive points (fifty-five). He shot early and low past Hubert Birkenmeier to level the scores. Ivan Buljan then had his chip saved, so after four kicks each it was 1–1.

Rudy Glenn stepped up. A few weeks earlier he had beaten Birkenmeier with a shot to his right. "The key is being precise and handling the situation," Glenn remembered. "I changed things a bit from before. In Chicago I went one way, and in the championship game I went the opposite way." It worked—Glenn scored, and Bob Iarusci now needed to hit the net to keep Cosmos alive. He didn't. The title went to Chicago.

The game marked the beginning of the end for the NASL. One day later, three teams—Atlanta Chiefs, California Surf and

Washington Diplomats—announced they were folding, and Dallas Tornado merged with the Tampa Bay Rowdies. By the end of the year, Minnesota Kicks had also folded. Woosnam was voted out as league commissioner the following season, and in 1983 the NASL folded.

Two years after hosting the 1994 World Cup, a tournament that Woosnam helped bring to the USA, Major League Soccer started up a new league and amazingly decided to keep the thirty-five-yard shoot-out in case of drawn games. "I don't think it hurts us to have something this controversial," said new commissioner Doug Logan. But when Don Garber replaced him in 1999, the first thing he did was get rid of the shoot-outs, bringing the MLS in line with other leagues. "You can see why he did it," said Toye. "But we felt it was an exciting way to end these games."

The simple word "drama," so common in soccer reportage, itself transports us back to the stage, to when actors were called "players" and the entertainment was introduced by a supposedly neutral chorus/narrator (the referee). We talk about a player "losing the plot," "reading his opponent," "showing character"—all these expressions have literary and dramaturgical undertones.

"In a way, a penalty shoot-out is like the epilogue of a Shakespearean play," Dr. Adam Smyth, Tutorial Fellow in English at Balliol College, Oxford, told me. "It continues the themes of the drama and gives meaning to what has gone before: but it also exists uniquely outside of it." Such epilogues break down "the fourth wall," as when Rosalind remains in character at the end of *As You Like It* but lays bare the theatrical nature of the production by directly addressing the audience. "It's an add-on to the main play, so what survives is the imposed truth, sometimes a false truth, of the shoot-out," added Smyth.

The idea of a "false truth" is fascinating. We often remember more about the shoot-out than the game itself, and certainly more about the villains of the piece than who may have deserved to win the game. We remember Southgate, not Shearer. It's the single moment that comes to represent the whole match, which also happens in drama—that moment on which the action hinges. Never mind that Italy actually were second-best after a brilliant Holland performance in 2000, that Red Star Belgrade were wretched against Marseille in the 1991 European Cup final, or that Argentina kicked Italy off the pitch in the 1990 World Cup semifinal; all of them won on penalties, so it didn't matter.

Take another Shakespearean example: *Othello*, Act III Scene iv, when Othello asks Desdemona for the white handkerchief he gave her, a charmed gift from his mother that represents his heritage and her chastity; when she cannot provide it, his suspicions are confirmed. The handkerchief is the most important symbol in the play; that scene is the shoot-out we remember regardless of the action around it.

The role of the referee fits into this idea of stage-drama. He leads out the players (our actors) before the match and is seen, at least before the game, existing outside the main action as the conveyor of truth. Before too long his position becomes ambiguous. Is he favoring one team over another? Does he want to stay outside the game or be sucked in and become a player himself? "The referee can become compromised as the action unfolds," Smyth noted. Shakespeare's narrators often proved unreliable, or at least partisan. That was the case with the chorus in *Henry V*. Very early in the play it reveals itself as pro-Henry, pro-England and anti-France, but "the idea that he is an objective outsider soon dissipates, and he begins to shape the action himself."

No penalty exists without a past. Even a player who has never taken or faced one before has a history, and will have forged alliances and hostilities with players on his or the opposing team. No game is as simple as Team A taking on Team B, and when there is a penalty, those allegiances, or otherwise, come into sharper focus. It becomes a moment of intimacy, as described by Joe Hart before Mario Balotelli's opening kick in the Euro 2012 quarterfinal: "Amid all the craziness at the height of the game, when that moment came, we disappeared into our own little world." Throughout the previous season, Balotelli, then a team-mate of Hart's at Manchester City, took ten penalties at the end of every training session and would laugh about the prospect of a penalty shoot-out between their two sides. "When it came around, we were having fun but we respected the situation."

This is when soccer becomes a true soap opera. The twenty-two characters all have different back-stories, and their individual relationships are put under strain. That's what happened when Greek champions Olympiakos took on Panathinaikos in January 2008. Panathinaikos striker Dimitris Papadopoulos had only been on the pitch for four minutes when, with the score at 1–1, Olympiakos's Paraskevas Antzas handballed in the area. Papadopoulos picked up the ball to take the penalty, and imme-diately the subplots kicked into action.

Papadopoulos was in the middle of a difficult season. He had scored seventeen goals in his first season at the club, 2003/04, and in summer 2006 a contract row ended with the player win-ning a hefty pay raise. As his wages and expectations grew, he struggled to deliver; when he stood over that penalty kick he had scored only once in fourteen league matches.

His opponent in the Olympiakos goal was Antonis Nikopolidis, a former Panathinaikos player and Papadopoulos's best friend. In fact, Nikopolidis was godfather to the striker's son Achilles. Nikopolidis saved the penalty, and Panathinaikos fans immedi-ately accused the pair of collusion.

Three days later, Olympiakos beat Panathinaikos 4–0 in a Cup tie. Papadopoulos was on the bench, and every time he warmed up he received dog's abuse from the fans. He accused coach José Peseiro of making him a scapegoat and as a result was fined €15,000 and forced to train on his own for a fortnight. He did force his way back into the side—he made nine starts and scored two penalties—but the damage was irretrievable. Later that year, with Panathinaikos refusing to let him join another Greek club for nothing, he moved to Lecce.

Papadopoulos always insisted that the penalty miss was an honest one—"even if my brother was in goal, I would always try and score"—but that one kick came to define his career. As if that wasn't bad enough, Nikopolidis knew as soon as he made the save that he was landing his friend in deep trouble. "When I made the save, I was happy and worried at the same time," he said. "I was sad because I could see what would happen afterward, how he would be treated until he left the club. It was so unfair."

The all-or-nothing, win-or-bust drama of the penalty does heap inordinately unfair consequences on the protagonists. Take Miroslav Djukic, who had a last-minute penalty to win a first ever league title for Deportivo La Coruña in May 1994. Their normal penalty taker was Bebeto, but he had missed two in the last month, including the previous week against Logroñes, so coach Arsenio Iglesias had nominated Donato as the new first choice. But Donato had been subbed off ten minutes earlier, which left Djukic with the responsibility.

Djukic was up against a Valencia goalkeeper, José Luis González, playing only his third game of the season. A week earlier, the Basque-born twenty-nine-year-old had saved a penalty with his first touch, stopping a Real Valladolid spot kick after José Manuel Sempere had been sent off. Valencia were at the end of a weird season. Coach Guus Hiddink had been fired after a UEFA Cup tie ended in a 7–0 loss to Karlsruhe. Two other coaches had been appointed since, but a change of president, Paco Roig replacing Arturo Tuzon, culminated in Hiddink's return.

"It would be horrible to row so far only to die on the shore," Depor midfielder Fran had said before the game. The Spanish TV commentator added, "A whole season depends on the taking of this kick from twelve yards, with the responsibility on Miroslav Djukic." Over in Barcelona, Johan Cruyff turned to his neighbors on the Camp Nou bench and said, "Relax, he's going to miss it." Barcelona had already chased down a six-point gap on Depor, and minutes earlier beaten Sevilla 5–2 to go two points clear at the top.

"You can't imagine a moment of more tension," remembered

Julio Llamazares, the Spanish novelist and poet who was watching the game in Oviedo, where he was promoting his new book, *Escenas del cine mundo* (Scenes from a silent film), at the literary city's Book Fair. "Two men facing each other, alone, face-to-face, just like an old-fashioned duel."

Llamazares could not tear his eyes away from the television. He watched as Djukic walked from his central defensive position to the Valencia penalty area.

Llamazares would imagine what was in Djukic's mind in his short story *El Penalti de Djukic*, which was published a year later. How his wife Ceca called him before the game and warned him not to take one; how pundits warned that Depor lacked a champion's mentality and would bottle it; how, when the penalty was given, his teammates put their hands to their heads in disbelief, or, in the case of goalkeeper Liano, crossed themselves. "In his sporting life, he had come through difficult times," wrote Llamazares. "He remembered making his debut for [FK] Rad Belgrade, winning promotion to La Liga but seeing a fire in the stands, and there were the other things life had thrown at him. The day he decided to devote himself to football against the will of his father, who practically disowned him; his marriage to Ceca and the birth of their two children; the death of his brother Miloslav in a car accident."

Djukic had been lucky at crucial moments in his career, not least when he played as a libero for the first time in his career against Zeljeznikar a few years earlier. It so happened that Juan Ballesta, Iglesias's assistant coach, was in Belgrade to see Partizan play Red Star. He was bored and had a few hours to kill, so watched FK Rad, another of the city's clubs, and saw Djukic play the game of his life. Djukic was holding out for a move to Paris Saint-Germain or Standard Liège but when Depor's offer came through, he accepted.

"He picked up the ball and pressed it in his hands," Llamazares continued. "He always did that, just to make sure there was enough air. Although the air had gone out of him. He felt as if his chest were closing in . . . He could not even hear the roar of the crowd, which had gradually silenced as the decisive moment approached. Djukic heard only the beating of his heart and his ragged breathing. Taking a deep breath for air, he felt the pressure on his diaphragm. He could not feel his lungs; it was as if he was locked out. Djukic tried again. He put the ball on the penalty spot, and stepped back. In front of him, the referee warned the Valencia goalkeeper and he imagined that he would be as nervous as him at that moment. It was not quite enough to reassure him, but at least it made him begin to think about the penalty. Until then, a lot of things had gone through his mind, but not how he would kick the ball."

"The TV pictures made a big impact on me when I watching them," Llamazares explained. "There was a league title on the line with this penalty, so it had a special and unique drama to it. The fact that someone would win and someone would lose—this is what a penalty is all about. It's always a tragedy for someone."

The tragedy, in this case, belonged to Djukic. He barely looked at the ball as he struck, or rather scuffed, it, and González was not even at full stretch when the ball lodged in his midriff. Djukic fell to the turf—"like a fallen boxer," wrote Llamazares. Iglesias pulled at his hair and looked to the heavens.

"The tension and fear got to him," wrote *El País* after the game. "Weather-beaten men sank to their knees and raised their hands in supplication. Utopia was just a few meters away, dependent on the toe of a boot. The silence that fell was from centuries of waiting. All the memory of a people concentrated on the flight of a leather ball. And it did not go in. The accursed fate had once again crossed with theirs. And the rockets which exploded in the Coruñesa night sounded like shots of rage against heaven."

Djukic walked off the pitch in a daze and was so upset in the dressing room, where he lay on the floor crying, that a teammate had to call his wife Ceca to help persuade him to get up. "There were a lot of tears, but I had great support from the people of La Coruña who helped me get over it," Djukic later recalled.

The story took another twist when it was alleged that the Valencia team had been offered a *malétina*—a "little suitcase," also known as a third-party payment *primas a terceros*—from Barcelona to win the game. A bonus of fifty million pesetas (€300,000) had been agreed one week before the game; one player anonymously told *El País* that a Valencia player met a Barcelona player in a motorway service station to hand over the money, which came to three million pesetas (€18,000) each. Lubo Penev, the center forward who missed the game as he was recovering from testicular cancer, thought Barcelona had under-paid. "Three million? A league is worth at least ten!"

Fernando Giner, then the Valencia center back and a future vice president at the club, called the payment "bitter money." He had wanted Deportivo to win as they had two ex-Valencia players in the side, Ribera Voro and Nando, and called Bebeto a coward for not taking the penalty. He remembered walking off the pitch and seeing hundreds of fans crying in the stands; others tried to attack the Valencia team bus as it left the stadium. The next time they played, the Valencia team was showered with fake 10,000-peseta notes.

The psychological scars of Depor's loss ran deep; even beating Valencia in the Copa del Rey final the following season did little to ease the pain. Only their first title win, which came in 2000, brought closure. "I'm happy for them. Now I can rest easy," said Djukic, who by then was, ironically, playing for Valencia.

Djukic spoke about the penalty eighteen years later when a guest on Spanish TV show *Punto Pelota*. He was asked if some of his teammates, more used to taking penalties, had hidden on the day.

"No," he replied. "Everyone thinks that about Bebeto, but Bebeto did not hide. I was the second penalty taker at the club. Donato was the first, but Arsenio had taken him off ten minutes before. Bebeto had missed a penalty and was not taking them. So I was the second penalty taker at that moment."

"How many times have you watched the penalty?"

"Many times, but at the start, no."

"Do you get tired of it?"

"It forms part of my past. I have it in some corner of my memory, but I do not keep harping on about it."

As they watched Djukic line up to take the penalty again in the studio, he provided his own commentary: "At this moment I take a deep breath to be relaxed and I am thinking about hitting it, waiting for the keeper. I always waited for the keeper to move and right then I was thinking, 'Well, I cannot wait anymore, I will have to hit it hard,' and I got to the ball without knowing clearly how I was going to hit it. And the worst is to have those doubts. Always, when I hit a penalty, you need to relax and to hit it.

"I was very sad, of course. You miss a penalty in the ninetieth minute and the dreams of so many people . . . and you are aware of all of that—a historic opportunity. It would have been the first trophy for us to win, it was a dream to win the title, and we were very close, but we did not manage it. The truth is it was the saddest moment of my sporting life. It was a very tough moment for me."

"But only the brave ones miss."

"Cristiano, Messi, me . . ." said Djukic, and he laughed.

The Djukic story has a German parallel, a penalty drama that took place during the penultimate round of the 1985/86 Bundesliga season. Werder Bremen were two points clear of Bayern Munich and needed to beat them to secure the title (it was in the days of two points for a win). The game was goalless after 89 minutes when Bremen's Rudi Völler burst toward the area and struck the ball against Soren Lerby. It cannoned off his chest but referee Volker Roth saw a handball and pointed to the spot. Völler said after the game he did not think it was a penalty.

Bayern were furious and assistant coach Egon Cordes kicked the ball away in anger. Seven Bayern players surrounded the referee, and the minutes ticked by before Michael Kutzop, an experienced defender and Bremen's regular penalty taker, was able to take the kick. "Apparently it took fifteen minutes until the penalty was ready to be taken [actually it was more like three]; to me it seemed almost an eternity," Kutzop said. He skipped up to the ball and left goalkeeper Jean-Marie Pfaff rooted to the spot. The effort went to his right, high, and struck the post. "Perhaps I had too much time to think," Kutzop reflected. "I did almost everything right, but not quite everything. I can't remember what happened after the ball hit the post. It felt like I blacked out." Kutzop looked stunned. He rubbed his face in disbelief and, at the urging of teammate Bruno Pezzey, moved into midfield. "I was running around aimlessly and in midfield I could do less damage."

Bremen could still have won the title on the final day of the season, but they lost 2–1 to Stuttgart and Bayern Munich beat Borussia Mönchengladbach 6–0 to triumph on goal difference. Kutzop continued to take penalties, successfully, for Bremen the following season. "I didn't get any insults thrown my way, from the fans, teammates or the coaches." But he did get phone calls, lots of them, from grateful Bayern fans, which forced him to change his number.

Two years later, Bremen won the Bundesliga, but by then Völler was at Roma. "I often him hear say 'I've won everything in football except the Bundesliga title, and all thanks to you,' although it's in jest when he's drunk a few beers," Kutzop said. "A lot of people say that if I hadn't missed it, nobody would have heard of me. I've no idea if that's true. But the fact is that even today I can still hear the ball striking the post."

You can see why Djukic's missed penalty caught the imagination of Llamazares. "Any missed penalty, and converted ones too, must stay with a player for a long time," the novelist told me. "They must replay them in their head over and over again—especially if they were big moments for the team. But the penalty suits the narrative form in culture because of the tension." And why do we spend more time focusing on those who miss penalties? "Easy: because losing is more romantic than winning."*

The old-fashioned ritual of the duel was about the preservation of honor, which, for a man, was the most important part of his identity. Its purpose was not so much to wound or kill but to demonstrate a willingness to be hurt (or killed) in defense of your reputation. This issue of honor was what compelled Hector to fight Achilles in Homer's *Iliad*, Sir Lancelot to fight King Arthur, and Robin Hood to take on Little John. In all those cases a respect grew between the combatants, which developed in the latter two cases into friendship. That sense of sporting idealism survives in soccer: mortal enemies one minute, embracing brothers-in-arms the next.†

---

*The idea of embracing defeat was taken one step further by Chile striker Mauricio Pinilla, who was an inch away from eliminating Brazil from the 2014 World Cup in the Round of 16 (and would have saved the hosts from the trauma to come, in the 7–1 semifinal loss to Germany). With less than one minute of extra time to play, the score 1–1, Pinilla's dipping volley beat goalkeeper Julio Cesar but cannoned back off the crossbar. The game went to penalties and Pinilla, shooting first for Chile, had his effort saved. Brazil won the shoot-out 3–2, but the story does not end there. Around thirty-six hours after that shot, Pinilla headed to his friend Marlon Parra's tattoo parlor back in Santiago. It was a Monday morning, and Pinilla was the first customer. "He was there before we even opened," said Parra, "and he was euphoric, very emotional. He had slept very little since the game, less than three hours per night, just going over the events of what had happened." Pinilla was clutching a newspaper cutting of his volley smashing the woodwork, and he wanted Parra to burn the image on his back. "It was an indelible memory for him, and he was both frustrated and proud about it." The missed volley did not only upset Pinilla; it traumatized the whole nation. That's why, on the day of the World Cup final, a young psychologist called Fabian Vallejos organized a public replay of the Brazil-Chile match with a doctored tape, in which Pinilla's shot crept in *under* the crossbar. Thousands of Chile fans watched the video on a loop and celebrated the "goal." Pinilla did not attend this group therapy session; instead, he embraced his new-found, nearly man status. Just below his new tattoo he had requested that Parra add the words: "One centimeter from glory."

†Believe it or not, soccer players have a code of honor too, and stepping forward to take a penalty for your team is its perfect manifestation. "You will never hear me criticize a player for taking a bad penalty in a shoot-out," Alan Shearer said, "because he had the balls to stand up and take one in the first place."

The duel, like the penalty, has attached to it a strict list of conventions that must be adhered to. The duelists take ten paces to reach their marks; goalkeeper and penalty taker retreat to their marks. They wait. No one starts moving too early. The uniform, too, is part of the code. The goalkeeper wears a uniform different from his teammates. This is his marker, the outfit that defines him as the keeper of the castle, the last line of defense. The idea of soccer as a battle is nothing new; the uniforms only enhance it. "In the era of the Normans and the Saxons, and even before then in Roman times, armies were made of people pulled off the street," Tim Angel told me. "People were illiterate and could only recognize each other by colors or symbols on their uniforms."

Angel is chairman of Angels Costumes, which dresses the entertainment industry and has the largest collection of costumes in the world housed in a breathtakingly huge warehouse space near Hendon in North London—eight miles of clothing rails, all with astonishing outfits on them. Angels have won thirty-four Academy Awards for "Best Achievement in Costume Design" and in 2008 supplied costumes to all five films nominated for the Best Picture Oscar (*Across the Universe*, *Atonement*, *La Vie en Rose*, *Sweeney Todd* and the eventual winner *Elizabeth: The Golden Age*). More recently, Angels have dressed the cast of *Downton Abbey*, *Boardwalk Empire*, *Call the Midwife*, *The Borgias* and *Wolf Hall*.

"From the 1910s onward, goalkeepers always wore a different color jersey from the rest of the team," Angel said. "That was so referees could see who was handling the ball, but it was also a marker to his own teammates as well. In the heat of the battle, you need to identify who is on your side and who has your back."

As we walked past rail upon rail of military uniforms, Angel pointed out the similarities to soccer uniforms: the chevrons on a sergeant's uniform to denote authority, like a captain's armband; armor, the equivalent of shin pads; medieval tabards—cloth vests with a symbol on them (like a red rose, or a St. George's cross) worn over armor—uncannily like a substitute's bib; insignia to denote regiments, similar to the "Premier League" or

"Champions League" badges worn on the arms of uniforms today; even rosettes, hats and scarves, adopted by peasants when joining the army, just like fans supporting their team.

"Look at any dug-out in a game and you can recognize the structure very easily," Angel, an Arsenal fan, continued. "The coach is the general, usually wearing a suit and prowling his touchline; behind him are the staff officers, with jumpers and initials on them, which serve to show their rank. Behind them are the rest of the team. But the hierarchy is clear—and it's all apparent from their costumes."

Every regiment had its own marching tune and they also had mascots, often animals around which they would flock and defend to the hilt. The most obvious example is the Roman army's eagle, its symbol of strength, courage and immortality. Today, Roman club Lazio parades its own version of that standard—Olimpia, an American golden eagle—around the Stadio Olimpico before every home match. Though she is used to her surroundings now, that was not always the case: on her third prematch appearance, rather than fly around the stadium, Olimpia perched on the roof and watched Lazio beat Cagliari 2–1. "The eagle was the soul of the legion and to lose it was a national disgrace," Angel told me. "In England, Henry I had a lion on his standard when he came to power in 1100, and when King Richard I sent his Great Seal of the Realm in 1198 there were three lions on the standard, which became the Royal Arms of England."* And now the three lions represent England's soccer team. What could be a better military metaphor than that?

Dr. Alex Gordon takes this vision of battle, one romanticized by Greek mythology and Renaissance literature, a step further. Gordon is a professional semiotician, and as chief executive of Sign Salad, a cultural insight agency, it's his job to look for

---

*The number of lions had increased because Henry I married Adeliza, whose father had a lion on his shield, so a second lion was added to Henry's standard. In 1154, Henry II married Eleanor of Aquitaine, who also had a lion on her family crest, so a third was added.

meaning in everyday events and symbols. "It's clear to me that international football is the modern-day replacement for battle," he said. "We see that not just with the language used in football reporting—'our man inside the camp,' 'gaining territory,' that kind of thing—but also with national anthems and exchanging of pennants before matches.

"A penalty shoot-out is critical to the way a nation views itself. Its whole cultural narrative is being written as it takes place, and the national myth is being reinforced or transformed. In England's case, it absolutely matters because every loss on penalties is a reminder of our loss of empire; the penalty defeat is about the loss of our global status. If we start winning on penalties again, maybe we will have a place back at the world's table."

If soccer reinforces national myths—Holland used to be creative liberals and Germany efficient but effective until the 2010 World Cup, when the two countries swapped styles of play to reflect changes in their own societies—the penalty takes it one step further. We no longer need to watch the full ninety minutes to learn that England has lost its former position as a global power-broker: all we have to do is watch a ten-minute shoot-out as six men struggle to do their job.

The clarity and simplicity of the penalty's one-on-one combat, especially in today's social-media-driven crowd-sourced landscape, have a romantic appeal that can be traced back to Hector, Lancelot and Robin Hood. "Historically the duel is about chivalry, romance, and with a subtext of homo-eroticism, all of which are true of the penalty," Gordon continued. "There's the respect of waiting till your opponent is ready; the romantic stories of penalty heroes and villains; and the hugs and kisses as part of the celebrations. And masculinity plays a huge role: only the brave take a penalty, but missing one is like losing your alpha-maleness. Like the lion who loses a fight and is banished from his pride, this is about the essential structure of the human and animal tribal system."

Andrea Pirlo experienced a simple moment of clarity before

he took Italy's first penalty in the shoot-out to decide the 2006 World Cup final. He described his walk toward the goal as "an endless and terrible walk into one's own fears." His mind was scrambled. He did not know where he would kick the ball. As he walked toward the penalty area, he looked down at the pitch and the grass looked different to any other pitch he had ever played on. He looked at the names of his sons sewn into his soccer boots and tried to walk calmly as though he was rocking them. Whenever he looked up, he was temporarily blinded by flash photography behind Fabien Barthez's goal. He worried that he would not be able to see the ball at his point of contact. He was out of breath when he reached the penalty area. He looked over at Gigi Buffon, just for a nod of support, but got nothing back. Pirlo described what happened next in his autobiography *Penso quindi gioco* (I think when I play):

> I breathed deeply. But that breath wasn't only mine. I felt like the worker who struggled to get to the end of the month. I even felt I could be the businessman who is a prick in his everyday life. I felt I was a teacher, a student, an Italian immigrant in Germany . . . I was all those people at the same time. Incredible as it may sound, only in that moment I realized how great it was to be Italian—a priceless privilege. It wasn't the politicians with their empty speeches who taught me that. It wasn't even my dusty history books. I never thought that, just a moment before I took a penalty, I could feel like the spoke in a superior apparatus that is so imperfect, flawed, poorly led, quite old yet so unique. I scored. But even if I had missed that penalty, the teaching would have still been there. It's incredible to feel that what you are feeling is going through millions of people's minds and souls at the same time. Looking back, I can say that the tepid shiver I felt before scoring was by far the truest feeling I've ever felt in my life.

The interplay between the fans and the players is unique in the construct of "soccer as drama." The audience does not, cannot, change the fate of the characters in a play, yet the soccer crowd thinks it can influence players, the referee, the opposition, even the managers, by making its feelings known. This is a world where the emotions and conclusions born out of the denouement are far less complex than those elicited by the best art, theatre, books, music and films: if your team wins, good; if your team loses, bad. The battle for survival makes one fan's happiness dependent on another's misery: *mors tua, vita mea*—your death, my life.*

The penalty brings this into clearer focus. The crowd/audience judges players on their theatrical performance on the pitch—and the soap opera version of their lives as presented by the media—but the beauty of the penalty is that it blurs the lines. The simple act of either scoring or missing should create clarity for a player and his "character archetype," but it is not that simple. Didier Six was haunted by his missed penalty for the rest of his career, and beyond; but did one bad kick really make him bad at his job, a fragile character not to be trusted? Did Dimitris Papadopoulos become a bad player just because his friend saved his penalty? The act of taking a penalty may appear straightforward, but the context and repercussions ensure that it never is.

In no country is this more resonant than Zambia. No one can remember who was the first to sing the Chipolopolo Song, the anthem of the national team, during the penalty shoot-out against Ivory Coast that concluded the 2012 African Nations Cup final at the Stade d'Angondjé in Gabon. What we do know is that after captain Chris Katongo scored Zambia's first penalty, a line of around twenty squad members, made up of substitutes and backroom staff, were singing it in unison. By the time Emmanuel Mayuka walked up to take Zambia's second penalty the players in the center circle, some of them waiting to take the single most important kick of their lives, had followed suit. The sight, and

---

* From Bromberger, C., "Football passion and the World Cup: why so much sound and fury?," in Sugden & Tomlinson (eds), *Hosts and Champions*, pp. 281–90.

sound, was astonishing. But that was far from the most inspiring element of the Zambia 2012 story.

Nineteen years earlier, current Zambian FA president Kalusha Bwalya was just about to go for a run in Eindhoven, where he played for PSV, when he took a phone call that changed his life. It was the Zambian FA accountant. Kalusha had never spoken to him before; normally he dealt with the general secretary. He assumed it was to discuss travel plans for the upcoming World Cup qualifier against Senegal. As the only Europe-based player, he would be traveling separately from his teammates, who had chartered a plane to Dakar via a series of refuelling stops.

The accountant finally managed to get out the bad news. "The boys didn't arrive, there was something wrong with the plane," he said. The plane had reached 6,000 feet and then crashed into the ocean, just over a minute after taking off from Libreville.* Everyone on board—eighteen players, two coaches, five Zambian FA officials, and the five-man crew—had died.

Kalusha only believed it when he turned on his television and saw it on the BBC.

The players had known for a while that traveling to games was a risky business. The country was struggling financially in the late 1980s and the Zambian FA could not afford to charter planes or pay for passenger flights, so instead borrowed a De Havilland C5 Buffalo military jet from the Zambian Air Force. That too was far from reliable. Before their first World Cup qualifier in 1992, the Zambian players were stuck on board for five hours at Malawi's Chileka Airport while a dispute broke out over what currency the Zambians would use to pay for their fuel. When the captain asked the players to put on their life jackets, they did so

---

*The flight captain Feston M'Hone's orginal plan, reported by Ian Hawkey in his excellent book *Feet of the Chameleon*, was to stop for refuelling in Brazzaville (Congo), Libreville (Gabon) and Abidjan (Ivory Coast) before arriving in Dakar (Senegal). But because the plane was a military aircraft, it had ben refused perission to fly over Congolese airspace. Its first stop, then, was Libreville's Leon Mba airport.

with smiles on their faces. "The boys always used to say, 'This plane will kill us one day,'" said Kalusha.

His teammates had given notice of their burgeoning talent by beating Italy 4–0 at the 1988 Seoul Olympics. They had been close to a first ever World Cup qualification. Now they were gone. Disbelief dissolved into grief. In Zambia, newsreader Dennis Liwewe cried for twenty minutes on air, shouting the name of each player as he did so. Zambian president Frederick Chiluba ordered a week of national mourning, and on the third day he wept as he delivered a eulogy in front of over a hundred thousand people at the national stadium. "We must not give up," said Kalusha.

An English coach, Ian Porterfield, was appointed to build a new team practically from scratch: the only surviving squad members were Kalusha, his brother Joel, and Charles Musonda and Bennett Mulwanda, both of whom were injured for the Senegal game. Incredibly, Zambia continued winning: they beat Morocco (1–0) and Senegal (4–0) and needed only to avoid defeat in Morocco to qualify for a play-off to reach the 1994 World Cup in the USA. They lost 1–0. The dream was over. For nineteen years, at least.

Kalusha played a crucial role in Zambia's route to the 2012 final. After failure in 2006 World Cup qualifying, he had put plans in place for a young squad to be put together. He'd also reappointed coach Hervé Renard, whose previous spell as Zambia coach ended in a quarterfinal loss to Nigeria in 2010. "When I was growing up in Kamuchanga, I dreamt that Zambia might win a major trophy," Kalusha explained. He did help Zambia's Under-20s win the East and Central Africa Challenge Cup, but the major continental prize had always eluded him. He played in six African Nations Cups and never won. "I gave my blood and sweat. I tried with my heart and soul to take Zambia to the World Cup. I was never deterred."

As the 2012 tournament went on, Zambia's confidence slowly grew. They beat Senegal and hosts Equatorial Guinea in the group stage, got past Sudan (3–0) and Ghana (1–0) in the knockout rounds, and faced favorites Ivory Coast in the final. Incredibly, the venue was Libreville, just a few miles from the 1993 plane crash.

The day before the final, Kalusha took the players to the crash site, where they all laid wreaths. They also sang the Chipolopolo Song. "That visit made an intrinsic connection to the boys," said Honour Janza, Zambia's technical director. He became emotional as he remembered that day. "The people who perished in that tragedy were our heroes, and the journey on which they died was about bringing glory to Zambia. It motivated them to pay tribute to the fallen heroes by winning that Cup. I think the boys also had a belief that the dead have a connection with those that are alive—that played on their minds."

The fans had adopted the Chipolopolo Song as the team's new anthem in Zambia's first game after the crash, a friendly against Malawi, three weeks after the players were buried. Singing the song tightened the connection with the lost generation. "We want to put the souls of our fallen heroes to rest," said goalkeeper Kennedy Mweene.

Mweene kept Zambia in the final. Something of a penalty specialist, he stood tall as Didier Drogba missed a spot kick in the second half. For Drogba, it was déjà vu. The striker went on to score Chelsea's winning penalty in a Champions League final, but he had also missed from the spot four years earlier, in Ivory Coast's African Nations Cup final loss on penalties to Egypt.

The game finished goalless. Penalties it was. And then the singing began.

Nga wumfwa ubwite bwamfumu,
Uyasuke muchinshi muchinshi,
Ati Kalombo Mwane.

When you hear the call of the Lord,
Answer with respect,
I am here Lord.

The players had practiced penalties after every training session. They'd invented individual competitions, every round a sudden death with any miss causing elimination; and team competitions, splitting into four teams of five and holding mock shoot-outs. Every time Mweene saved a penalty he would demand $100 from the player who missed. The players spent a lot of time working on prekick routines, so they knew what to expect if called upon.

And the singing? "The team was very spiritual, and usually singing is key for team spirit," Janza said. "Before every training session we would pray and sing to ask God to be on our side. We believed we had done our best and had left the rest to God to help us win."

The shoot-out was a long one. Both teams scored their first six kicks, though Ivory Coast had a let-off when Sol Bamba's saved effort had to be retaken. Mweene, the keeper, stepped up. He was first-choice taker for his club Free State Stars, and he had never missed for them. His confidence was high after the Drogba miss. As a goalkeeper, he also felt he had an advantage when taking penalties. "I like to place it in the corner, regardless of where the goalkeeper will move," he explained. "But with penalties the more you take them the better you become. I felt it was easy in that game, because I wanted to motivate my friends by scoring." This time, Mweene waited for Boubacar Barry to dive and slowly passed the ball into the other corner. Barry was so impressed, he shook Mweene's hand after the kick. "When I'm trying to save penalties, I look at the taker, and in that little time you can see how scared or confident he is," Mweene said. "Some are predictable to read. There is not much time to judge where to dive but if you see any hesitation in the player, it's possible."

The score was now 7–7. "The penalty execution by the boys was fantastic," said Kalusha. "I could not believe we were that good on the day." The Zambia players were still singing the Chipolopolo Song.

Kolo Touré stepped up for Ivory Coast. He mumbled to himself, gave a nervous smile to the referee. Just as he started his run-up, the referee called a halt and ordered Barry, sitting just inside the eighteen-yard box, to stand up and move out of the area. The pause was only five seconds, but it might have been a lifetime. Touré stayed where he was rather than return to his mark, and side-footed it to his right, where Mweene dived to punch it out.

Rainford Kalaba only needed to score his penalty to win Zambia's first African Nations Cup. As his teammates dropped to their knees to sing, Kalaba smashed the ball over the crossbar.

"When Rainford missed that penalty we thought that we might lose," Janza confessed. It was still 7–7. "Even guys who never dreamed that they would take penalties had to step up— you can imagine how they felt," Kalusha, a penalty expert in his playing days, said.

Gervinho was next for Ivory Coast. He had already refused to take the previous penalty, which Touré missed. That told its own story. The spot was a mess and Gervinho, opening his body, hit it over the bar. After fourteen successful penalties in a row, three in a row had been missed.

Now it was Stoppila Sunzu's chance to win the game. A defender, relatively new to the team, Sunzu was three years old when the 1993 team perished. As he walked to the spot, he carried on singing. He spotted the ball and stepped backward to his mark, still singing.

Nga wumfwa ubwite bwamfumu,
Uyasuke muchinshi muchinshi,
Ati Kalombo Mwane.

The Chipololopo Song had become a force for unity back home. Just a few months earlier, parliamentary and general elections had divided Zambia along ethnic lines: the Patriotic Front—the party that won the elections—was predominantly supported by Bemba-speaking groups, the Movement for Multiparty Democracy by Nyanja-speaking groups, and the third political party—the United Party for National Development—by Tonga-speaking groups. The tension this created cooled as Zambia progressed to the final; after every victory, in bars, in homes and on the streets, the country united in singing the song (it helped that Chipolopolo is a neutral dialect that captures Bemba, Nyanja and other Zambian tongues). The song is thought originally to have had a political edge to it: the story goes that Chris Chali, one of the country's most popular musicians, wrote it in praise of the United National Independence Party when it came to power in 1964. Its leader was Kenneth Kaunda, and before the national team was called the Chipolopolo, it was KK11—Kenneth Kaunda's 11. That nickname died with the 1993 generation. Ever since then the team had been called Chipolopolo.

"I had to look to God to help me deliver for my country," Sunzu said. He too grew emotional as he remembered that day. "I was not really thinking about that penalty: I surrendered everything to the hands of God. We had thought how wonderful it would be to win the Cup for the nation. You just have to know where to place the ball, and if you strike it well, you will score even if the goalkeeper dives the right way. Leaving it in the hands of God was the best option."

And so, just a few miles from the tragedy that wiped out a whole team and devastated a nation, Sunzu channeled the power of song, of prayer, of belief, and scored his penalty. Zambia won the African Nations Cup. Coach Renard carried an injured player, Joséph Musonda, as a father would a sleeping toddler, to join the celebrations. Kalusha, watching from the sideline, quietly wept.

PENALTY ICON—
MARTIN PALERMO

Awkward. That's the only word to describe the atmosphere on July 3, 1999, in the antidoping room just off the players' tunnel in the Estadio Feliciano Caceres in Luque, Paraguay, after Colombia had beaten Argentina 3–0 in their Copa America group match. On one side of the room was Colombia goalkeeper Miguel Calero, and on the other Argentina forward Martin Palermo. The pair did not exchange a single word while they were waiting to be called.

Perhaps both of them were in shock: Palermo had just taken, and missed, three penalties in one match. "I remember that every day, and particularly the anguish on Martin's face after each of the penalties," said Calero, who would tragically die in December 2012. "But when I saw him in the doping room, he wasn't able to speak. He couldn't believe what had just happened."

Nor could anyone, although two months earlier Palermo had caused much hilarity in a league game when his standing leg gave way before he struck a penalty for Boca Juniors against Platense. His right foot somehow connected with the ball, which then cannoned into the goal off his left shin. Referee Fabian Madorran was happy to allow it, and after the game the Argentine FA sent the video of the incident to FIFA asking if it should have been allowed. FIFA said yes, because Palermo had not intended to strike the ball with both feet.

Argentina coach Marcelo Bielsa gave Palermo his international debut in 1999 because regular forwards Gabriel Batistuta and Hernán Crespo, playing in Europe at the time, had said they were too tired to play in the Copa America. Palermo had won the El País award for South America's best player in 1998 and, in his first competitive international match, scored two goals as Argentina beat Ecuador 3–0. "I'm confident in my ability, I feel no pressure," he said.

Even though Palermo missed the next two penalties he took after his "double-kick," against Independiente and San Lorenzo, Bielsa had designated the striker as the team's penalty taker against Colombia. He was called into action after just five minutes. After a very straight run-up, he smashed his shot against the top off the crossbar. Within three minutes Colombia went ahead when Ivan Cordoba scored—from the spot.

In the second half, Hamilton Ricard won a penalty for Colombia, only for goalkeeper Germán Burgos to save his spot kick. With a quarter of an hour left to play, Juan Roman Riquelme crossed for Palermo, but a Colombian defender brushed the ball away with his hand. Another penalty.

At this point, Bielsa—who, like Palermo, was nicknamed "El Loco"—ran out of the dug-out and told Hugo Ibarra to get Roberto Ayala to take the penalty. Ayala, whose only spot kick before then had been against England in the 1998 World Cup shoot-out, tried to talk Palermo into giving him the ball, but without success. Palermo went wider for this run-up but used the same style: blasting the ball with his laces. It was the same outcome too. The ball flew over the bar.

As the Argentine commentator shouted "For the love of God, how can this happen?" Palermo pulled up his shorts on either side and roared in anguish. It was an instinctive reaction, captured in an iconic image. But things were about to get worse.

Just as they'd done after his first miss, Colombia scored soon after, Edwin Congo doubling their lead; then Jhonnier Montaño, only sixteen, made it 3–0. With two minutes left to play, Palermo fell over in the box and referee Ubaldo Aquino generously awarded another penalty. This time Ayala did not even have time to talk Palermo out of it; Palermo picked up the ball and spotted it while Ayala was running upfield. "Ayala looked like Forrest Gump running to prevent the inevitable," remembered Argentine sportswriter Federico Bassahun.

Still Palermo did not change his style. He laced the ball and at least got this one on target. But Calero dived the right way, to his left, and the ball was at the perfect height for him to punch it clear. Palermo wandered around in a daze for the last two minutes and at the final whistle still looked lost when his Boca teammate Jorge Bermudez, playing for Colombia, asked for his shirt.

Back in the dressing room, Bielsa was furious and laid into a tearful Palermo, shouting, "You selfish idiot!" "Bielsa was a tough guy," Palermo remembered. "He told me that I had put my own interests before those of the team. I kept on crying."

In public, Bielsa tried to deflect criticism away from Palermo. "I'm responsible for this loss," the coach stated in the postmatch press conference. "I'm the only one responsible. Palermo has a good history with penalties and he is a confident forward, that's why he scores so many goals. He took that responsibility over and again during the match because of that quality, because he is optimistic. It was not his fault." In private, Bielsa banned Palermo from ever taking penalties again.

After his doping test, Palermo hid himself away in his room in the team hotel, with his head under the pillow: "I was sad but also embarrassed." Diego Simeone tried to talk to him, but Palermo sent him away. "I was convinced Bielsa would sack me from the team."

"Is he the only guilty one?" asked the headline of Argentine paper *Olé* after the game. "Palermo hit rock bottom and now it's complicated for us to reach the next stage of the competition." *El Gráfico* blamed the coach. "El Loco is the culprit" was its headline. "Bielsa is most to blame, because he decided the penalty takers."

Three days later, Argentina needed to beat Uruguay to stay in the competition. Palermo faced the press before the game and performed far better than he had on the pitch. "I'm not ashamed by what happened to me," he said. "OK, so it's rare, I realize it doesn't happen every day, but let's forget it. I've forgotten it. I'm fine emotionally and I would have no problem taking another penalty again. But I need to think about what's best for the team. I'm not selfish and if a teammate wanted to take it, then he could. But if he wanted me to do it, I would be happy to."

He did not realize it then, but he was the talk of the soccer world. Atlético Madrid had wanted to sign him; their general secretary Miguel Angel Ruiz said, "He was not super before he missed three penalties and he's not a disaster now." Former Argentine heroes like Oscar Ruggeri and Abel Balbo both praised "his character" and, unsurprisingly, he won support from Brazilians too. "I've never seen such a strong personality," said Ronaldo. "Where were his teammates?" asked Roberto Carlos. "I didn't see any of them trying to take one." "I couldn't have done that," added Cafu. Argentine president Carlos Menem listed great players who had missed penalties in the past. "And even Carlos Menem," he added.

Bielsa did not sack Palermo, not straight away anyway, and was rewarded when the forward scored in a 2–0 win over Uruguay. But there was to be a twist in the tale. In the quarterfinal, Argentina were 2–1 down to Brazil when they won a penalty. Ayala took the ball. His effort was weak, and Dida saved it. Argentina were out.

"Palermo had to take that penalty!" said Maradona at the time. "The only person who can miss three penalties in one match is the guy with the balls to take the third one after missing the first two."

Palermo missed his next penalty after the Copa America too, when Newell's goalkeeper Norberto Scoponi stopped his effort for Boca. Coach Carlos Bianchi took him off penalty duties. He never played for Argentina under Bielsa again, but ten years later, just after breaking Boca Juniors' all-time professional scoring record (he beat Francisco Varallo's seventy-year-old tally of 195 but had had to wait six months to get the final goal while he recovered from a cruciate ligament injury), he was called into Maradona's Argentina squad before the 2010 World Cup.

Palermo completed his redemption with a 93rd-minute winning goal against Peru to seal Argentina's place in South Africa. He was thirty-six when he scored at the World Cup, his late effort against Greece allowing him to supplant Maradona himself as the oldest Argentine player to score in the tournament.

CHAPTER 5

BIG DATA, BIG DECISIONS

Over the space of five weeks between August and September 1833, French writer Honoré de Balzac published his "Gait Study" in the pages of *Europe Littéraire*. His weekly articles were the result of his observations from the local coffee shop. He would analyze the customers and, simply by looking at their pitch and poise—noting "a stern immobile face," or observing that "the body is in constant motion"—guess their profession.

The study of body language is nothing new. For most goalkeepers, watching a player's approach to the ball is still the preferred method to decide where to dive. Felice Accame, a student at Milan's Università Cattolica, presented a paper in March 2011 based on 122 penalties taken in the 2009/10 Serie A season.* He noted that 74% of penalties were scored, 26% missed; that players shot to the goalkeeper's right 51% of the time, to the left 39% and centrally 10%; and that players did not look at the goalkeeper before kicking the ball 69% of the time (and made eye contact 31% of the time). His most significant finding concerned the angle of the run-up:

---

*The paper was called *"Neuroscienze e sport—il calcio di rigore."*

Figure 10: Angle of approach to penalty

Run-up Angle (approx.)	Scored/Missed	Conversion Rate
15°	11/7	61%
30°	59/15	80%
45°	20/10	67%

For Accame, it was clear that players whose angle of approach was either too wide or too straight had less chance of scoring.

The Norwegian professor of sports psychology Geir Jordet also believes that body language plays an important role in the success of shoot-outs. In his office in Oslo he showed me a video of two players walking back to their marks after a penalty, and asked me to guess what had happened seconds earlier.

The first was from Sweden against Holland in Euro 2004, the game Jordet focused on in the academic study that made his name.* Christian Wilhelmsson is walking back to the center circle, his brow furrowed, his eyes cast down. "If you are in a room and this guy is walking toward you, would you think he had good or bad news?" Jordet asked. "Very bad news," I said.

It turns out that Wilhelmsson had scored.

The other player was Diego Maradona in the 1990 World Cup semifinal against Italy. Like Wilhelmsson's, his penalty was taken in the middle of the shoot-out, with the scores level, and could not win or lose the game for his team. Maradona celebrates as if he has just won the World Cup: he jumps up, pumps his fists above his head, and roars in delight. (The context here is relevant: he had missed a penalty in the previous round's shoot-out against Yugoslavia, and the semifinal was in Naples, where he played his club soccer.) "Good news or bad news?" Good news. And the Italian kicker after Maradona, Aldo Serena, missed.

---

*Jordet, Elferink-Gemse, "Stress, coping and emotions on the world stage: the experience of participating in a major soccer penalty shoot-out" (*Journal of Applied Sport Psychology*, 2012).

Jordet's findings still came as a surprise. If a player converts his penalty when the scores are level and he celebrates with one or two hands raised over shoulder height, his team is 82% more likely to go on and win the shoot-out than if he doesn't celebrate.* "That makes sense," Jordet explained, "as it can affect the outcome in two ways, firstly by giving your team a boost—and it gives the next opponent a higher probability of missing." The effect is similar to that of a converted Panenka, then, with just one slight difference: there is no downside to raising your arms.

The search for extra knowledge that will give them an edge is nothing new for goalkeepers. Romanian keeper Helmuth Duckadam used his understanding of game theory to save all four Barcelona penalties for Steaua Bucharest in the 1986 European Cup final. A regular, and very good, poker player, Duckadam faced Barcelona captain José Ramon Alexanko first up after Steaua's Mihai Mejearu had missed his kick. Duckadam dived to his right to save it.

Laszlo Bölöni then missed for Steaua, and Angel Pedraza was next for Barcelona. "If my first save was a guess, now it was about thinking as if I was the opposition player," said Duckadam. He thought about what he would do if he was in Pedraza's shoes. "I went to the right again, and saved it again." It was 0–0 after four penalties.

After Marius Lacatus scored for Steaua, Pichi Alonso stepped up for Barcelona. Duckadam quickly calculated the odds. "He must have thought that after going to the right twice, I was going to change sides, so I kept to the same side and the ball hit me on the chest."

Gavril Balint put Steaua 2–0 up, so Marcos Alonso needed to score to keep the game alive. Now Duckadam wondered what Marcos would be thinking. "I think he believed that I was always

---

* Moll, Pepping & Jordet, "Emotional contagion in soccer penalty shootouts: celebration of individual success is associated with ultimate team success" (*Journal of Sports Sciences*).

going to throw myself to the right, so after three times I changed: I went to the left, and again, I saved the ball." Duckadam had saved four penalties in a row. He was so focused on the game theory that he had not kept score in the shoot-out. "I had no idea the game was over and Bölöni had to tell me that we were European champions."*

Game theory is all about strategic decision making, in this case when two people have a choice to make (which way to kick/dive) and neither knows what the other will do. The most celebrated illustration of game theory is the Prisoners' Dilemma. Two people who committed the same crime, together, are arrested and kept apart. If they both keep silent, they will both get lenient sentences; if one talks, the other will get a

---

*Duckadam is not the only Romanian goalkeeper to go down in European Cup history. In the final qualifying round for a place in the 2014 Champions League group stage, one of the richest games in club soccer, Ludogorets Razgrad center back Cosmin Moţi saved two shoot-out penalties to beat Steaua Bucharest. Moţi was in goal because the Bulgarian champions' goalkeeper Vladislav Stoyanov had been sent off in the final minute of extra time, and his side had made all three substitutions. Moţi, who had spent seven years of his career at Steaua's fierce rivals Dinamo Bucharest, took Ludogorets's first penalty and scored. He then dived the right way for five of the seven kicks he faced and saved two of them as the Bulgarian side, only formed in 2001, won the shoot-out 6–5. "I relied on my instincts and was just taking last-second decisions on where to jump," said Moţi after the game. Stoyanov added, "I was not worried when I saw him putting on the gloves. There is no guarantee I would have done any better." Moţi is not the only outfield player to save a penalty: memorably, Niall Quinn kept out Dean Saunders's spot kick for Manchester City against Derby County in 1991, while Felipe Melo (for Galatasaray against Elazigspor, 2012) and Eric Viscaal (for Gent against Cercle Brugge, 1993) have done the same. None were quite as unlucky as former England captain Bobby Moore: in a January 1972 League Cup tie for West Ham United, he kept out a spot kick from Stoke City's Mike Bernard, only for Bernard to smash the rebound past him. "I wouldn't like to endure that again," Moore said after the game. "There I was, stand-in goalkeeper, trembling—and who doesn't?—in the face of a penalty. I don't think I've ever felt so sick in my life when the ball came back over my head. I know now about the ups and downs of life. I was very much up and very deeply down. I think from now on I will just carry on as sweeper Moore, and leave the goalkeeping to somebody else."

long sentence; and if they both talk, they will both get medium-length sentences. Just like goalkeeper and penalty taker, neither prisoner knows what the other will do. The most likely scenario is they both talk, because each assumes the other will, and end up with longer sentences than if they had kept quiet.

But there are ways to gain an advantage in games like this. Jens Lehmann found one in 2006, for Germany's World Cup quarterfinal against Argentina. His goalkeeping coach Andreas Köpke gave him a piece of hotel-headed notepaper on which he'd written down the opposition players' preferred kicking corners.* Lehmann referred to it before every penalty. It read:

Riquelme: Left
Crespo: Long run-up, right
    Short run-up, left
Heinze: Left low
Ayala: 2 [shirt number] waits long time, long run-up, right
Messi: Left
Aimar: 16, waits long time, left
Rodríguez: 18, left

In the event, Ayala and Rodríguez were the only players from the list who took penalties. Lehmann followed his instructions, and saved Ayala's; he also went the right way for Rodríguez, but the

---

*Lehmann's traditional method of looking at a piece of paper will not be overtaken by the digital revolution any time soon. In response to the 2009 Carling Cup final shoot-out, when Manchester United goalkeeper Ben Foster looked at penalties taken by his Tottenham Hotspur opponents on an iPod just before the shoot-out began, FIFA amended its rules to exclude the use of digital technology while a game is in progress. FIFA's 2013/14 version of the Laws of the Game, subheading "Interpretation of the Laws of the Game and Guidelines for Referees, Law 4, The Players' Equipment," reads "The use of electronic communication systems between players and/or technical staff is not permitted" (though medical staff may use "electronic communication systems"). Foster, by the way, saved three penalties in that shoot-out.

shot went in. Germany were 4–2 up when Esteban Cambiasso approached.

I asked Lehmann about that save. He remembers studying the list for a long time before the kick, and making sure that Cambiasso saw him looking. It was written in pencil, it was barely legible, and Cambiasso's name wasn't even on it, but Lehmann believes Cambiasso thought the goalkeeper knew where he was going to kick the ball. In truth, Lehmann had no idea. He waited until the last minute, and only at that moment remembered that he had faced a free kick by Cambiasso some years earlier and that the angle of his standing foot suggested the ball would go the same way.

"You had time to compute all that information at such an important moment?" I asked. "Seriously?"

"Seriously," Lehmann replied, and he did not look like he was joking.

Of course, it's far too simplistic just to write "Heinze, left" or "Crespo, right." The best takers mix up their penalties, but for most, patterns can be detected. That's where Ignacio Palacios-Huerta, the Professor of Game Theory, comes in.

Palacios-Huerta's in-depth analysis helped Chelsea prepare for the 2008 Champions League final; he then featured in the book *Soccernomics*, which was published in 2009. Since then, I have worked with the authors to set up a soccer consultancy with the same name. One of the first services we offered to clubs and national teams was Palacios-Huerta's penalty analysis.

The process of selling his analysis was eye-opening. I met goalkeepers and finance directors, goalkeeping coaches and performance directors, strikers and chief executives. They loved the idea of discovering recurring patterns in kickers and goalkeepers in order to give their team a competitive advantage. But the money-men found it difficult to put a value on something so hard to quantify. Here's an example to explain why that is.

Before the 2010 FA Cup final, Palacios-Huerta provided a full penalty analysis of the Chelsea players for Portsmouth. He could see that Chelsea's main penalty taker, Frank Lampard, had developed a habit that season of repeating a kick to his natural side—which for a right-footed player like Lampard is to the keeper's right (ten out of thirteen kicks, or 77%). Also, Lampard always scored when the goalkeeper moved early. Portsmouth goalkeeper David James had another advantage: he was a current England teammate of Lampard. In game theory parlance, even if James did not know which way Lampard might kick the ball, Lampard might think that James knew because of their shared history. Lampard has a poorer conversion record against keepers who have been his England teammates: Rob Green and Joe Hart have both saved his penalties. Sure enough, Chelsea were awarded a penalty in that Cup final. James dived the correct way, to his right. Lampard missed the target, on that side of the goal.

"If there is a perceived advantage in the match-up, it will always help the goalkeeper, not the taker," Jordet said. The taker might know the goalkeeper's preferences, but that is far less important than the goalkeeper knowing the preferences of the taker. A similar advantage might come into play if the same player took two penalties in one game, and had to decide whether to pick the same spot again or a different one.

The basic question that every potential Soccernomics client wanted to know was: what difference did our analysis make, given that Lampard's penalty was off-target? Sure, the goalkeeper dived the right way, but how do we not know that he might have gone that way anyway? In short, what is this analysis worth? For most people, these questions are impossible to answer. For a game theorist, they are just a challenge.

Palacios-Huerta came up with a calculation to place a value on one goal for a home team, which was typically worth 0.70 point in the average game, and one goal for an away team, worth 0.85

point.* He then assessed that over a season a club is involved in an average of twelve penalties. His conclusion was that his analysis can help a team save three more penalties and score two more penalties than it otherwise would. The value of that is as follows:

(a) 2 more goals scored (one at home, one away) are worth 0.70 + 0.85 = 1.55 points

(b) 3 fewer goals conceded (1.5 as a home team and 1.5 as a

---

*This is how his calculation ran:

On average, the home team:

(a) wins around 50% of games (25% by one goal and 25% by more);

(b) draws around 30% of games;

(c) and loses around 20% of games (10% by one goal and 10% by more).

So if the home team:

(a) scored one more goal in a game it won (50% of all games) it would have earned 0 more points;

(b) scored one more goal in a game it drew (30% of the games) it would have earned 2 more points (from 1 to 3);

(c) scored one more goal in a game it lost by one goal (10% of the games) it would have earned one more point (from 0 to 1);

(d) scored one more goal in a game it lost by two or more goals (10% of the games) it would have earned 0 more points.

So the weighted average value of one goal for a home side is:

$(0.50 \times 0\text{pts}) + (0.30 \times 2\text{pts}) + (0.10 \times 1\text{pt}) + (0.10 \times 0\text{pts}) = 0.70$ point

If the away team:

(a) scored one more goal in a game it won (20% of all games) it would have earned 0 more points;

(b) scored one more goal in a game it drew (30% of the games) it would have earned 2 more points (from 1 to 3);

(c) scored one more goal in a game it lost by one goal (25% of the games) it would have earned one more point (from 0 to 1);

(d) scored one more goal in a game it lost by two or more goals (25% of the games) it would have earned 0 more points.

So the weighted average value of one goal for an away side is:

$(0.20 \times 0\text{pts}) + (0.30 \times 2\text{pts}) + (0.25 \times 1\text{pt}) + (0.25 \times 0\text{pts}) = 0.85$ point

The weighted average values are the same for conceding one goal fewer as one goal scored. So if a home side concedes one fewer goal, its average value would be 0.70 point; for an away side, 0.85 point.

visiting team) are worth $(1.50 \times 0.70) + (1.50 \times 0.85) = 2.32$ points

Total value: 3.87 points

3.87 points would have been the difference between one team being relegated or staying up in seven of the ten Premier League seasons running from 2003/04 to 2012/13.

One Premier League chief executive told me his team spends more than any other club on data and sports science, but felt the analysis wouldn't work because the players forget information during games. "We do a spot test at halftime, give each player one word to remember, and by full time they have forgotten it, because of tiredness, concentration, all sorts of things," he said. "So it might be hard for kickers and goalkeepers to remember trends in the heat of the game." Palacios-Huerta can deliver his analysis up to three days before every game, so the information is designed to be part of the prematch preparation rather than a midgame memory test. In any case, it's understandable that players wouldn't bother to remember a random word they were told at halftime: they know it has no conceivable relevance to winning or losing. A goalkeeper told about a penalty kicker's preferences might make more of an effort to remember them.

A few days before the 2010 World Cup final in Johannesburg, Simon Kuper, one of the authors and a Dutch fan (he grew up in Holland), contacted a member of Holland's backroom team to see if they would be interested in a detailed breakdown of the Spanish players. They were, so Palacios-Huerta worked all night to crunch the numbers. Some of the results were fascinating and, with his permission, can be reproduced for the first time here. This is an abridged version of what the Dutch learned about Spain's goalkeeper, Iker Casillas, and two of their potential penalty takers, David Villa and Fernando Torres. (Rival teams, bear in mind the numbers used for this report are now out-of-date and so will no longer be significant.)

Most goalkeepers, just like most kickers, have a tendency to go for the natural side more. The average split is 60–40, so Casillas's tendency, 54–46, is weaker than most goalkeepers—especially against right-footed kickers, when he is closer to diving 50–50. Despite this pattern, his success rate when the

Figure 11: Iker Casillas

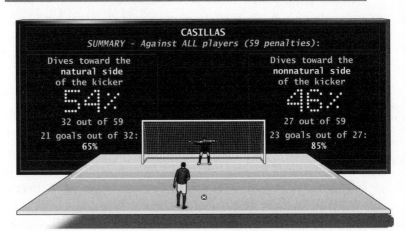

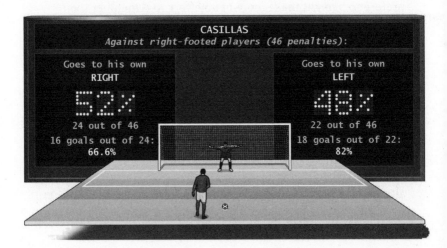

penalty is struck to the kicker's natural side is far better than when the kicker aims for the nonnatural side. He also has a tendency to repeat his previous choice. (This was interesting data when compared to reserve goalkeeper Pepe Reina: over 58 penalties, the scoring record against Reina was 75%, while his diving tendency was 67–33 to the kicker's natural side, and up to 93% for left-footers, against whom he has never saved a penalty.)

Figure 12: David Villa

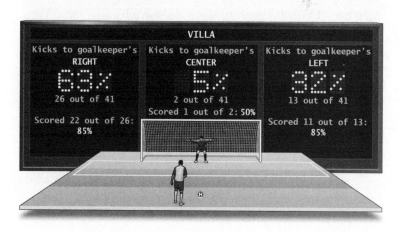

Villa—41 penalties
Scoring rate: 83% (34 out of 41)

Palacios-Huerta recorded that Villa was excellent at random-
izing his penalties but did have a tendency to avoid choices that
had not worked for him in the past. It was noted that he had
missed a penalty against Honduras in the group stage of the
competition, aiming to his natural side; and that against Belgium
in the World Cup qualifiers, he missed with a kick placed centrally.

Figure 13: Fernando Torres

Torres—35 penalties
Scoring rate: 71% (25 out of 35)

The stand-out element in Torres's numbers is the fact that he
kicks more to his nonnatural side than his natural side. The
scoring rates are similar on either side but it is very rare for that
tendency to emerge.

"It was a very detailed and helpful analysis," Holland's goalkeeping coach Ruud Hesp told Kuper before the game.

In the game itself, Villa and Xabi Alonso, two of Spain's most regular takers, were replaced, which would have left Spain with Torres as their only player with more than five penalties to his name. Could Holland have shaken off their negative penalty DNA to turn it around? Andrés Iniesta's extra-time goal means that we will never know.

Palacios-Huerta now spends much of his time as a board member and Head of Talent Identification for his team, Athletic Bilbao, whose policy is only to recruit Basque players. Palacios-Huerta had no qualms about writing the Spain report. He wanted Holland to win on penalties because he believed it was a unique opportunity to demonstrate the power of scientific analysis. "I can't believe we came so close," he said when we met in a London pub over three years later. Unlike Gyuri Vergouw, the Dutch consultant who caused such a stir in his homeland, Palacios-Huerta thinks Holland would have won the penalty shoot-out had they been able to hang on just another few minutes.

Palacios-Huerta sent another Premier League club a preliminary report about Carlos Tévez's main penalty preferences. Again, with his permission, here is part of it. This does not feature the Routine of Execution, a section that clubs like which covers any specific movements or changes to look out for in a kicker's routine that may point to one direction over another.

1. Tévez has kicked to the goalkeeper's Right (R) 45.6% of the time, Center (C) 27.2% and Left (L) 27.2%, with a success rate above 90% in all cases.

Conclusion: he kicks far less often than the typical player to the R (the natural side), and much more often to the C.

2. A mistake that goalkeepers facing Tévez make is that they too often choose R against him (around 73%, whereas he kicks R just above 45%).

3. He tends NOT to repeat what he does from one penalty kick to the next.

4. He tends not to repeat what he does against the SAME goal-keeper. For instance, in February 2011, he kicked two penalties in the same game, against WBA. One went L and the other R.

5. He almost never kicks midheight. All of his kicks, with one exception, are low or high.

6. He has faced this [club name] goalkeeper before and on that occasion he scored, kicking L. This suggests the probability that he will not repeat L (and choose instead C or R) against this goalkeeper is much higher than against another goal-keeper. In particular the statistical models said that AGAINST THIS GK in the next game (and again this just applies to the match-up of THIS GK–Tévez) the probabilities are that:

   – he will kick L with a 15% probability
   – he will kick C with a 40% probability
   – he will kick R with a 45% probability

7. There is another factor. Most players tend NOT TO REPEAT what did not work in the past (at least for the next 3 or 4 penalties). Tévez has not missed many penalties, and so it is difficult to tell. But if he is like the others, the fact that he missed against Blackpool in January 2011, when he kicked R low and missed [this game took place quite soon after that], means the adjusted statistical probabilities are:

   – he will kick L with a 21% probability
   – he will kick C with a 45% probability
   – he will kick R with a 34% probability

The calculations may seem complicated, but what's left for the goalkeeper is not: all he needs to know is the fundamental advice, in this case not to dive to his left, instead to go right and keep his legs in the middle.

*

There is one other goalkeeper who, like Helmuth Duckadam, went the right way for every kick in the shoot-out of a major competition final. In 2012, Petr Cech dived correctly six times out of six to help Chelsea beat Bayern Munich in the Champions League final. I wanted to know how he did it.

"Don't look, but there's a lady over there on your left. What is she wearing and what is she doing?" asks Christophe Lollichon, his eyes on me. I have no idea as I hadn't noticed her—and that's just one reason (there are many others) why I would never make a top goalkeeper. Lollichon talks me through her full outfit, and tells me she's rummaging in her handbag. "It's all about peripheral vision, which is essential for a goalkeeper who has to spot dangers coming from all sides," he explains.

Lollichon is Avram Grant's greatest gift to Chelsea. After José Mourinho left the club in September 2007, taking his backroom staff with him, his successor Grant needed a goalkeeping coach. Petr Cech recommended Lollichon, his coach at Rennes. By the time Mourinho returned to Stamford Bridge in summer 2013, Lollichon had become so indispensable at Chelsea that Silvino Louro, Mourinho's preferred goalkeeping coach, was shifted to a new role and given the catch-all title "assistant coach."

Lollichon is obsessive about knowledge. He and Cech share a love of learning languages and of military history. When we first meet in a hotel near Chelsea's training ground, I listen to them having an intense discussion about Bahrain's human rights record. "Petr is very intelligent, his IQ is 138, and his memory, wow, it's like a computer," Lollichon tells me later.

The Frenchman is constantly on the look-out for new ways to challenge and improve Cech. In recent seasons he has invested in a machine, originally developed to improve anticipation for table-tennis players, which fires out three different colored balls at a time for him to save. "Without above-average anticipation skills, there is no way you can stop a genius like Messi from scoring. If you're only relying on your reactions, you're dead," says Cech. The difference he alludes to is clear: the reaction save comes after the opponent has struck the ball; the anticipation save prepares you before the shot has been struck.

The Chelsea goalkeepers also work with a giant color screen to improve peripheral vision. They stand in front of it for a twelve-minute session. There are five hundred lights on the screen and the aim is to hit a light as soon as it flashes. For Lollichon, this was too one-dimensional, so he asked the Australian manufacturers to develop a version with different colored lights, and more than one light flashing at the same time. "It helps us determine if a goal-keeper reacts quicker on his left or his right side." The screen, which is also used by pilots, McLaren Formula One drivers and the USA basketball team, improved Cech's reaction time by 26%, to 253 milliseconds, or about a quarter of a second. Hilário scored 275 milliseconds and Ross Turnbull 299 milliseconds.

Lollichon is always taking inspiration from other sports. He watches a lot of ice hockey, was a regular at handball matches when he was at Rennes, and is a big fan of France's record-breaking handball goalkeeper Thierry Omeyer. "His reflexes, reading of the game and speed reactions, all exceptional!" At Chelsea, he encourages his goalkeepers to play head tennis and peteca, a Brazilian sport which is like badminton with hands. "*Plusieurs disciplines*—the more the better," he comments.

Lollichon's buzzword is "influence." He wants his goalkeepers to influence the play around them. He cites two examples: Cech pushing his defenders ten yards higher up the pitch against Blackburn Rovers, so that when keeper Paul Robinson launched a ball forward, Cech had more room to claim it; and against Stoke, to counter Rory Delap's long throw-in, Cech's starting position on the corner of the six-yard box to punch the ball clear. "Robinson ended up playing it short and Delap threw the ball back to the halfway line. Ha, they didn't know what to do!" he laughs.

Just before our second meeting, at the same hotel, Lollichon has been teaching Chelsea's young goalkeeper Jamal Blackman to influence the play around him. In a training session, wingers fired in crosses to Demba Ba, and Blackman had to disrupt the striker. "He was like a big handball goalkeeper, putting Demba off, and he was good. Oh yes, he was very good."

As the man who influences the influencers, Lollichon never stops working. When I mention his name to people who know him, they talk in awe about his work ethic. One said he is often still on the training ground at two in the morning; another that more than once last season he ran out of Stamford Bridge as soon as the final whistle went, jumped in a cab to the airport and flew to Madrid to watch Thibaut Courtois, Chelsea's goalkeeper on loan at Atlético Madrid, play three hours later. On his way to the airport he would debrief Cech about his performance; then he would be back at the training ground the next day.

On May 19, 2012, Lollichon enjoyed his greatest success. That was the day when Cech, who had saved an Arjen Robben spot kick in normal time, dived the right way for all six of Bayern's penalties, saving two to clinch Chelsea's first Champions League title. "You have to approach every game with a plan in mind and know what the opposing players like to do," said Cech before the game. "Your aim is to be surprised as little as possible."

For that, Cech had Lollichon to thank. His coach put in "massive, massive, massive work" before the game analyzing the Bayern kickers. He also made it a collaborative project, presenting the Chelsea squad goalkeepers with a thirty-minute video featuring every Bayern penalty since 2007. Lollichon asked each of the keepers to focus on one Bayern player—Cech was exempt: his job was not to single out any one player—and present their findings the following week. A few days before the game, the four men sat in Lollichon's office at Cobham, pulled down the projector screen that takes up a whole wall, and went through the analyses. Turnbull spoke first, using notes that he had prepared, and Lollichon was impressed. "It was an excellent analysis, very professional." Hilário was next. "Also superb." Then the discussion opened out. "We had a very interesting chat, everyone participating, talking all as equals. We would spot something and pause the video, and talk through the ideas. That meeting: wow. It's something I will remember for all my life."

Lollichon did his analysis as usual on each Bayern player but is wary about revealing too much. "We are talking now about some special information, and I know that Mr. Abramovich would be very upset if I told you all our secrets."

I understand, I say. "So just tell me this: does every taker have a tell?"

"Yes. Every penalty taker has something, and when I find what it is, I put it in the analysis and make sure Petr knows about it."

Lollichon has a checklist when he analyzes penalties. There are thirteen points on it, and he checks off each one. He says Cech does the same before every penalty he faces. Later, I wondered what they might be, and could only come up with twelve. (Please note, Mr. Abramovich: this is my own list.)

1. Left or right foot.
2. Length of run-up.
3. Angle of run-up.
4. Speed of preparation.
5. Gaze behavior.
6. Preferred corner.
7. State of the game.
8. Important penalties converted.
9. Important penalties missed.
10. Angle of standing foot.
11. Other patterns.
12. Previous history with keeper.

I was skeptical about Cech being able to tick off all these categories in the short time it takes for a new taker to appear in a shoot-out. Most likely he looks for two or three cues from each individual player, and they come from this long-list. Either way, Cech does have an impressive ability to retain and process information at moments of high tension. "His mental power, it's incredible, high, high, high," Lollichon confirms. He uses bio-feedback methods to control tension, which as Lollichon put it "is using your mind to control your body."

Against Bayern Munich, the Chelsea team felt confident as soon as the game went to penalties. In training before every Champions League game, each Chelsea player had taken three penalties against three different goalkeepers, moving across from goal to goal. The coaches had observed the players and discussed which of them should take a penalty and in what order.

Before the players took their place in the center circle for the shoot-out, they headed to the touchline for some water. In the match footage you can see Lollichon speaking to the takers, reminding them about Manuel Neuer's penalty preferences, then going with Cech over to the bench to talk to the other goalkeepers. Lollichon remembers the conversation well.

"OK, guys, say something to me," said Cech.

Hilário replied, "Petr, you know everything. Now you just have to do it. That's all."

And Cech said, "OK, let's go. Let's do this."

"It was Hilário," Lollichon tells me. "He found the right words. He was an important guy for us, a great person."

Even before a kick was taken, Lollichon felt that this was Chelsea's moment. Not only had Cech saved Robben's penalty in the first half, but in the semifinal, when Messi had missed a penalty at Camp Nou, Cech had dived the right way. "We could see the Bayern players didn't want to take a penalty. You can see it in their faces. They did not want it. The body language of some of their players was very visible. Robben had his head down, *pfffff*. You could feel their disappointment and I think that influence can be important. You can transfer your bad mental feeling to your teammates."

I bring up the shoot-out on my phone, and am stunned when Lollichon tells me he has never watched it before. Really? "Too busy," he smiles. He twitches every time a Bayern player takes one, pushing his chest forward as though about to dive full-length across the coffee table, and when Cech comes close to saving one, he groans. "Ooooooohhhhhh, Petr, so close . . ." Cech, he tells me, is brilliant at moving on if he fails to save, or even if he does save, a penalty. "What's gone is gone, it's over."

Lollichon was not too worried when Juan Mata missed Chelsea's first kick, even if the Spaniard had done the opposite of what he had been advised. "It can happen, the emotion of it all, but my job is to reduce that uncertainty." Mario Gomez, David Luiz, Manuel Neuer ("because no one else wanted to take one") and Frank Lampard all scored before Ivica Olic stepped up. Then Cech did something I had never seen him do before: he kept his left arm by his side, and waved his right up and down as though pointing to the right corner. "I know you're going that way" the message seemed to be. "There is something special with this player, we knew it and we worked on it," Lollichon comments. Olic kicked to the opposite corner to where Cech was pointing, and the goalkeeper saved it.

Ashley Cole scored, and then up walked Bastian Schweinsteiger, the Bayern vice-captain. On my phone he looks nervous and tired and yet every time I watch this penalty I think he will kick to his natural side. "You do?" asks Lollichon. "You can't see the tell? Look, look! It's clear. We can see it. Petr saw it, and that's how he saved it." Schweinsteiger went the same way as Olic, with the same outcome.

"Tell me the tell!" I shout.

He's not telling.

Every time a goalkeeper dives the right way in a penalty, he increases his chances of saving it by 30%. In the last two years, Cech has dived the right way for penalties 75% of the time. Lollichon is convinced that his analysis has made the difference. But there is room for improvement. He wants that 75% to reach 80%, and then 90%. He is excited about a new product that can help contact lens wearers like Cech to see more clearly. There is also a two-year project in development with a London-based French ophthalmologist to improve focus and concentration. "It may help us improve by maybe 1% on the penalties, but that's all it takes. It's all about the details. I really feel that it's important for us to get better, and we can do it, I know it." And with that, he's off, back to the training ground, looking for more knowledge, more answers.

Chelsea's victory against Bayern Munich was even more impressive for another reason. Not only were Chelsea playing in Munich, they lost the toss to kick first, so went into the shoot-out at a disadvantage. Why so? Palacios-Huerta analyzed the results of 212 penalty shoot-outs, taking in 2,106 penalties, and concluded that the team kicking first win 61% of the time (compared to 39% for the team kicking second). "The coin toss to choose who goes first is not a fifty-fifty toss but nearer a sixty-forty toss," he said, "where the team kicking first has a 22% probability advantage over their opponents."*

The figures are more pronounced in the Champions League than in World Cup games, though the differences aren't huge:[†]

Figure 14: Kicking order in penalty shoot-outs

Competition	Kicking First Wins	Kicking Second Wins
World Cup	59%	41%
Champions League	63%	37%
UEFA Cup	56%	44%
Finals & semifinals	60%	40%
International club competitions	59%	41%
Domestic cups	61%	39%

---

*This information had clearly not made its way to Greece captain Giorgios Karagounis, who was reported to have won the toss in the 2014 World Cup Round of 16 tie against Costa Rica. Karagounis chose to kick second, and, after the first seven kicks were scored, Theofanis Gekas, a former teammate of Costa Rican goalkeeper Keylor Navas at Levante, had his shot saved. Gekas had reacted to the referee's whistle quicker than any other player in the shoot-out and had perhaps tempted fate pre–World Cup by starring in a Vodafone advertisement in which a young fan saves his penalty.
[†]The following table (Figure 14) appears in Palacios-Huerta's book *Beautiful Game Theory*.

To make things fairer for both teams in a shoot-out, Palacios-Huerta wants to reduce that 22% probability margin to a smaller figure, and he believes he has found a way to do it. In his 2012 paper "Tournaments, fairness and the Prouhet-Thue-Morse sequence," he writes: "If the order AB offers *any* kind of advantage to *either* player, then by reversing the order in the next two rounds we will tend to compensate for that advantage."

The closest scenario to that is the tennis tiebreak, where Player A serves first, then Player B serves twice, until the winner gets to seven points (and leads by two). The tennis sequence, therefore, is as follows: ABBA ABBA ABBA etc. Palacios-Huerta thinks that can be improved by reversing the original order, "to compensate for any potential advantage that might have been given to either one of the players until then." His ideal penalty order, then, is: ABBA BAAB ABBA BAAB. The single A and B serves/kicks at the end of each sequence of four would be far too confusing to work in tennis or soccer, but the idea of soccer adopting a tiebreak method would certainly make things interesting. Palacios-Huerta sent his recommendation to the eight members of the International Football Association Board (IFAB) and received six replies. His proposal is still under consideration.

One thing Petr Cech said stayed with me. He told me that he never liked to stay in the middle for a penalty because it might look, to the fans, as if he wasn't trying. I was surprised that a goalkeeper with his status would be concerned about something like that. Then I learned that he was not alone.

The idea that goalkeepers will dive for a penalty because less blame might be attached if they don't save it is known as "action bias." It was examined in a 2007 study headed by Israeli economist Michael Bar-Eli for the *Journal of Economic Psychology*.[*] The study's conclusion was that the same negative outcome (i.e., a

---

[*] Bar-Eli, Azar, Ritov, Keidar-Levin & Schein, "Action bias among elite soccer goalkeepers: the case of penalty kicks" (*Journal of Economic Psychology*, 2007).

goal) is perceived to be worse when it follows inaction rather than action. "Because the negative feeling of the goalkeeper following a goal being scored is amplified when staying in the center," the study reported, "the goalkeeper prefers to jump to one of the sides, even though this is not optimal, exhibiting an 'action bias.'"

But why is it not optimal? Bar-Eli took a sample of 286 penalties and compared the direction of the kicks to the direction of the goalkeepers' dives. (The "left" and "right" in the following table refer to the goalkeeper's left and right.)

Figure 15: Kicking and diving direction

	Left	**Center**	**Right**
Kick direction	92 (32%)	82 (29%)	112 (39%)
Dive direction	141 (49%)	18 (6%)	127 (44%)

It is clear that of these kicks, taken from a random sample of the top four leagues in Europe and some Israeli matches, the option to kick down the middle is almost as popular (at 29%) as going for either side. Yet goalkeepers only choose the middle as their preferred decision 6% of the time.

Bar-Eli and his team then looked into the goalkeepers' attitudes and opinions about their decisions. They asked thirty-six keepers playing in Israel—two from every first division side and one from each second division side—the same questions. The first was:

When goalkeepers try to stop a penalty kick, what is the most normal thing they will do (in order of preference)?

Jump Right
Jump Left
Stay Central

They received thirty-two answers:

Right/Left/Central—16
Left/Right/Central—9
Central/Left/Right or Central/Right/Left—7

Jumping either left or right is perceived as the normal option for goalkeepers.

They then asked the goalkeepers about regret.

How bad will you feel, on a 1–10 scale (1 = won't feel bad at all, 10 = feel very bad), in each of the following situations, which present the outcome of a penalty kick in an important game?

You jumped right and a goal was scored
You jumped left and a goal was scored
You stayed in the center of the goal and a goal was scored

Fifteen of the thirty-two respondents marked down 10 to all three outcomes—making their results inconclusive for the study's purposes—but eleven said they would feel worse about a goal being scored if they stayed central and the ball had gone to either side.

So Cech is not the only one.

There's a great photo taken from the halfway line during the 2007 Community Shield shoot-out between Premier League champions Manchester United and FA Cup winners Chelsea. The game, the first at the newly opened Wembley, had finished 1–1. The picture shows Chelsea's first kicker, Claudio Pizarro, standing over the ball on the spot, with the number 14 on his back, facing an empty goal. That's right: the goal was empty. United's goalkeeper Edwin van der Sar was trying out a new tactic: walking incredibly slowly to his position, and keeping Pizarro waiting.

The goalkeeper had learned that any kind of break in routine for the taker could be disruptive. He was right. Van der Sar saved Pizarro's kick. Then he kept Frank Lampard waiting for Chelsea's second by speaking to the referee about the penalty spot, seemingly just to waste time. Lampard's shot was saved too. Van der Sar went on to save Shaun Wright-Phillips's penalty too, and United won the shoot-out 3–0—a rare scoreline.

Van der Sar tried a similar trick in the 2008 Champions League final shoot-out against the same opposition. He dragged his feet, making the Chelsea players wait for him to take his mark. On average, Petr Cech made the United players wait 0.4 second to take their penalties; van der Sar upped that to 6.4 seconds. The one player who didn't fall for it was Salomon Kalou. Interestingly, once van der Sar was ready, Kalou respotted the ball and went through his prekick routine while the goalkeeper waited. Kalou's kick was probably Chelsea's best.

Geir Jordet wondered if van der Sar was actually gaining an advantage from these tactics, so he did some analysis.

Figure 16: Waiting time and shot performance

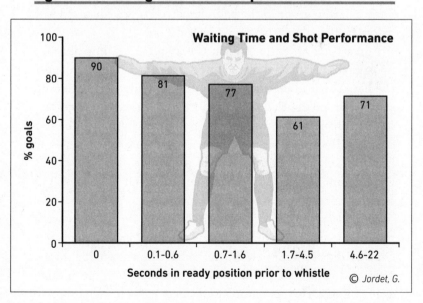

© Jordet, G.

The result is clear: strikers who have a short waiting time after spotting the ball and before the referee blows his whistle have a far better success rate from penalties, as much as 90%, than if they had to wait up to 4.5 seconds, when the conversion rate drops to 61%. Anything longer than that and it would seem the tactic is too obvious to the striker and, like Kalou, he might spot what's going on and restart his prekick routine.

Every player I spoke to about penalties said the same thing: they would prefer the goalkeeper to be ready and waiting for them, standing still on the goal line, rather than being slow to take his position or moving around on the goal line. The two most famous examples of goalkeepers putting off kickers in this fashion involve Liverpool number 1s in European Cup finals: Bruce Grobbelaar against Roma in 1984 and Jerzy Dudek against Milan in 2005.

The Roma game was the first European Cup final to be decided on penalties. The Italians were furious that Liverpool's opening goal, scored after 15 minutes by Phil Neal, had been allowed (it looked as if Ronnie Whelan had impeded goalkeeper Franco Tancredi, who dropped the ball). Roberto Pruzzo equalized just before halftime, and the game finished 1–1.

Roma took an early lead in the shoot-out when skipper Agostino di Bartolomei scored after Steve Nicol hit the ball over the bar. The lead did not last long. Phil Neal scored, then up stepped Bruno Conti, Roma's favorite son. He seemed uncertain of his run-up and smashed the ball against the top of the crossbar. He later described his miss as "unspeakable pain—my heart shrank to nothing and I was psychologically destroyed." Graeme Souness and Ian Rush netted to put Liverpool 3–2 ahead.

Then it was the turn of Francesco Graziani. He and Conti were the only two 1982 World Cup winners in Roma's squad. But Graziani did not want to take one: he had missed penalties in the 1980 and 1981 Italian Cup finals for Torino—both, ironically, against Roma. He was waiting for someone else to step forward:

"I felt there were other leaders who could take the responsibility of the penalty. Those guys had more charisma than me, so why give me that burden? But what else could I do?"

As Graziani approached the spot, Grobbelaar performed his spaghetti-legs routine: his arms went floppy, his legs wobbly, and his tongue hung out as he minced to his goal line. It became an iconic moment, and representative of Liverpool's success, but Graziani barely noticed Grobbelaar's buffoonery. He was focusing on his own routine: kissing the ball, spotting it, walking back to his mark, crossing himself and kissing his knuckle. There was only the briefest glance up, at which moment Graziani caught Grobbelaar's final leg-twitch before he started his run-up. No more than that.

Grobbelaar's natural position for penalties was a bizarre one, crouching down with his hands by his ankles. He may have been poised to pounce into a corner but he looked shrunken and made the goal look bigger. Not to Graziani, who like Conti hit his shot over the crossbar. Grobbelaar ended up the hero, but he did not make a single save.

More significant, at least in Rome, than the goalkeeper's antics was the identity of "the other leaders" Graziani mentioned—specifically Brazilian midfielder Falcão. The star of the team, Falcão had flat-out refused to take a penalty. "I only said that my legs hurt and that if someone was feeling in better shape, it was better that he took it instead of me," he claimed later. "I'm not a penalty taker, I know my limits. Other teammates are better than me at penalties—anyway, if I had taken one, it would have been the last one." It may have been the effect of Falcão's refusal, or Graziani's rotten penalty past, or the fact that Pruzzo and Toninho Cerezo, who would have taken penalties, had both gone off injured, or even the additional pressure on Roma given they were playing at home, that cost them from twelve yards.

Reports that di Bartolomei and Falcão came to blows in the dressing room after the game were denied. "We were too shocked, we sat there for an hour and said nothing," said Tancredi.

"Falcão is alone and wounded," wrote *Corriere dello Sport*. "Half of the Roma squad has turned their back on him. Bitter fans have been unforgiving. Everyone, in those decisive moments, was waiting for him to appear on the penalty spot, but Falcão stayed in midfield with his tracksuit on his shoulders. He didn't move, just gazed into the distance, looking hopeless."

There was a tragic postscript to the story. Di Bartolomei later suffered from depression and committed suicide, shooting himself on the tenth anniversary of this game. He had been Roma's captain, the heart of the team, and was devastated to be sold that summer to AC Milan, where he joined his former Roma coach Nils Liedholm. The moving documentary *11 Metri* charts his astonishing career, and questions the significance of the date of his death. In it, his son Gianmarco claimed the date was a mere coincidence, though journalist Michele Plastino disagreed: "It certainly has too strong a connection and meaning. One would think it's a message: defeated in the most important day of his career and defeated in life as well." In his diary, on that date's page, there were two pictures: one of the Curva Sud, the Roma fans' stand, and the other of Padre Pio, a saint in the Catholic Church. "I think di Bartolomei knew well what day it was," said author Andrea Salerno. "I don't believe in coincidences: that game represented the end of a dream, and of the rise in his football career."

If Grobbelaar's influence was overstated in 1984, the same cannot be said of Dudek's role twenty-one years later. This was the match in which Liverpool looked dead and buried, 3–0 down at halftime. Then came that astonishing comeback, three goals in seven minutes, the third a rebound from a missed penalty.

Dudek entered the shoot-out buzzing with confidence after an incredible last-minute point-blank double save from Andriy Shevchenko, but Jamie Carragher was worried that the Pole was too passive, and told him to get nasty. "I thought he'd stand in the goal being dead polite and nice," Carragher told Guillem Balague in *A Season on the Brink*. "I told him to do anything to put them off. He hadn't been booked, so kick the ball away and get booked if you like, just do anything to gain an advantage. Whatever you wanna call it, gamesmanship, cheating or whatever . . . fuck it . . . he's got a European Cup winner's medal now."

Liverpool coach Rafa Benitez had been meticulous with Liverpool's preparations, organizing for a DVD of the 2003 Champions League final shoot-out (in which Milan beat Juventus) to be flown over from Spain. Despite that, he only correctly predicted that Serginho and Andrea Pirlo would be taking penalties. "All you have to do is be Dudek," Liverpool's goalkeeping coach José Manuel Ochotorena reassured his goalkeeper before the shoot-out. "Allow your instincts to guide you, and do everything with self-belief."

Dudek took on all the advice. Before the first penalty, he bounced along his line, waving his arms like a windmill. If Grobbelaar's move was for the cameras, this one was designed for Serginho. It worked: the Brazilian leaned back and hit the ball over the bar.

First up for Liverpool was Didi Hamann, who scored despite having a stress fracture in his toe. Benitez wanted his two most reliable kickers, Hamann and Steven Gerrard, first and last. Milan Baroš, the other regular kicker during the season, had been substituted and Benitez had turned down three other requests to take one: from Xabi Alonso, who had missed the penalty in the second half; Luis García, whom Benitez nominated as number six; and Carragher. Benitez had also asked Djimi Traoré to take one, but the Frenchman declined.

Second up for Milan was Pirlo, and again Dudek windmilled his arms and bounced along the line. For this penalty he also leapt forward just before it was taken, and pushed the ball out clearly in front of his goal line. The referee let it go but Milan's keeper Dida had not been so lucky two years earlier, being booked for the same offence. It was obvious in 2005 that he was much more static on his line.

When Dida dived to his right but could not keep out Djibril

Cissé's kick, the Liverpool players realized that the goalkeeper had been going the same way for every kick. Jon-Dahl Tomasson pulled one back for Milan, and Dida dived right, again, to stop John Arne Riise. When Kaká's high shot hit the back of the net, Dudek was already five yards out of his goal. Vladimir Smicer, suffering from cramp, scored by kicking to Dida's left, and after four kicks each, Liverpool led 3–2.

For Milan's fifth attempt, Dudek again did his thing, hopping, bouncing, waving. Now he was facing Shevchenko, who had scored Milan's winning penalty two years earlier; but this time Shevchenko had just seen his side lose a three-goal lead, and watched in amazement as Dudek kept out his eight-yard header and two-yard rebound. Dudek dived to his right, Shevchenko went down the middle; the goalkeeper stuck out an arm and kept it out. He only realized Liverpool had won the competition when he saw Carragher running dementedly toward him.

Dudek was credited with continuing the tradition established by Grobbelaar, but there were clear differences, not least that Dudek saved three penalties to Grobbelaar's none. Grobbelaar was crowned the Clown Prince, but Dudek's achievement was greater.

The name Marco Weichert will mean nothing to soccer fans, but in summer 2011, he was crowned the Penalty King of Leipzig. Weichert wore his crown proudly, for he was a sixth division player at SV Naunhof who had beaten thirty-nine other participants, many playing at a higher level of soccer, in a shoot-out competition that was the brainchild of German sports psychologist Dr. Georg Froese.

Froese had wanted to examine the personality of successful penalty takers and was hoping to find a link between personality and strategy in penalty kicks. To do so, he invented an award, Der Elfmeterkönig von Leipzig, and invited forty players from Bundesliga 2 all the way down to division eight for a day of questions and penalties.

First, each participant had to fill out a questionnaire with five categories:

i. Soccer Ability: what their standard of play was—a self-assessment of their level
ii. Competition Anxiety: how they normally reacted to the pressure of competition
iii. State/Action Orientation: how well they focused on a single action as opposed to the more general state around that action
iv. Personal Perceptions: how they assessed their own ability to manage difficult situations
v. Regulatory Focus: similar to State/Action Orientation, it asked whether, in reaching a target, a player was prevention-focused, i.e., determined to "not fail" (state-oriented), or promotion-focused, i.e., determined to succeed (therefore action-oriented).

Each player then took twelve penalties in a qualification round, on a rotation of four kicks at three different goalkeepers, six at each end of the pitch. There was a crowd of about fifty people watching which neared a hundred when you included the other penalty takers, who knew that there was a prize at stake.

Each player was given a strategy before each penalty (the three keepers were not given any information). This could have been where to put the ball, or whether to wait for the goalkeeper to move, or to hit the ball independent of the goalkeeper's movement. Froese had broken down penalty strategies into the two methods "Independent" or "Goalkeeper-Dependent" and wanted to know which was more effective. As he put it, "Are there two totally different psychological processes at work for the two main strategies in penalty kicks?"

The best eight players from the qualification round then faced off against each other in a sudden-death shoot-out, from quarterfinals through semifinals and on to a final. The most striking result was not that a sixth division player won—in fact, soccer playing ability and how many penalties each player had taken in the past had no impact on the results—but that the Competition Anxiety factor had such a large effect on the outcome. "It was so strong that you could predict each player's success rate up to 40 percent based on that criterion alone," said Froese.

I met Froese in a café in Berlin soon after his dissertation "*Sportpsychologische Einflussfaktoren der Leistung von Elfmeterschützen*" (Sports psychological factors influencing the performance of penalty takers)—published as a book—won him the 2013 Science Award from the German FA, and a €30,000 award. As his young children played hopscotch on the street around us—and his father Michael, the Potsdam-based psychoanalyst who spoke of England's issue with "magical rationalized avoidance," listened in—Froese told me about an incident from his own playing career.

He was once suspended by his club SV Babelsburg for having a Panenka penalty saved in an important Cup game. Not only that, but as soon as the goalkeeper caught his lofted effort, he threw the ball downfield and the opposition scored. Froese is now player-manager of his own team in the German lower leagues and has taken himself off penalty duties. "One thing I learned from the Elfmeterkönig von Leipzig was that I don't have the personality to take penalties," he said.

He found two other interesting results. One was that the factors in the Personal Perceptions category had no bearing on the outcome: the self-confident players did no better than the less confident ones; indeed there was no clear evidence that any personality factor was more successful. This is significant for those who link the penalty-taking success of the likes of Matt Le Tissier and Mario Balotelli to their extrovert personalities. It also brought to my mind a comment by Pierre van Hooijdonk, who once spoke of the etiquette of penalty takers moving to a new club. "You can't demand to take penalties when you're a new signing, even if you are a specialist," he said.

"You have to discuss it with the coach first and the decision has to come from him. It's important there is no discussion on the pitch about it."

The other result was that over a long series of penalty kicks, the Goalkeeper-Dependent method was much more effective than the Independent method. "The Independent is more common, as in scary moments the kicker will take the most secure path he can. 'At least I know what I'm going to do,' he can say," Froese explained. "And the more important a penalty is, the bigger the probability that he will shoot Independent. For important games like in a World Cup, fewer penalties are placed and more are blasted. 'Close your eyes and hope.' In this case, players don't stick to their usual routines and have more chance of missing. But Goalkeeper-Dependent is more effective. If you miss it looks worse, but if the player is trained to do it in the right way, it works. It's the King's Way!"

There are not many Goalkeeper-Dependent penalty takers. Balotelli is one. He approaches the ball slowly, waits for the goalkeeper to move first, then places his kick accordingly. He has also been extremely successful, scoring the first twenty-one penalties of his career (a run that ended in September 2013 when Napoli's Pepe Reina saved his effort). Balotelli copied his method from Diego Maradona, whose highlights DVD—a gift from his mother—he watched when he was twelve. "From there I started to shoot penalties like that," Balotelli told Grant Wahl in *Sports Illustrated*. "It's mental. You have to be calm and wait for the goalkeeper to move. If the goalkeeper stays, he doesn't have time to go to one of the corners. If he moves, I see him before. It's kind of impossible for him. The only two ways I can miss a penalty are if I'm not concentrating or I shoot out."

Yasuhito Endo, Japan's most-capped player, uses the same method but is even slower than Balotelli in his approach. He walks up to the ball and rolls his shot away from the goalkeeper if he dives too early. Even when the keeper knows the strategy and waits, as Edwin van der Sar did in Manchester United's Club World Cup win over Gamba Osaka in December 2008, there is little he can do: Endo passed the ball into the corner of the net. Van der Sar went the correct way, but could not stop it. Endo scored twenty-five of his first twenty-eight penalties in twelve years at Osaka.

In Japan, Endo's method is known as the *korokoro*, an ono-matopoeic word meant to conjure a picture of something rolling slowly along the ground. For example, a six-year-old might roll a bowling ball *korokoro* down his lane; a heavy wheelbarrow is pushed *korokoro* across a field; an acorn might roll *korokoro* into a pond.* A scored *korokoro* penalty makes the goalkeeper look helpless, but Endo is adamant that is not his intention. "Tactics are very important in penalties, just as they are in the game," he told me. "If you look carefully at the goalkeeper, and especially at his legs, then outsmart him, it becomes easy to score." Endo thinks he can tell where the goalkeeper's balance will take him and just aims for the opposite side. "I never feel pressure from it, but with my present kicking style, that look at the goalkeeper is pretty much everything, that's how important it is."

The one time Endo did not take a penalty *korokoro*, in Japan's World Cup qualifying defeat to Jordan in March 2013, Amer Sabbah saved his effort. Japan's FA complained to FIFA that two players, goalkeeper Eiji Kawashima and Endo, had lasers shone into their eyes from the crowd at key points in the game. Endo admitted that the laser was on him as he prepared for the penalty, and that may be why he changed his tactic, though (possibly

---

*This is the subject of "Donguri Korokoro," a popular Japanese nursery rhyme about an acorn (*donguri*) that falls into a pond and plays with a fish until it starts to feel homesick.

to calm tensions between the sides) he claimed it did not affect his kick.*

The Goalkeeper-Dependent method was perfected by one player who did it so well that he made a mockery of any advantage goalkeepers who knew him might have had. Gaizka Mendieta used his eyes to trick the goalkeeper into diving a certain way, then would roll the ball in the other direction. It frustrated his Spain colleagues Iker Casillas and Santiago Cañizares in equal measure.

Casillas was on the receiving end in October 1999, when Valencia beat Real Madrid 3–2 at the Bernabéu. Mendieta had opened the scoring from the spot. "He did not take his eyes off me!" Casillas said. "He does not look at the ball! Jesus! What a guy!" Mendieta ended that season by netting two penalties in successive games at Euro 2000, on his way to scoring twelve out of twelve in the calendar year. France only beat Spain in the quarterfinal when Raúl missed from the spot in the last minute; Mendieta had been subbed off.

Cañizares spent eight years practicing penalties with Mendieta at Valencia, where Predrag Mijatovic was the nominated taker. Mendieta would work on his technique with Oleg Salenko, who used the same method, and after "Mija" left in 1996, Mendieta stepped in. "I looked at the ball just to place it on the penalty

---

*This was not the first time there had been penalty trouble between these two sides. In the 2004 Asian Cup quarterfinal, in a hostile atmosphere in Chongqing, China, Japan drew 1–1 with Jordan and the game went to penalties. The right side of the penalty spot was a muddy mess and Japan's first two shooters, Shunsuke Nakamura and Alex Santos, both left-footers, slipped and missed their shots. Japan captain Tsuneyasu Miyamoto asked referee Subkhiddin Mohd Salleh to inspect the pitch and the shoot-out was moved to the other end, but his appeals to restart the shoot-out at 0–0 were denied. Jordan were 2–0 and 3–1 up but missed two successive penalties that would have put them through. In sudden death, both teams missed in the first round; Miyamoto then scored for Japan, and Jordan's Bashar Bani Yaseen hit the post. Jordan had missed four penalties in a row. Japan got past Bahrain in the semifinal and went on to beat hosts China in the final.

spot and then fixed my gaze on the keeper. In that way I controlled my movement. I used my eyes and balance and it normally worked."

Valencia faced Bayern Munich in the Champions League final in 2001. It was a match of penalties: three in normal time and then a shoot-out. Mendieta scored in the third minute, beating Oliver Kahn. Cañizares then saved from Mehmet Scholl before Stefan Effenberg equalized from the spot. In the shoot-out, Mendieta kicked first for Valencia and scored again; but Zlatko Zahovic, Amedeo Carboni and, crucially, Mauricio Pellegrino all missed for the Spanish side, and Bayern won the game. "We knew we were a team who might miss one or two, we were not a team who always scored all five," remembered Cañizares. "We had so many doubts about how we were going to take the penalties, that's why we sent our best takers up first to try and get ahead."

Spain coach José Antonio Camacho had other ideas: he preferred to use Mendieta as the fifth taker in the shoot-out, and in the 2002 World Cup that had mixed success. In the Round of 16, Mendieta scored the winning penalty against Ireland after Casillas had saved from David Connolly and Kevin Kilbane. "Gaizka is a specialist, he does not get nervous, he controls it very well. He is mentally very strong," said Camacho. In the next round, against South Korea, the strategy backfired: youngster Joaquin missed Spain's fourth and the Koreans scored all five, leaving Mendieta waiting in vain. "I gave it to the kid because he wanted it, and there were four players who didn't," the coach explained.

All those years of practice with Cañizares did the goalkeeper no good at all in June 2003 when, as a Barcelona player, Mendieta won and then took a penalty. Back at the Mestalla, where he made his name, against his former teammate, he had no problem waiting for Cañizares to move and then placing the ball the other way. When I asked Mendieta about it, he moved his small eyes left and right and said, "Yeah, it was all in the eyes, nothing else."

I had some other data-related penalty questions that demanded answers, so I asked James W. Grayson to run more analyses to see if perceived wisdom about penalties could be backed up with numbers.* My first question was: if the World Cup is meant to be the competition with the best players, does it have the best record when it comes to penalty conversion—notwithstanding that it also has the best goalkeepers, of course?

1. Which competition has the best penalty conversion record?

The anti-international soccer lobby likes to claim that the Champions League, not the World Cup, is where the best soccer is now played. It makes for a compelling debate as to whether or not Spain would beat Bayern Munich or Barcelona (in the latter case, that would practically be Spain taking on Spain plus Lionel Messi). I wondered how penalty records fluctuated across competitions, and if the greater the pressure, the lower the conversion rates. Grayson threw up some interesting findings. First, he broke down the success rates of penalties in open play across leagues and competitions:

Figure 17: Successful penalties in open play

Competition	Sample Size	Conversion Rate
La Liga	521	80.2%
Eredivisie	418	79.9%
Serie A	597	79.2%
Bundesliga	366	78.7%
Ligue 1	424	78.3%
Premier League	487	76.8%
Total	2,813	78.9%

*As before, Grayson used data from Infostrada Sports, which was taken from every World Cup (1930–2010) and European Championship (1962–2012), every penalty taken in the top league in England, Italy, Germany, Spain, France and Holland from 2007/08 to 2012/13, and Champions League penalties from 2002/03 to 2012/13.

Competition	Sample Size	Conversion Rate
World Cup	203	80.3%
Champions League	528	79.2%
European Championship	59	74.6%
Total	790	79.1%

© Infostrada

He ran the same analysis for shoot-outs only, and the picture was very different:

Figure 18: Successful penalties in shoot-outs

Competition	Sample Size	Conversion Rate
World Cup*	202	71.3%
Champions League	189	69.8%
European Championship	153	82.4%

© Infostrada

The sample size is not huge—especially for open-play penalties in the European Championship—but you can see the drop in conversion rate for the World Cup and Champions League competitions. When the stakes are this high, for reasons of either national prestige or for financial prizes, players struggle. On the other hand, the European Championship conversion rate is far higher for shoot-outs than for open-play penalties.

2. Is a home team more likely to be awarded (and score) a penalty?

When the referee is described as "a homer," it's because he has given decisions that appear to favor the home side. This is tricky

---

*The reason why the ratio between open play and shoot-out penalties is almost 1:1 in World Cups and 1:3 in the European Championship is because the World Cup data goes back to 1930, whereas shoot-outs only started in 1982. With the European Championship, the data begins in 1962 with shoot-outs starting in 1976.

to assess, because that home side, given its natural advantage (in the majority of cases, anyway), is more likely to be an attacking force and to demand more decisions in the penalty area in the first place.

Grayson broke down the numbers by attendance to see if there was any correlation between penalties awarded to the home side and crowd size.

Figure 19: Penalties and home advantage

Attendance	Total Pens	% of Pens Awarded to Home Side
0–17,499	1,028	60.0%
17,500–27,499	820	61.3%
27,500–42,499	893	65.3%
42,500+	851	65.6%

© Infostrada

There is a clear jump from 61% to 65% in the proportion of penalties awarded to home teams once the attendance passes 27,500. It follows that better teams are likely to have larger crowds, more attacking possession and therefore be expected to win more penalties. But is this related to the greater noise of a crowd trying to convince a referee to award a penalty? We will investigate this further when we look at the role of referees in the penalty drama.

Grayson broke down the numbers further, as I wondered if the crowd size played any role in the success of penalties.

Figure 20: Penalties and crowd size

| Attendance | HOME | | AWAY | |
	Pens	Conversion	Pens	Conversion
0–17,499	617	80.4%	411	76.4%
17,500–27,499	503	79.9%	317	75.1%
27,500–42,499	583	78.7%	310	78.7%
42,500+	558	82.3%	293	75.4%

© Infostrada

There is no real pattern to the numbers here, though it is noteworthy that the home conversion record is best when the attendance is highest, and that the record of away teams' shooters drops when the crowd is highest.

3. Is the team that scored last most likely to win the shoot-out?

There are some obvious examples of momentum seemingly pushing a team on to an inevitable victory on penalties, most often when defeat seemed certain during normal time: the 2005 Champions League final, when Liverpool came back from 0–3 down against AC Milan, and the 2012 Champions League final between Chelsea and Bayern Munich. Going into those shoot-outs, given the boost that Liverpool and Chelsea clearly had by getting themselves back into the game, they had an advantage—or did they?

Figure 21: Last scorer before penalty shoot-out

	No. of Pens	Conversion	Win Ratio
Scored last in match	185	78.4%	61.1%
Conceded last in match	184	72.8%	38.9%

© Infostrada

Scoring the final goal in the game clearly has an impact on the conversion rates and the subsequent winning ratios. If a team scored last and kicked first in the shoot-out, it would be expected to go on and win.

4. Does wearing the captain's armband make any difference to penalty success?

The captain may not always be the best player, but when it comes to taking responsibility from the spot, is it easier for the man wearing the armband to hide? The numbers suggest that is exactly what happens: captains take 13% of open-play penalties but only 8% of penalties in shoot-outs. Given that there are eleven players per team, there is an 8.8% chance of any player taking a spot kick (that rises to 10% if you exclude goalkeepers), which shows that, from this data sample, captains are less likely than the average player to take a penalty in a shoot-out. As for whether they are successful . . .

Figure 22: Captains and penalties

Status	OPEN PLAY		SHOOT-OUTS	
	Sample	Conversion	Sample	Conversion
Captain	479	80.5%	42	71.4%
Noncaptain	3,096	78.5%	477	73.0%

© Infostrada

The result of this analysis is interesting, even if it's not too surprising. Captains who score penalties in open play have a slightly better record than noncaptains, but the picture is different in a shoot-out scenario. In that instance, the captains' success rate drops to 71.4%. Captains may be less likely than other players to take penalties, but are those who do pushed into spot-kicking duty by virtue of wearing the armband?

5. Is a substitute more likely to score in a shoot-out than someone who's played the full 120 minutes?

I held a long-standing theory, based on nothing but a hunch, that bringing on a penalty specialist in extra time might help teams in a shoot-out. Geir Jordet captured this data and it seems to back this up—though I am mindful of Rickie Lambert's comment about the feel of the turf helping a player's confidence. So this theory may work best if the penalty specialist came on not one minute before the shoot-out, as Jamie Carragher did against Portugal in 2006, but nearer thirty minutes.

Figure 23: Playing time and penalty shoot-out conversion

Playing Time	Sample Size	Conversion
1–30 mins	15	86.7%
31–90 mins	72	81.9%
91–120 mins	322	78%

The numbers show that the chances of shoot-out success decrease the longer a player spends on the pitch. The sample size for players brought on in extra time who then go on to take a penalty is very small—only fifteen players, and you would expect them to have more expertise if they are taking a penalty in that scenario. It's a table, therefore, that economists would say is "not statistically significant." Nonetheless it strengthens my belief that all coaches should take a penalty specialist to major tournaments and keep him on the bench until required. It may only be for one kick, but as Matt Le Tissier put it, "You only need one missed kick to get knocked out, so why take the chance?"

6. Where should a coach pick his best penalty takers in a shoot-out?

The common perception is that your best taker should take the fifth penalty; but sometimes being chosen fifth means the shoot-out will be over before it's your turn. Matt Le Tissier and Steven Gerrard may have been relieved when that happened, but not so Cristiano Ronaldo, whose Portugal side lost on penalties to Spain in Euro 2012 before he could take one; nor Mendieta, who could do nothing as South Korea scored their five in 2002.

Palacios-Huerta looked in detail at the ideal kicking-order in a shoot-out.* He took into account the "sample bias" of every

---

*Palacios-Huerta & Apesteguia, "Psychological pressure in competitive environments: evidence from a randomized natural experiment" (*American Economic Review*).

penalty—which depends on the score, the team and the round of shooting—to produce an "index of importance." The variables make the index complicated to decipher but a pattern does emerge: that for the most frequent paths (when the score is level when the first team is kicking, and when the second team is behind), the importance variable drops from the first round to the second for the first team, and from the first to the second and third for the second team, before it rises for the fourth and fifth penalties.

We all know that penalty numbers four and five are important, but Palacios-Huerta's index shows they are important in a stand-alone sense as well as because of what's occurred in the penalties that took place before them. "In round 1, for instance, the first team begins with a 60.2% chance of winning," he explains. "If it scores, this probability increases 7.1% to 67.3%, and if it misses the probability drops 26.9% to 33.3%. The corresponding figures for round 5 are +17.6% and −35.7% respectively. Thus, the cumulative impact of any scoring rate differentials over five rounds can be substantial."

The basic shape of Palacios-Huerta's "importance" variable is a U-shape, with the more important penalties at numbers one, four and five, though number four is marginally more important for the team kicking first than second. Maybe next time Portugal are in a shoot-out, Ronaldo might want to bear that in mind.

PENALTY ICON—
RIK COPPENS

Rik Coppens was past his best when he pulled off a penalty trick that no one had dared try before. It was 1957, and Belgium were leading Iceland 4–0 in a World Cup qualifier. Coppens said *"Twee tijden"* ("Two touches") to teammate André Piters, hoping he would understand what he meant. The pair had never before discussed or practiced the penalty.

Coppens ran toward the ball, on a seven-step run-up, then, opening his boot, rolled it into the path of "Popeye" Piters. The ball did three revolutions and Piters had to dive to get there before the goalkeeper, but he made contact. The ball rolled back toward Coppens, who side-footed it into the goal.

"It was my decision," Coppens explained to me. "We were well ahead, so nothing could go wrong. I wanted to do something special for the public. I was a show-off, loved being creative. Coming up with something like this was normal for me." Belgian FA officials were not so enamored with Coppens's choice of penalty. He was not selected for the return match between the two sides.

Coppens was one of the best players Belgium ever produced. The tragedy was that he never won a trophy and his peak years,

1950 to 1954, were before European club competitions began. Not that he would have played in many of them: he spent most of his career at his local side Germinal Beerschot, whose idea of success was finishing fourth in the Belgian first division (which they did, thanks to him).

His parents owned a fish-shop and Coppens would duck out of serving there to train. His diet helped him. "I had strong bones, sturdy legs, because of all that protein I ate as a kid," he said. "Even now, nothing beats a bit of stockfish with mustard sauce, or skate. Turbot! A good piece of cod. Haddock. Eel. I like fish twenty times more than meat!"

If the Iceland penalty was his most audacious moment, his best performance had come three years earlier, shortly after Belgium drew 4–4 with England in the 1954 World Cup. "We played against West Germany in their first game after they had been crowned world champions and we beat them 2–0. That was the best game of my career." Coppens was up against Werner Liebrich, Germany's best defender, and he ran him ragged. "Coppens made a fool out of him," said Frank Raes, who cowrote a biography of Coppens, *Ik, Rik Coppens*, and played for Beerschot in the one season Coppens was coach there. "Coppens would dribble round Liebrich and then do it again. He was the 'King of Dribble,' technically so good: a hero, a rebel, and an icon." And as a coach? "He was better as a player."

In 1954, Coppens was the first Belgian to win the country's Golden Boot. By then, Beerschot had fought off interest from foreign clubs wanting to sign him: Napoli, Inter Milan, Espanyol and Barcelona, who had just missed out on Alfredo di Stefano, were all interested. "Beerschot kept saying no to any club that wanted me, they just wanted to keep me," said Coppens. "I was never angry with them for that." One agent offered him a blank check, but he had no idea what club he was representing. "In those days, you stuck with your club, and that's what I did."

Coppens is now eighty-three, and he lives in Wilrijk. He can see the Beerschot stadium floodlights from his apartment. I asked him if he gets bored of talking about the "two-touch" penalty. "Yes," he replied. I can see why: his legacy deserves to be about more than a gimmick penalty that Johan Cruyff repeated twenty-five years later.

"I heard Johan Cruyff call it unique," Coppens said. "I didn't like that, Johan Cruyff shouldn't have said that."

Cruyff probably didn't know that Coppens had invented the penalty: he was ten years old when the Iceland game took place, and it was hardly likely to have been shown on television. Some highlights of matches were shown on news bulletins in the local cinema, but Cruyff had been a professional for nineteen years before he tried it. Surely he would not have waited so long to copy it?

In 2005, Arsenal's Robert Pires tried to reprise the "two-touch" penalty. His job was to pass it to Thierry Henry, who was not going to pass it back, but score himself. Arsenal were leading Manchester City 1–0, ironically through a Pires penalty (Henry had been brought down in the box but did not want to take the spot kick). The day before the game Henry had persuaded Pires to try the routine at the end of a training match. Penalties were rarely given in training, but on this occasion Pat Rice was the referee and he awarded one. Significantly, Henry took the first touch and Pires ran on to score.

"When he first explained it I laughed and thought, 'Only Titi could come up with that,'" Pires explained. "But as far as I was concerned, that was it. It was over and done with. Never in a million years did I think we'd be doing the same thing the next day."

Pires then explained what happened against City, and how he succumbed to peer pressure from his compatriot. Ten minutes after the first penalty, Arsenal won another. "Titi came up to me and said, 'OK, we'll do our special.' I said, 'You've got to be joking! Not in a real match!' But he said, 'Come on, yeah, yeah, yeah, this is the time to do it, we're winning.' I really didn't want to do it but he convinced me.

"The problem was that we've now reversed the roles. In training he touched the ball to me and I scored, but now he was asking me to take the penalty and he was going to run in and score. I can tell you, in my head things were not going very well. I said, 'We shouldn't do it.' The last thing he said was, 'Don't worry, I'll be there.'

"So I step forward and put the ball on the spot. I turn back and look to see where Thierry is. He was behind two City players! The last image I have of him in my mind is that, so now I'm even more in two minds: should I do it or not? OK: I do my run-up, stand in front of the ball, and in all honesty from then on it's a total black-out. I still can't see what I did. Everything went black. My foot went over the top of the ball, I don't think I even touched it, then I see Titi next to me saying, 'What are you doing?' I felt so stupid. It was a terrible feeling knowing I'd mucked it up. One of their players gave me a real mouthful, it was Danny Mills: he came up and shouted in my face how I was taking the piss and I was an arrogant Frenchman. I couldn't even answer back. I was frozen. I just felt terrible."

Pires only learned after the event that Cruyff had done something similar before, and it was when we spoke that he heard the name of Coppens for the first time. Would he have felt disrespected if someone had tried the same move against his team? "Honestly, no. If that happened against us and they scored, I think I would have applauded. It's a daring thing to try and we need fantasy in football. I just wish we'd managed it."

Coppens, though, was the original showman. When he returned from a long injury lay-off after fracturing his ankle, 10,000 fans turned up on a Sunday morning to a reserve team game against Beringen. Beerschot won 9–1. Coppens didn't score. "He was like Maradona without the drugs," said Raes. "A unique talent." He would dribble round a goalkeeper twice just to make sure, and once lay down on the goal line and pushed the ball over the line with his nose.

He thought penalty taking was a simple art, even if he did sometimes respot the ball four or five times before he was ready to strike. "A penalty is just for technical players," he added. "I didn't really practice them, but I don't understand how you can miss a penalty. They are so simple."

CHAPTER 6

STATUS ANXIETY

The 2012 Champions League semifinal second legs were more dramatic than anyone could have expected. On the Tuesday night, Bayern Munich won a shoot-out against Real Madrid after Cristiano Ronaldo and Sergio Ramos both missed. The following night, Chelsea overcame Barcelona in an incredible match at Camp Nou, the most surprising element of which was Lionel Messi missing a second-half penalty. Had he scored, Barcelona would have been 3–1 ahead and, with Chelsea reduced to ten men after John Terry's red card, surely on their way to the final.

In the space of twenty-four hours, the two best players in the world, possibly among the best that have ever played the game, each missed a penalty. I buy into the argument that over the years their personal rivalry has pushed them to improve—without Messi, I doubt Ronaldo would have reached the level he has, and vice versa—but following each other's penalty misses? That was too weird.

We all know that these things can happen. Anyone can miss a penalty. And big players will miss big penalties, because they are usually the ones who take them. But this was the Champions

League semifinal, the most important game of that season given that both clubs had made the competition their priority and, arguably, were just a penalty away from reaching the final. So why did they miss in this particular game?

Geir Jordet thinks he has the answer. He looked at thirty-seven shoot-outs from World Cup, European Championship and Champions League games. There were 298 different players taking 366 kicks. He divided the players into three categories: current-status players, no-status players, and future-status players. By current-status he was referring to players who have won individual recognition for their performances, either a top-three place in FIFA's World Player of the Year awards, the Ballon D'Or vote, South America's Footballer of the Year, the World Cup Golden Boot, or a place in UEFA's Team of the Year: 41 players, taking 67 penalties, fell into this category. No-status players were those who had not won and never did win awards; future-status were those who had not won awards when they took their penalties, but would go on to win awards in the future.

Figure 24: Status and performance

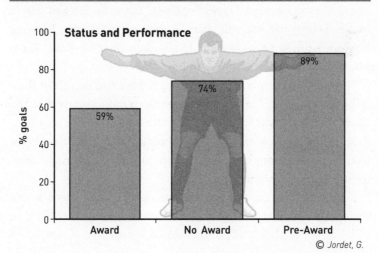

© Jordet, G.

His results were surprising: overall, 74% of the penalties were scored, but the current-status players only scored with 59% of their kicks; the no-status players scored with 74% and the future-status players with 89%. The current-status players also missed the target more often than the others, on 13% of their kicks, compared to 7% for future-status players and 5% for no-status players.

Jordet named examples of players whose penalty records changed after winning awards. Frank Lampard scored for England against Portugal in 2004. In 2005, he came second in FIFA's World Player of the Year award and the Ballon D'Or. In 2006, against Portugal again, he missed a penalty. Ronaldo, in that same game in 2006, scored the winning penalty for his country; by the time he stepped up for Manchester United in the 2008 Champions League final he was Ballon D'Or silver medalist (he would go on to win gold, among many other awards, that season) and had been named in UEFA's Team of the Year. He missed his penalty against Chelsea.

OK, two players do not make an analysis stand up, but there are others who have missed important penalties. Messi, as we know. Steven Gerrard. David Beckham. Clarence Seedorf. Paolo Maldini. Diego Maradona. Jaap Stam. Didier Drogba. Roberto Baggio. Andriy Shevchenko. Marco van Basten. Raúl. Zico. Michel Platini. What is going on here?

"Current-status players have more to lose and therefore their fall will be bigger," Jordet explained. He recommends that the coach identifies which players have the highest public status or most inflated public expectations, "because these individuals are likely to experience extra performance pressure" and might need to be taught coping mechanisms.*

Jordet also found that the current-status pattern occurs on a team level as well: teams with more superstars are more likely to

---

*"When superstars flop: public status and 'choking under pressure' in international soccer penalty shootouts" (*Journal of Applied Sport Psychology*).

perform badly in penalties. He noted that teams with 20–50% of current-status players scored 67% of their penalties compared to teams with no-status players at 86%, and 1–20% of current-status players at 71%.*

I wanted to look deeper into his results and see if the pressure of expectation for current-status players really is the common factor explaining why big players miss big penalties. There was only one place for me to start: when the best player in the world missed a penalty in the biggest game in the world.

The headline was short and sweet. It ran on April 7, 1991, in *Gazzetta dello Sport*: "*Baggio, il gran rifiuto*" (Baggio, the great refusal). It was a clear nod to the country's most famous literary *gran rifiuto*, which is how the poet Dante referred to Pope Celestine V's abdication of the Papacy in 1294 in his most celebrated work, the *Divina Commedia* (Divine Comedy). Celestine was the first Pope to formalize the resignation process, and Dante wrote of a nameless figure he saw in Hell: "*Vidi e conobbi l'ombra di colui che per viltade fece il gran rifiuto*" (I saw him and I knew his soul, he whose cowardice had made the great refusal).†

The day before the *Gazzetta dello Sport* pronouncement another deified figure had abdicated his responsibility.‡ Roberto Baggio, after five successful years at Fiorentina, had returned to Florence for the first time with his new club Juventus. He was nervous. He had scored all thirteen penalties for Juventus that season, but when his coach Luigi Maifredi asked him the night before the game if he wanted to take a penalty against Fiorentina, his eyes betrayed the answer.

---

* "Why do English players fail in soccer penalty shootouts? A study of team status, self-regulation, and choking under pressure" (*Journal of Sports Sciences*).

† "Inferno" III, lines 59–60.

‡ *Gazzetta*'s headline writers had made a mistake: April 6 is indeed St. Celestine's Day in Italy, but the day commemorates Pope Celestine I, not Pope Celestine V, whose feast day is May 19. They had the right headline, but the wrong saint.

Fiorentina fans had made no secret of their displeasure at the club selling their star player to hated rivals. Baggio, then twenty-three years old, knew his career was about to take a big leap forward, but he was suffering inside. As he reportedly told a friend a few days before the return to Florence, "It's about time I decide what I want to do when I grow up."

A few years earlier, Nicolà Berti had been so upset at the abuse he received from Fiorentina fans when he first returned to the club after joining Inter Milan that he was taken off after half an hour. Baggio lasted longer than that, despite the incessant taunts: "*Baggio puttanà, l'hai fatto per la grana!*" (Baggio, you whore, you did it for the money!)

When Stefano Salvatori brought down Baggio five minutes into the second half, referee Rosario Lo Bello had no hesitation in awarding a penalty. Baggio had already told his teammates before the game that he would not be taking a spot kick, so Luigi de Agostini, penalty taker the previous season, stepped up. As Baggio walked away from the goal, his teammates Julio César and Marco de Marchi embraced him, understanding what this moment meant. Fiorentina goalkeeper Gianmatteo Mareggini saved de Agostini's effort. Diego Fuser went on to score the only goal of the game, and Fiorentina won 1–0.

Had de Agostini scored, had Juventus won the game, this story would be different. If, when Baggio was substituted ten minutes later, a female fan had not thrown a Fiorentina scarf at his feet, this story would be different. Maybe if Baggio, on seeing the scarf, had not picked it up and, clutching it, applauded his former fans, this story would be different. But he did.

Baggio had embraced his great friend at Fiorentina, Stefano Borgonovo (who tragically died in the summer of 2013), before he left the pitch. Borgonovo did a double-take when he saw Baggio bend down to grab the scarf: "He would never have picked up the scarf if he remembered he was playing for Juventus."

Fiorentina president Mario Cecchi Gori led a standing ovation as Baggio walked off. That started the turnaround from whistles to cheers, as the crowd, briefly, fell back in love with its former hero. One set of fans unfurled a banner that read "The war is over, give us back the hostage."

If anything, it was a moment of closure between the player and the club, a final gesture before Baggio could move on. Not that he had much sympathy from the press, or indeed his own teammates. De Agostini said he didn't mind stepping in because "I'm a guy who takes responsibility." Maifredi understood Baggio's decision but "still hoped he would take the penalty." Juventus president Gianni Agnelli wanted Baggio kept on the bench all game, brought on just for the penalty and then taken off again.

A poll of *Gazzetta* readers voted 81% that Baggio was wrong to avoid taking the penalty. Its journalist Alfio Caruso wondered if the decision hinted at a mental weakness: "Baggio started to behave like a luxury nonleaguer . . . It's a paradox but this is the transfer that might damage his career the most as it has shown how vulnerable he is, how weak his character and how fragile his psychology."

"Baggio was scared, silent, still, nonexistent, he had shrunk," wrote *Gazzetta*'s Claudio Gregori. "Not taking the penalty was a proper desertion. He was a victim of that psychoanalytic group session where one takes his own past. He probably needed Freud more than Maifredi."

Two years later, in 1993, the "deserter," described by former Fiorentina teammate Giancarlo Antognoni as "just a man like anyone else," was FIFA World Footballer of the Year and Ballon D'Or winner. By the time the 1994 World Cup came around he was the star of Italian soccer. He had two problems, though: one, he went into the tournament with two injuries, a knee that had bothered him all season and tendonitis in his right foot. The other was coach Arrigo Sacchi, whose adherence to a compact 4–4–2 system left little room for a *fantasista* such as Baggio.

Sacchi had tried out over seventy players in the build-up to the tournament—so many, in fact, that one magazine ran pictures of the Pope, Rambo and Popeye under the headline "Arrigo, have you forgotten anyone?"

Italy lost their opening match, against the Republic of Ireland, then beat Norway after Sacchi had controversially taken off Baggio on 20 minutes following goalkeeper Gianluca Pagliuca's red card. "This is crazy," lip-readers claimed Baggio said as he trudged off. So much for Sacchi's promise that Baggio was as important to Italy as Maradona was to Argentina. "His creativity often felt trapped in Sacchi's system," said teammate Gigi Casiraghi, who'd expected to be withdrawn instead. "He had some problems with the coach." Casiraghi proved a better option for the team a man down, and Italy won 1–0. But there was more collateral damage: early in the second half, captain Franco Baresi went off injured.

Italy drew 1–1 with Mexico in game three, and Group E ended like this:

	P	W	D	L	F	A	Pts
Mexico	3	1	1	1	3	3	4
Ireland	3	1	1	1	2	2	4
Italy	3	1	1	1	2	2	4
Norway	3	1	1	1	1	1	4

Italy sneaked into the next round as one of the four best third-placed teams, having scored one more goal than Norway. They faced Nigeria next, and the pressure was mounting on Italy's star man. Agnelli had called Baggio a *"coniglio bagnato"* (wet rabbit) after the Mexico game. Baggio laughed it off, and changed his answer-phone message to say he would return calls "once I have dried my ears."

He had last scored for the Azzurri in April 1993—a drought that had now lasted fourteen months. His family could see that he was feeling the pressure so, against his wishes, his wife Andreina, daughter Valentina and parents Matilde and Florindo flew to Massachusetts for the Round of 16 game against Nigeria. "He's a sensitive guy and I could see he needed reassurance. When he saw us, he cheered up," said Matilde.

Nigeria took the lead, but with two minutes left (and shortly after Gianfranco Zola had been sent off), Italy's campaign came to life: Roberto Mussi jinked past two defenders, cut the ball back to Baggio on the edge of the area, and he drove the ball home to equalize. Ten minutes later, Baggio scored again, this time from a penalty. He waited for Peter Rufai to take a step to his left then smashed it hard to his right, in off the post.

He scored again in the quarterfinal win over Spain with two minutes left, a dramatic winner from Giuseppe Signori's lobbed pass to make it 2–1. Then, in the semifinal against Bulgaria, again Baggio was the hero. His first goal was sensational: a run from the left, past two defenders, before curling a shot into the far corner; the second, five minutes later, secured the 2–1 win. Baggio went off with twenty minutes left with a hamstring strain, leaving Sacchi to complain, "It's a pity he gets himself injured just as he finds his form."

There were four days until the final. Baggio was injured, Baresi had undergone arthroscopic surgery on his knee, and Italy were without defenders Alessandro Costacurta and Mauro Tassotti, both suspended. There was also the travel factor: their opponents Brazil had played their semifinal in Pasadena's Rose Bowl, the final venue, while Italy had played in New York and needed a six-hour flight to get to LA.

Baggio did not train for three days and on the morning of the final gingerly tested his leg in the wedding-reception room at Torrance's Marriott Hotel. Sacchi named the team but was still not sure whether to include Baresi and Baggio. His initial team sheet read:

Pagliuca
Bennarivo
Baresi (Apolloni)
Albertini
Maldini
Mussi

Donadoni
Berti
D Baggio
R Baggio (Signori)
Massaro

Sacchi had made all his players take penalties at the end of every training session. Signori and Baggio had not missed a single kick. Three hours before kick-off, after drinking a coffee, Baggio told Sacchi, "I'm ready to play."

Brazil hit the post when Pagliuca fumbled Mauro Silva's shot, Romário dragged wide from four yards, and Baggio had two glimpses of goal, one sliced over, the other hit straight at Claudio Taffarel. "I could have scored but I missed the chances because I was not calm inside myself," he later said. "In other circumstances and in better physical shape, I'm sure the real Baggio would have made the most of that pass from Massaro. But my World Cup was over when I got injured against Bulgaria."

The match, played in searing heat, ended goalless. It was the first ever World Cup final to be decided on penalties and it did not go down at all well. "Imagine listening to [Abraham] Lincoln and [Frederick] Douglass debate for two hours and then having them step down from their podiums to decide a winner on belches," wrote Alex Wolff in *Sports Illustrated*. FIFA president Sepp Blatter promised it would be "the first final, and the very last" to be decided on penalties, and claimed it was not a sporting way to end such a game. "Football is a collective sport, while penalties are an individual skill," he pointed out.

Italy gathered in the center circle, and Baggio could sense the tension. "We were all feeling the same before the penalties. We could see the fear in each other's eyes. When you're taking penalties, you need to be focused and clear-headed, but we weren't."

Baresi kicked first for Italy. His performance had been heroic, especially given the speed of his recovery from injury. Nine years earlier, Baresi had taken two and a half months to recover from the same operation on his left knee; this time he was back on the field in less than four weeks. His penalty flew over the bar. Brazil did not take advantage: Pagliuca saved from Marcio Santos. The next four penalties—from Demetrio Albertini, Romário, Alberigo Evani and Branco—were all scored.

Up stepped Daniele Massaro, the Milan striker who was top scorer for the Italian champions that season. He had also scored twice in the Champions League final, a 4–0 demolition of Barcelona. His form had earned a late call-up, though before the tournament he had not played for Italy for eight years (he and Baresi were the only players who had been part of Italy's 1982 World Cup-winning squad). Massaro had only recently been converted into a striker: he'd started out in midfield for Fiorentina and as a winger for Sacchi at Milan. Fabio Capello moved him to center forward when he was thirty-one, and he was a popular impact sub whose availability and lack of moaning won the fans over. He called himself soccer's first *aziendalista*, or company man, whose motto was always "Put the team first."

"It was my moral duty to take a penalty," Massaro recalled almost twenty years later. "I saw some of my teammates try to hide, but I felt I was one of the leaders of that team, and those are the times when you have to prove yourself in front of others. Just before the penalty I didn't feel so bad, I was pretty confident of scoring. But the next ten seconds, it's like there's been a black-out in my mind. Like I lost myself when the kick happened, like it was a dream."

More like a nightmare. Massaro hit it poorly and Taffarel saved.

"My first feeling was one of surprise. How could I have made such a big mistake? I then felt sorry, not for me but my teammates. But I never felt guilty. Never! You can only make a mistake if you step up in the first place. I'm proud that I took responsibility. No regrets."

Brazil captain Dunga scored to make it 3–2, and Baggio was next. He was a specialist. He had scored a penalty on his Vicenza debut, when he was just sixteen, against Brescia. He liked to wait for the goalkeeper to move before choosing his corner, and his penalty record—108 goals out of 122 kicks (a success rate of 88%)—remains an Italian record.

He described what happened next in his autobiography, *Una Porta nel Cielo* (A Goal in the Sky):

At times, you intend to do one thing and another thing happens altogether. I don't want to exaggerate but I haven't missed many penalties in my career. And even when I didn't score, it's because they were saved, not because I shot over the bar.

This is to make you understand that what happened in Pasadena doesn't have a simple explanation. When I went to the spot I was relatively lucid—well, as much as you can be in those moments. I knew that Taffarel always dived. I knew him well. So I decided to go down the middle, half height, around half a meter or little more than that, because Taffarel never managed to make saves with his feet. It was an intelligent choice because Taffarel effectively threw himself to his left and he would never have got to the central trajectory that I had in mind. Unfortunately, and I don't know how, the ball rose three meters and flew over the bar.

Was I up to it? Well, I was the first-choice penalty taker. There wasn't a reason why I wouldn't take one. The only players who miss penalties are those who don't have the courage to take one. That time I missed. It affected me for years. I still dream about it. Getting over that nightmare was difficult.

"Baggio had spent his entire career telling us that poetry in football doesn't exist in the penalty, but that miss in Pasadena told us a lot of things," said Vanni Santoni, author of *L'Ascensione di Roberto Baggio*, a novella that paints Baggio as a sainted figure often talking to God, while Sacchi sits in a chemical bath in Coverciano, Italy's national training center. "It embodied Italy's struggle to combine beauty and victory. It portrayed him more than scoring would have done. He came out of it purified."

It also summed up the many contrasts of his career. Baggio was one of the best players of his generation, yet only ever won a UEFA Cup and a Coppa Italia. He scored in three World Cups, but Italy lost on penalties in all of them. He was a Buddhist, yet obsessed with hunting. Later in his career he took the trouble to write a nine-hundred-page document on how to improve Italian soccer, but resigned from his position at the Italian FA as "President of the Technical Department" after a year. As he whispered during a rare interview in 2013, "It's true, victory always just eluded me."

That image of Baggio, hands on hips, looking down at the spot as Brazil burst into celebration, is one of the most iconic in soccer. But for the Italians, Baresi summed up the moment of yet another World Cup elimination on penalties. The warrior-defender could not stop crying, and the more his teammates tried to console him, the more he wept. "He was like a sad baby out there on the pitch," wrote Giorgio Tosatti in *Corriere dello Sport*. "After winning so many wars, he lost his last battle. In many years he had never lost control, his cool, his pride. He once played with a broken arm but we never saw his tears despite the huge pain. It was like watching Rambo cry.

"What can you say to such players? What can you say to Roberto Baggio, if he wanted to play and make another miracle for Italy despite the injury, but he missed a couple of chances and a penalty instead? Hadn't somebody criticized him for not being brave enough? He was certainly brave this time around. What can you say to Massaro, tired to death, if Taffarel saved his penalty? Their pain is just bigger than ours."

There was no criticism, just sadness, in the days that followed. Over a thousand Lazio fans went to Fiumicino airport to welcome back Beppe Signori, and he hadn't even played in the final (though he probably should have done).

The idea held that penalties were unfair, and Baggio was adamant that the golden goal, which was introduced in time for Euro 96, or even a replay, would be better. "Does it seem [right] to you that four years of sacrifices come to be decided by three minutes of penalty kicks? Not to me. It's not right to lose in that way," he said.*

Massaro doesn't agree. "It's true that the best team doesn't always win, but I really can't see a better option," he said. "They are definitely cruel and maybe a bit unfair—but penalties are the only solution."

As for the theory propagated in Brazil that the spirit of Ayrton Senna, the Brazilian racing driver who had died earlier that year,

---

* After the game, Blatter set up a FIFA Task Force, called Football 2000, to look at alternatives to the shoot-out. Options included awarding the win to the team with the most corners, or with the fewest fouls; or playing on until someone scores; or taking off a player every ten minutes to create more spaces. This eventually morphed into the "golden goal," the professional equivalent of "next goal wins," which settled one match at the 1998 World Cup (France's win over Paraguay) and three in 2002 (Senegal beating Sweden and South Korea beating Italy in the Round of 16, and Turkey beating Senegal in the quarterfinal). The finals of the 1996 and 2000 European Championships were also won by golden goals, Germany's Oliver Bierhoff and France's David Trezeguet the respective match winners. But UEFA was not happy with the system. In its technical report following the 2000 tournament, it made these complaints about the golden goal:

1. It is an untidy way to finish a match.
2. It puts too much pressure on the referee—the match officials can decide the game.
3. It is unfair from a sporting perspective—there should always be an opportunity for the losing team to fight back, even if it is only for a few minutes.
4. It can create unnecessary conflict among the players and provoke spectator unrest.

FIFA's plan to create attacking soccer in extra time had not worked: rather than seeing teams go for it in an attempt to score the golden goal, it led to more defensive soccer as teams tried to avoid conceding. After the 2002 World Cup, FIFA abolished the rule and reverted to the standard extra time and penalties. The latest Task Force, Football 2014, has made no further amendments to the penalty regulations despite Blatter's promise twenty years previously.

had lifted the decisive kick into the sky, Baggio was not convinced. "It's the romantic explanation for a technically inexplicable act. That is, if it wasn't for my tiredness."

Massaro is now working as an ambassador for Milan, and he added, "It's true that because Baggio and Baresi missed, people tend to forget I missed mine too. But there's a clear reason for that: these guys were among the best Italian players ever. It's normal people are more interested in talking about them."

Nevertheless, that did not help him come to terms with his miss. After the final he sat silent in the dressing room for over an hour, and noticed on his return to Italy that no one ever mentioned penalties when he was around. "It was like a taboo subject, a wound that never healed." Even now, Massaro is still not comfortable talking about it. He still dreams about the moment. "The penalty is with me every day, but the nightmare in my sleep is all about the long walk to the spot. It took me ages to get there from the center circle, and even though it was so hot, I could feel shivers down my back. I have given a lot of thought to what I could have done differently, but I haven't found the answer. Some say don't change your mind, others kick it hard and true. The reality is that only those who have taken a penalty in a World Cup final can know what it's like, and there is nowhere to hide. You just need cold blood and good luck."

And what about Baggio? Should he have been on the pitch? Should he have taken a penalty? "It's simple: he was the guy that got us to the final," said Massaro. "I will always thank him for that because he gave me that opportunity. You don't see much gratitude in football, but on the day of the final, Sacchi showed the world that he was first a real man and second a football coach. Baggio was in no condition to play, but he had got us there. He had to play. What can you blame Baggio for? He missed his penalty. So? I missed mine. We were brave, we took the responsibility, we didn't run away. Maybe it seems different from the outside, but these are things that your teammates recognize."

There might have been another factor behind Baggio's missed

penalty: the fact that he *needed* to score to keep his team alive. The most significant finding, Geir Jordet believes, in all his analysis is the psychological effect of the "negative valence" kick—in other words, the kick to stop your team from losing.

In his analysis of World Cup, European Championship and Champions League shoot-outs, he noted that the penalty success rate when it came to stopping a team from losing the shoot-out drops to 62%, while the rate to win the shoot-out rises to 92%. Remember Andreas Möller, who was desperate not to take a penalty in the Euro 96 semifinal shoot-out against England, but as soon as he had seen Gareth Southgate miss he ran out of the center circle to take the kick?

James W. Grayson ran an updated analysis, taking into account more recent competitions and over four hundred shoot-out penalties. He got similar results, with a 94% rate "to win" and a 64% "to not lose" rate. "This shows how big the differences are when you put psychology into the mix," said Jordet. "It basically shows the power of thinking about positive, as opposed to negative, consequences when taking these shots."*

Baggio was one of the best players of his generation; Maradona one of the best of all time. He also missed some key penalties for club and country, including the decisive shoot-out spot kick for Napoli in their 1987 UEFA Cup defeat to Toulouse, and one for Argentina in their shoot-out win in the 1990 World Cup quarter-final over Yugoslavia (he did score in the semifinal shoot-out against Italy, on his "home ground" in Naples).

Maradona's most famous penalty record, however, has become a regular refrain among amateur players in Argentina. When a friend of mine missed a penalty in a park game in Buenos Aires, he was told, "Don't worry about missing that penalty. You

---

*This happened twice at the 2014 World Cup. First, when Mauricio Isla missed for Chile when taking the final kick in the shoot-out against Brazil, and also for Costa Rica's Michael Umaña, who had scored to win the shoot-out against Greece, but had his sot saved when kicking to avoid defeat against Holland.

know, Diego once missed five in a row!" That's right, Diego Maradona, the great Diego, failed from twelve yards five times in succession. Francis Cornejo, the man who spotted Maradona as a ten-year-old and was his first coach, recognized his talent but never allowed him to take penalties. He later explained why: quite simply, he wasn't very good at them.

In the last season of his career, 1996/97, Maradona was back at his former club Boca Juniors, who were trying to build a dream team. Carlos Bilardo was coach and among Maradona's team-mates were Claudio Caniggia, Juan Sebastian Verón and Kily González. The team finished second in the league, but Maradona was left wondering what might have been. "Would we have done better if I hadn't missed those five penalties in a row during that awful period?" he asked in his autobiography *Yo soy el Diego de la Gente* (I am Diego of the People). "Those five curses signaled the end of my football career."

The poor run began on April 13, 1996, against Newell's Old Boys. Boca were unbeaten but Maradona kicked his penalty wide of Sebastian Cejas's goal midway through the first half, and two minutes later Hernán Franco scored the only goal of the game to win it for Newell's. Maradona was taken off with a foot injury, and the crowd booed him as he limped off the pitch. "I went off because it was really painful, but there were some idiots that booed me: they didn't believe I was injured!"

By June 9, Maradona was fit again, and up against Belgrano. There was another penalty, and this time goalkeeper César Labarre saved it. Labarre barely celebrated—he was worried because Belgrano were playing badly and his team were fighting relegation—and Maradona couldn't bear to look to the stands, where he knew his wife and daughters would be in tears. Soon it was forgotten: in the same game, he scored an outrageous lobbed goal from the corner of the eighteen-yard box and Boca won 2–0.

On June 9, Boca faced Rosario Central. Maradona was still on penalty duty, but again his effort from twelve yards was saved, this time by Hernán Castellanos. "We won, the team played well, so did I, and we were still in the running for the title . . . but I missed another penalty, the third in a row! It was a disgrace; it was breaking my balls!" Boca won 1–0; later in the game Verón took over penalty duties and also missed.

Two weeks later, Boca welcomed fierce rivals River Plate to the Bombonera. Before the game, River goalkeeper Germán Burgos said he wanted Maradona to take a penalty in the game. "Even if he doesn't want to take one, I will ask him to do it," he said. The mind trick worked. Boca were 3–1 up when they won a penalty. Maradona stood over it. Burgos readied himself. The penalty hit the post. Another failure. At least this time the rebound fell to Caniggia who scored for his hat-trick. Boca won 4–1.

The title race with Vélez Sarsfeld was going down to the wire but Boca's hopes ended on August 7 after a 1–0 defeat to Racing. Once again, Maradona missed from the spot. Boca ended up in sixth place, while Vélez clinched the Torneo Clausura on the last day of the season.

"I wanted to win that title with Boca so badly," he said. "When I got into the dressing room, I started to cry as I knew that was my last chance. Once we had lost that title, I wanted to kill myself. My family had never seen me so sad. I took responsibility for everything Boca did that year—the good things, yes, but also the bad as well."

Maradona had once scored fifteen penalties in a row for Napoli; back home, as the light faded on his controversial career, he was struck by what he called "this penalty curse." "The thing about penalties," he said much later, "is that they are fifty-fifty. You can get it on target, or you can miss." If you're the best player to ever have played the game, though, your chances should be greater than fifty-fifty.

Raúl is another player who fits the Jordet template. By the time he was twenty-three he had won plenty of individual accolades, including (just for 1999/2000) UEFA's "Best Forward of the Year," a place in the European soccer writers' Team of the Year, Champions League top scorer and *Don Balón* magazine's Player of the Year.

Spain had gone into Euro 2000 as one of the favorites; they were certainly playing some of the best soccer on the continent, exemplified by a 9–0 win over Austria in qualifying. But their tournament began with a shock defeat to Norway, then a stuttering win over Slovenia, before a miraculous come-from-behind 4–3 victory over Yugoslavia thanks to two goals in injury-time (one from Gaizka Mendieta from the spot).

World champions France awaited in the quarterfinal in Bruges. France took the lead with a curling Zidane free kick before Mendieta, again, scored from the spot. Youri Djorkaeff put France ahead before halftime, and France held on as the clock ticked past 90 minutes. When goalkeeper Fabien Barthez fumbled a back-header near his six-yard line, Spanish defender Abelardo lunged for the ball and tumbled as his foot touched the diving Barthez's shoulder. It looked like Abelardo had made contact with Barthez rather than the other way around, but referee Pierluigi Collina awarded a penalty.

The problem for Spain was that Mendieta, the team's specialist, had been taken off. Fernando Hierro, next in line, was on the bench. Real Betis striker Alfonso Pérez wanted to take it, but he was overruled. Raúl stepped up. He was tired, so much so that midway through the second half he had walked toward the touchline, thinking he was being replaced when in fact Ivan Helguera was making way. He had played fifty-seven games for Madrid that season, which included a February trip to Brazil to play in the Club World Cup, and during that time had missed three of his six penalties.

Raúl leaned back as he hit the ball with his left foot and it sailed over the corner of crossbar and post, smashing into the netting that separated the fans from the pitch. As French fans, who had chanted "Vive le coq!" to put him off, celebrated, Pep Guardiola rubbed his beard hard with both hands and Raúl trudged away from the penalty area. There was time for substitute Ismael Urzaiz to head over with the goal gaping. When the final whistle came, so did the tears. Raúl cried on the pitch, and later confessed he cried in the dressing room and in the team hotel. Once again, he had failed to score a decisive goal for his country.

Raúl's miss was compared to famous Spanish errors in history: Julio Cardenosa, who missed an open goal against Brazil in the 1978 World Cup; Luis Arconada, who let Michel Platini's free kick slide under his body at Euro 84; Julio Salinas, who squandered a chance against Italy in 1994; and Andoni Zubizaretta, who allowed Garba Lawal's shot to squeeze in at his near post in the 1998 group-stage defeat to Nigeria. *Marca* showed a picture of the miss under the headline "It's all over! Raúl sends Spain's dream into the clouds," while *ABC* blamed the weight of history—"the same as always"—and wrote, "Spain cries with Raúl." The paper even claimed the national team was cursed and made the link between the venue for the game, Bruges, and the Spanish word for witches, *brujas*.

The idea that Raúl represented the traditional values of Spain, and was therefore untouchable, was broken only by journalist Diego Torres, who pointed out that the striker had also missed a penalty for Spain Under-21s in their 1996 European Championship final defeat, in a shoot-out, to Italy. "Behind his mask of an introverted and shy kid is hidden a dominant character who intimidates his teammates, and even his coaches," Torres wrote in *El País*. "His self-esteem is colossal, fed without a break by uninterrupted success and praise. This was the night of his first great defeat. The first setback for a footballer launched on a geometric progression. A long apprenticeship which maybe had its culmination against France. The real initial test: the one which brings you to disaster or excellence."

Raúl missed his next penalty as well, in the last minute of a 3–3 draw against Málaga that September, but Real Madrid coasted to the league title and he was top scorer with twenty-four goals.

But Bruges summed up Raúl's misfortune at major tournaments: he had ended the 1998 World Cup as a substitute, was injured and missed the 2002 World Cup quarterfinal loss to South Korea, and at Euro 2004 was blamed for Spain's group-stage elimination after defeat to Portugal. His presence in the side, as a number 10, meant that Juan Carlos Valerón and Xavi Hernández were left on the bench. "Nobody personifies Spain's failure better than Raúl," wrote *El País*. His status had held the team back.

When he was dropped from the Spain squad in September 2006 for the first time in ten years, there was an outcry from the Madrid press. "He is a big star but to keep talking about it is ridiculous," moaned coach Luis Aragonés. Raúl never played for Spain again, despite the calls, even just before Euro 2008, for his inclusion. Aragonés got it right: Spain won the tournament thanks to Cesc Fabregas, who was selected instead of Raúl.

What do the stories of Baggio, Maradona and Raúl have in common? The players all missed, but it was the coach who took the flak for them. There are differing views as to how much responsibility a coach can take for a missed penalty, but it's easy to forget that in any penalty situation, and especially a shoot-out, the stress is not just on the player. The coach is the one whose career lives or dies by the result. A player won't lose his job after a shoot-out defeat. A coach might.

"It doesn't happen just like that, you brainstorm who your penalty takers will be for months in advance," said Aimé Jacquet, whose France team beat Italy in a quarterfinal shoot-out on their way to winning the 1998 World Cup.*

Jacquet gave an interesting insight into the psychology of the coach in this situation. "It's better to be direct, there's no time for the guys to think. The players are tired, the game has taken a lot out of them. It's the coach's responsibility to make the arrangements. So you never ask, 'Will you take one?' That's the worst. I say, 'You,

---

* Not everyone would agree with Jacquet: in fact, his captain in France's World Cup-winning team, Didier Deschamps—France coach at time of writing—stunned reporters on the eve of France's 2014 World Cup qualifying play-off second leg against Ukraine when he said his players had not practiced or even considered the prospect of penalties. France were 2–0 down at the time, and though they won the second leg 3–0, there was a time, at 2–2 on aggregate, when Deschamps's lack of preparation might have haunted him.

you, you, you and you: one, two, three, four and five.' The player has the hard job: to take the penalty. So you must make it easy for him."

In other words, the coach has to manage his status players. Before the penalties against Italy, one of Jacquet's chosen five, Youri Djorkaeff, specifically asked not to take one as he felt that Italy's goalkeeper, his Inter Milan teammate Gianluca Pagliuca, knew his patterns too well. Jacquet said it was fine and smiled, because he didn't want to worry the others.

He knew at this stage that two of his most senior players, Deschamps and Marcel Desailly, also did not want to take a spot kick. As the pair stretched alongside each other, Marcel turned to his teammate and said he should take a penalty before him. "You're the captain, it's your responsibility."

"But you're a defender, you've hardly run, and I'm knackered," came the reply.

As it was, Jacquet had his five, and had told Fabien Barthez he would be next if it went to sudden death. Barthez's goalkeeping coach Philippe Bergeroo told him, "We have been studying the Italian kickers—" Barthez cut him off and said, "I don't want to know anything." He was a goalkeeper who preferred to rely on his instinct. "That's the best way to be," agreed Laurent Blanc.

Each team's star men went first—Zinedine Zidane for France, Roberto Baggio for Italy—and scored. Both kicks were significant. Zidane always went the same way, to his natural side, but had complete trust in his ability. "I don't know if it helped me or not but I always knew where I was going to shoot," he said. "I never even asked myself the question. If I hit it right, the goalkeeper could not stop it." That was regardless of the level of tension as well. Against England in Euro 2004, France were awarded a late penalty with the score at 1–1, and Zidane spotted the ball and then crouched down, holding his ankles with his hands. The referee blew, Zidane stood up, seemed to scratch his nose, took a pause before beginning his run-up and scored, kicking to his usual side. The replay showed that Zidane was crouching down because he had been vomiting heavily on the edge of the area.

"For most of us, the question would be, 'How do you deal with that?'" Jordet remarked. "That's when players are more likely to fail and they will do stupid things, like rushing to get it over with quicker. It's OK for Zidane to have the discomfort but it is his response to it, the fact he's saying 'I have to do this, so that's what I'm going to do,' which is spectacular." Jordet and I had just watched the vomit video in his office. "Even when he throws up, he's gracious," said the Norwegian commentator.

Back to Jacquet, one of whose dilemmas, once he had told the two twenty-year-olds Thierry Henry and David Trezeguet that they would be taking penalties, was the right order. "I thought about going: experience, youth, experience, youth." Instead, he picked Bixente Lizarazu to go second. His poor kick was saved. Lizarazu usually kicked third in shoot-outs, and Jacquet blamed himself. "I think he was upset, and I felt a bit guilty when I thought about it afterward."

Barthez saved from Demetrio Albertini, then the teams exchanged goals until Blanc stepped up, fifth for France. He scored, and as Luigi di Biagio walked toward the spot, French full back Vincent Candela turned to his teammates on the touchline and said, "He's going to miss." He was right: di Biagio hit the crossbar, France were through, and the brainstorming had taken Jacquet another step closer to winning the World Cup on home soil.

There was redemption for di Biagio, though. Two years later, he stepped up for Italy in their Euro 2000 win over Holland. "I played a great tournament in 1998 and was certain I'd score that penalty against France," he told RAI TV show *Sfide*. "But I missed, and when I stepped up against Holland, I was shaking with fear." Di Biagio had promised his wife the night before the game that he would not take a penalty, and just before he walked to the goal, Totti turned to him and said, "Don't worry about being scared, it's normal. Have you seen how big van der Sar is?" Di Biagio was intimidated by the orange-clad fans behind the goal and as he spotted the ball he had no idea how he was going to take it or where he was going to put the ball. He went for precision over power and scored. "It was an amazing feeling. The only thing I don't like is that di Biagio will always be remembered for the mistake in 1998, not for that penalty scored two years later. But I guess that's normal."

When Marcello Lippi led Italy to victory in the 2006 World Cup final on penalties, it was the third shoot-out in a final that he had been involved with, and he predicted the correct outcome before each of them. His first was with Juventus in the 1996 Champions League final against Ajax. "I could see my players were desperate to contribute to the victory. With their eyes, they were telling me: 'Let me take one.'" It was a different story seven years later, when Juventus faced AC Milan in the Champions League final at Old Trafford. "When I was picking the five, all the players were looking in the stands, searching out their wives or girlfriends, or focusing somewhere else. I said, 'Guys, they don't allow me to take a penalty, you have to take them.' So I don't think it was a coincidence that we lost."

Against France in 2006, Lippi knew his five before the game: Pirlo, Materazzi, de Rossi, del Piero and Totti. But Totti had gone off and Lippi had to choose another player. He turned to Fabio Grosso.

"You take the fifth penalty."

"Why me?"

"Because you are the best man in the last minute," replied Lippi, referring to the injury-time penalty Grosso had dubiously earned against Australia and the late winner in the semifinal over Germany.

"I think those words gave him some extra confidence," Lippi said.

Lippi's choice of Grosso was a good example of picking the person over the player; he could have pointed at a bigger name—Fabio Cannavaro, Gennaro Gattuso, Luca Toni and Vincenzo Iaquinta were all available—but he felt that a player of lower status would do the job.

"I was astonished when he asked me," Grosso admitted. His last penalty had been five years earlier in Serie C2, Italy's fourth division. "I don't remember my penalty very well: my run-up, the way

I hit the ball, nothing's very clear. I just remember having a huge responsibility, and I forced myself to maintain my calm inside.

"Experience counts for nothing in moments like that. Of course you have to have the technique but above all it's about reaching a very specific mental state in the seconds preceding the shot. I will always remember that I ended a curse, the curse on Italy for penalty shoot-outs and extra time: there was the 1994 World Cup final, the 1998 quarterfinal, Euro 2000. The same thing worried us before the final but this time we had the resources to stay calm. Lippi helped transcend us with his confidence."

On the evening before the game, France coach Raymond Domenech had watched Trezeguet and Sylvain Wiltord practice their penalties. He'd laughed and told them, "Of course you're going to score if you take one now; but what about tomorrow, when you're tired, eighty thousand people are in the stadium and the World Cup is at stake?" Trezeguet insisted that he still wanted to practice. Wiltord scored. Trezeguet scored. "Enough now," Domenech said. "Do that again tomorrow and we'll be happy."

It didn't quite turn out like that. Pirlo, Wiltord and Materazzi all scored so Italy were 2–1 up when Trezeguet stepped up to face Buffon, his teammate at Juventus. Buffon had conceded a Panenka to Zidane earlier in the match and was not feeling at all confident. "I was not in tune with what was happening; it seemed to me that France could have taken two thousand penalties and scored all of them." Trezeguet knew that Buffon was used to facing his penalties (the pair would practice after training sessions at Juventus) so he aimed for one of the toughest areas of the goal: the top left corner.* He hit it wide, while Buffon had

---

*The concept of aiming for the top half of the goal made no sense to Rik de Saedeleer, who played for Racing Mechelen and Belgium in the 1940s. He knew that mathematically it reduced the likelihood of success. "If you aim for the top corner, you increase your chances of missing the target because you can hit it wide or you can hit it high," he said in a biography of him (*Rik De Saedeleer*). "It's simple math: at least if you hit it along the ground, you can't hit it too low. But you can hit it too high."

dived the other way. "For me, it was a logical consequence of the fact that he had played for several years with Buffon at Juventus and thought he knew where he was going to shoot," said Willy Sagnol, who stepped up for France's fourth penalty.

Sagnol did not want to take it, and he remembers Domenech saying to him, "You shoot." But he was not sure if it was a question or a statement. "I said yes as naturally as I could but then I doubted myself and said, 'Ach, it's too late now.' It's important to have an ego as a player, and to know how to control that in a World Cup final."

The French players returned home empty-handed, but they were greeted as heroes. A homecoming parade was organized, and as the players emerged one by one on to the balcony of Hotel Crillon, on the Place de la Concorde, Trezeguet was in tears, and was supported by Thierry Henry. Trezeguet considered his appearance on the balcony a major achievement: "It showed I was strong mentally."

This penalty miss did not define his career, partly because Trezeguet had scored France's golden goal winner in the Euro 2000 final against the same opposition and partly because France overachieved in reaching the 2006 final. Years later, Trezeguet told Canal Plus that his relationship with Domenech was complicated. "I did not feel important. I felt that the technical staff had no trust in me at that time."

Again, this ties in with the question of status and hierarchy in the squad. Trezeguet did not feel enough support, yet Domenech trusted him to take a penalty in the World Cup final. The coach's job is to prepare the players to perform at their peak. In a shoot-out, that means leaving as little as possible to Lady Luck.

PENALTY ICON—
SEBASTIÁN ABREU

"*Recordar é viver, Loco Abreu acabou com você*" (Remember and live, Loco Abreu destroyed you). That was the song Botafogo fans sang at their Flamengo counterparts in the years after Sebastián Abreu scored the most significant goal in the club's recent history. For the previous three seasons, Flamengo had beaten Botafogo to the Carioca state championship—in fact, Flamengo had won the last eight when the title had come down to those two sides—and the Botafogueses were hurting.

Abreu was nicknamed "El Loco" mainly because he was outspoken. The fact his opinions were often intelligent was beside the point. He disregarded convention, and chose the number 13 shirt on joining his new club in January 2010. Now thirty-four, it seemed he was just winding down his career. Three months later, Botafogo needed to beat Flamengo at the Maracanã to be certain of the title.

At halftime the score was 1–1. In the second half, Botafogo were awarded a penalty, and Abreu stepped up. He ran at pace, Flamengo goalkeeper Bruno dived early, and Abreu lofted a left-footed Panenka down the middle so smartly that it shaved the underside of the crossbar and with so much backspin that it did not even touch the back of the net. There was time for Adriano, of Flamengo, to miss a penalty before Botafogo won 3–1. Abreu's place in club folklore was sealed. He remains a club idol. Botafogo even adopted a sky-blue shirt to represent Abreu's Uruguay shirt for away matches.

In South America, the Panenka is called the *cavadinha*—the literal meaning is "little dig"—and Abreu had seen it at close quarters, from Djalminha, the Brazilian forward. Djalminha's first *cavadinha* was in October 1995, for Guarani against Internacional, whose goalkeeper Andoni Goycochea was famed as a penalty specialist. There were four key rules Djalminha laid down for his perfect *cavadinha*:

1. Observe the goalkeeper's behavior and if he waits until you kick the ball to dive, then avoid the *cavadinha*. If he goes early, try it.
2. It's all about the speed as you approach the ball. You have to run fast.
3. Don't try it every time, as the goalkeeper will soon notice. I never did it two penalties in a row.
4. The above is all theory. What matters is your personality, your intuition and your emotion.

Abreu spent only six months at Deportivo La Coruña alongside Djalminha, but it was long enough to learn from the Brazilian. The pair would stay behind after training and hone their technique in front of Deportivo's two African goalkeepers, Jacques Sango'o and Peter Rufai.

It was ironic, then, that another African goalkeeper, Ghana's Richard Kingson, was the victim of Abreu's ultimate penalty. Kingson had clearly not seen Abreu's spot kick against Flamengo. He hadn't watched Botafogo play Fluminense either, when Abreu had one *cavadinha* saved and three minutes later took another penalty, another *cavadinha*, and scored. He didn't know about Abreu's first successful *cavadinha*, in 1999, when he was at Tecos and needed one more goal to finish top scorer in the Mexican league; or five years later, the *cavadinha* that Deportivo Toluca's Hernán Cristante saved as Tecos fought to avoid relegation. Abreu was vilified, but one week later scored the headed winner against Puebla that kept Tecos up. He left the club straight after the game, accusing the fans of hypocrisy. In all, Abreu had taken twenty-four *cavadinha* penalties and he had scored with twenty-two of them.

When Uruguay faced Ghana in that controversial 2010 World Cup quarterfinal, after John Mensah and Dominic Adiyah had missed in the shoot-out, and as Abreu stood over the ball, needing to score to send Uruguay into the last four, still Kingson didn't know. Everyone in the Uruguay team knew, though.

Abreu had taken, and missed, three penalties in training the day before the game. One was to the left, one to the right, and one down the middle. Sebastián Eguren, his teammate, had shouted over, "Hey man, stop mucking around, we might need you tomorrow."

"Don't worry, tomorrow we will win with my signature penalty," came the reply.

"Please don't do that to me!" Eguren said. "Or at least let me know first: I will need to take a tablet to calm my heart!"

As the shoot-out progressed, Abreu had noticed that Kingson was moving early. He'd turned to his neighbor Jorge Fucile after Diego Forlán scored Uruguay's first penalty and asked, "Did you see what I just saw, Jorge? He moved before the shot, right?"

"Yes, Loco, he moved early then."

After Mauricio Victorino scored: "He dived early again, didn't he?"

"Yes."

Fucile also agreed after Andrés Scotti scored the third penalty. But that was enough for him.

"Hey, Loco, kick the *cavadinha* if you want to, but stop breaking my balls with these damn questions," he said.

As Abreu walked to the spot, Forlán turned to his teammates and muttered, "Please don't try a *cavadinha*, please, please, please!"

Uruguay coach Oscar Washington Tabarez had asked Abreu to take the third penalty, but he wanted to take the fifth. Abreu remains convinced that Tabarez knew what he was going to do.

He spots the ball slowly, deliberately, and takes seven steps back. He never looks at the goalkeeper and appears in total control. His run-up is long, starting outside the area, and one step before Abreu reaches the ball, Kingson makes his move, slightly forward and to his right. Abreu has read it perfectly. His *cavadinha* is not as high, or as slow, as against Flamengo, but it has the same outcome.

"I tried to be logical in an illogical situation," Abreu explained. "It was the last penalty and I thought that Kingson would be logical and dive to one side. I thought there was no way he would think that I would take such a risk with the last penalty in such a game."

That's the kind of lucidity and composure under pressure that lands you with the nickname "El Loco."

"People think I'm crazy but I have never heard anyone say the same of Zinedine Zidane when he took his penalty in the [2006] World Cup final," he reasoned. "Zidane was a genius, but Abreu, man, he was crazy."

CHAPTER 7

THE GOALKEEPER TURNS POACHER

One comment stuck in my head after my trip to the Algarve to visit England's penalty nemesis Ricardo. The Portuguese goalkeeper said that as a goalkeeper who takes penalties, he automatically had an advantage in any penalty scenario: as a shooter, because he understood the goalkeeper's strengths and weaknesses; and as a goalkeeper, because he understood the routine of execution involved.

I wondered at the time why more goalkeepers didn't capitalize on this competitive edge, and Ricardo blamed it on the coaches. "For a start, the goalkeeper's teammates would find it hard because the dressing room is a competitive place and some players want to fight for top scorer awards and not let anyone else score cheap goals," he said. "But then there's the other risk: that if a goalkeeper misses the [open-play] penalty, his goal is wide open. So I think the coach that lets the goalkeeper take penalties has to be a bit crazy too."

The key word that jumped out at me was not "crazy" but "too." It seemed that Ricardo was saying that goalkeepers who take penalties are crazy. "Well, those guys like José Luis Chilavert,

Jorge Campos, René Higuita, they are crazy, yeah. I am not crazy like them. But I did put my mark on history."

Ricardo was right: he is not crazy. But I wondered if he was an exception among penalty-taking goalkeepers. I wanted to know if there was something different about this breed of goalkeeper, and there was only one player to start with, one whose antics combined on-field violence with political posturing off the pitch. I needed to speak to Chilavert.

The first time he took a penalty during open play, it did not end so well. The Paraguayan goalkeeper had scored for his first club Sportivo Luqueño in two shoot-outs before, both when he was only eighteen. He moved to Spanish side Real Zaragoza in 1988, when he was twenty-three, and not long after that watched four of his teammates miss penalties in a Copa del Rey shoot-out defeat to Valencia.

In their next match, Zaragoza played Real Sociedad, and were awarded a penalty. The crowd knew that Chilavert had scored from the spot before, and chanted his name. The coach, Radomir Antic, told him to take it. As he walked upfield, Chilavert asked defender Isidro Villanova to cover his goal. "Don't move from the goal line," he said.

Chilavert scored, but Sociedad restarted the game while the goalkeeper was still running back to his position. Villanova had deserted his post to celebrate with a teammate. From inside the center circle, Jon Andoni Goikoetxea lobbed the ball straight back into the Zaragoza goal for an immediate equalizer. "I went to Villanova and shouted at him: 'If your mother tells you go to the market, would you just ignore her and play at a friend's house?'" Chilavert recalled. "But we had never seen a goalkeeper take a penalty before," Villanova replied. "It was funny!" Chilavert never took another penalty for Zaragoza. "I don't know why that is," he dead-panned.

Chilavert was not the first goalkeeper to take a penalty, but he sees himself as a pioneer for all future keepers who took them.

Arnold Birch was one of the first to take penalties on a regular basis: he scored five goals for Chesterfield in division three (north) in 1923/24.* Around the same time, Romanian goalkeeper William Zombory was a regular scorer for Chinezul Timisoara. Zombory was a former striker who begged to take penalties after moving between the sticks when the Chinezul youth team were short of a goalkeeper. He ended up scoring five goals for Ripensia Timisoara, with whom he won four Romanian league titles between 1932 and 1938. Zombory was also the first player in his country to play wearing a cap, and his popularity grew with each penalty he scored, as every time he would commiserate with the opposition goalkeeper by shaking his hand.

I was surprised (and had my doubts) when Chilavert said that he had heard of Zombory. But he knew that the generation of goalkeepers that followed him—the likes of Campos, Higuita, Nacho González and Carlos Roa—did not start taking penalties because of William Zombory. "I am convinced that when a goalkeeper takes a penalty nowadays, it's because of me and my legacy," he said. "I was a revolutionary. Those goalkeepers, they have told me that I was a reference for them. I was their guide. And I'm proud of that."

Chilavert became a regular penalty taker at his next club, Argentine side Vélez Sarsfeld. He would stay behind after every training session to take penalties—120 a week, and double that number for free kicks—which was noted by coach Carlos Bianchi. His breakthrough moment came in 1993, when Vélez needed to draw with Estudiantes to win the title for the first time in twenty-five years. Before the game, Bianchi asked who fancied taking a penalty if there was one. He was met with silence.

"There are two types of people out there," Chilavert said as he

---

*Birch was on trial at Sheffield Wednesday when the First World War broke out. He joined the Royal Navy and was interned at Groningen, where he ended up playing one season for Be Quick. After the war, he spent a year at Wednesday before moving to Chesterfield.

recounted the story, "successful people and mediocre people. Successful people don't think about failure. A mediocre person thinks: 'What would happen if I missed?'" This called to mind the importance of Geir Jordet's strategy for failure, which is not the same as preparing to fail. Coaches have to consider it, even if the players can't bear to.

So Chilavert put up his hand and said, "I do!" Immediately two of his teammates, Turu Flores and Gallego González, also asked Bianchi to take it. "OK," said Bianchi. "Turu will take it. Or González. If not, then Chilavert takes it."

Estudiantes were 1–0 up when Vélez won a penalty. Flores looked at González. González looked at Flores. "They didn't want to take it! Bianchi told me to take it, so I did." Chilavert scored, and Vélez won the title.

Chilavert became the first-choice penalty taker for Vélez and he scored over fifty goals for the team. He scored a hat-trick of penalties in a 1999 game against Ferro Carril Oeste, and graduated to free kicks, scoring one from inside his own half against River Plate past Germán Burgos.

Much of the credit, Chilavert believed, should go to Bianchi. "To let your goalkeeper take a penalty, the coach has to be brave, but also intelligent. Bianchi knew that I was a goalkeeper who won matches. I think that European coaches are more cautious. I don't know why, but they are definitely more conservative."

That is not a label that has ever been pinned on Chilavert, who became infamous during his playing days for punching journalists, spitting at opponents (including Roberto Carlos) and attacking fellow goalkeepers. He once accused Argentines of assuming Paraguayans only belonged on building-sites or were only fit to be housekeepers, and claimed Brazil should return territory it took from Paraguay during the War of the Triple Alliance in the 1860s. He also accused the Australian national team of taking drugs, and boycotted the 1999 Copa America in Paraguay because he wanted his government to spend the money on public education.

Chilavert's reputation gave him a psychological edge over opponents. He rarely changed where he kicked the ball. He was left-footed and always struck it with power to his natural side. "If you hit it well, no one will stop it," he asserted. On the odd occasion he felt anxious before a penalty, he would aim for the goalkeeper's face and smash the ball down the middle. "No one would stay in their spot then, everyone would dive."

If he had the chance to destroy an opposing goalkeeper, he would take it. For a while his rivalry with Boca Juniors goalkeeper Navarro Montoya inspired him. In one game, he scored a free kick past Montoya. Late on, there was a penalty, and Chilavert ran as fast as he could to take it. "Relax, dude," one of his teammates said, "you've already scored once."

"You should always give your enemies a second chance," Chilavert replied.

Chilavert scored, and Vélez won 5–1.

His strategy for saving penalties was all about studying the run-up. A long run-up with a wider angle suggested to him a hard kick to the kicker's natural side; a shorter run-up or straighter angle suggested a softer kick to the nonnatural side.

In the 2001 French League Cup final, when he was at Strasbourg, Chilavert used that strategy but failed to save any of the first three kicks. Next up was Jean-Paul Abalo, a Togolese defender. Chilavert tried to psyche him out. He held on to the ball longer than he should have, and laughed when Abalo swore at him. As he faced him on the goal line, Chilavert shouted "I'm going to dive this way!," pointing to his right. Abalo was on a short run-up, so Chilavert dived the other way, and saved it. He was due to take the fifth penalty, to win the match, when Amiens goalkeeper Julien Lachuer tried to trash-talk him. "He did just what I did to Abalo, but I told him, 'Sorry, mate, this isn't going to work.' And then I scored and we won the Cup."

It's true that Chilavert seems calmer now. These days he lives in Buenos Aires, in the middle-class district of Caballito, but he divides his time between properties in Miami and Asunción in

Paraguay. He sees himself as an entrepreneur, and has built an eye hospital for children in Paraguay. He still dreams of one day being president, but said he enjoys his life away from the spotlight. The only hint of the old Chilavert arrogance was when he occasionally referred to himself in the third person; otherwise, he seemed very happy out of the headlines.

He remembered his toughest penalty opponents—Ronald Koeman ("his shots were like missiles, they could kill you"), Michael Laudrup and Ronaldo—and the 1997 game against Unión when he missed two penalties, both smashed against the bar.

There were two other questions that had been bugging me. First, should more goalkeepers be taking penalties today? "Yes!" he exclaimed. As the self-styled pioneer of the penalty-taking goalkeeper, he should be upset. But whose fault is it: coaches, for being too cautious, or goalkeepers, for not going for it? "It's the goalkeepers," he answered. "They are not good enough with their feet anymore." It's a strange logic given that the abolition of the back-pass rule in 1992 forced goalkeepers to improve their ball skills. "Also you have to train for penalties. You have to work really hard for it. That's my secret to penalties: just pure hard work."

Then there was the "crazy" question. I wondered if taking penalties was an extension of his personality, demanding attention and being, well, a little crazy. He didn't buy it. "No, that's unfair," he said. "We were not eccentric at all. In fact, I was always calm. A good goalkeeper has three characteristics. One, personality, because it's not true that there is pressure in football. We have responsibility, not pressure. Two, he has to know how to use psychology against his opponents. And three, technique. I had all of them."

But what about the bad guy image? And, in fact, the bad guy behavior?

"I was playing a role on the pitch because I wanted to win. I had to be the villain. Look, I could hardly be the hero with this face! But I'm a quiet person, and always was. It was just a role."

I was not convinced by Chilavert's play-it-straight routine, especially when I heard about his reaction to the only goalkeeper to have scored more goals in professional soccer than him. In 2006, Brazilian keeper Rogério Ceni scored his sixty-fourth goal, breaking Chilavert's record. Chilavert's response was to tell *El Gráfico*, "I'm better than Rogério Ceni. I scored eight goals for Paraguay and did it in four different World Cup qualifying campaigns.* Ceni didn't score a single goal for his national team. I love that a Brazilian is still behind Chilavert. The number one is the Paraguayan: me."

It's hard to imagine, but when Rogério Ceni started his professional career, he was so bad at kicking that his teammate Sergio Baresi would take goal kicks for him because his could barely reach the halfway line. Telê Santana, then São Paulo coach, taught him to turn his body away from the ball and keep his standing foot close to it.

Ceni quickly improved. He honed his accuracy by trying to hit the crossbar from all over the pitch, a challenge set up for him by Valdir Joaquim de Moraes, one of the first full-time goalkeeping coaches in Brazil. By 1997, five years after Ceni's debut, Muricy Ramalho had replaced Santana, and he spotted that Ceni was turning up half an hour early for training to hit a hundred free kicks. "I knew that Rogério was the best guy we had for free kicks," he said after the goalkeeper curled in his first ever goal, on February 15, 1997, in São Paulo's 2–0 Paulista Championship win against União São João. "It was not an irresponsible decision."

"Why don't you take penalties as well?" Ceni was asked.

"We have a good penalty taker," he said, referring to Serginho, who would go on to miss a Champions League final penalty for Milan, "but no one for free kicks."

---

* This is true: Chilavert scored winning goals against Colombia in 1990 qualifying and Peru in 1994 qualifying; he scored the equalizer in a draw against Argentina in 1998 qualifying; and in 2002 qualifying, he scored four goals, against Colombia, Peru, Bolivia and Argentina.

He scored two more that season but was taken off dead balls by the next coach, Mario Sergio, an old-school former midfielder who felt Ceni would get too tired running the length of the pitch every time a free kick was awarded. Sergio lasted only ten games, and after he was sacked, Ceni gave him a signed shirt and thanked him for his honesty. Was this the behavior of, as Ricardo might put it, a player who is a little bit crazy?

In April 1999, Ceni took his first penalty, against Palmeiras goalkeeper Marcos, the man who would become a penalty legend himself. He shot to his natural side; Marcos dived the wrong way. Goal. The following week, when São Paulo got a penalty against União Barbarense, the fans demanded that Ceni take it, even though Serginho was playing. Ceni, with the blessing of his coach, Luca Carpegiani, took it, scored again and celebrated by hugging Serginho. São Paulo won 2–1. And the other goal? A Ceni free kick.

Despite his success, it was not until 2005 that Ceni became São Paulo's official penalty taker. By then, he had already scored twenty-nine free kicks. In that record-breaking season in 2005, São Paulo won the state championship, the Copa Libertadores and the FIFA Club World Cup. Their top scorer? Rogério Ceni, with twenty-one (ten penalties and eleven free kicks). He scored in every round of the Libertadores except the final: free kicks against Universidad Católica and Tigres, penalties against Palmeiras and River Plate. São Paulo beat Tigres 4–0 but Ceni was not happy. He scored two free kicks but missed a penalty, which greatly upset him. This was Ceni's year, though: he saved a penalty from Atlético Paranaense midfielder Fabrício in the final's second leg, which São Paulo went on to win 4–0. "At that point, I was not in the real world," Ceni said. "When the full-time whistle blew, I knew I could die in peace."

São Paulo gave up on the domestic league in the second half of the year, just focusing on their Club World Cup preparations. In Japan, Ceni scored in the 3–2 semifinal win over Al-Itihad to set up a final against Liverpool. Ceni was inspired against the

Champions League winners, who won seventeen corners to São Paulo's zero. After Mineiro's first-half goal, Liverpool had three efforts disallowed for offside, and Ceni saved brilliantly from Luis García, Harry Kewell and Steven Gerrard, whose free kick was pushed away at full-length. Ceni later explained that he "inverted the wall" for Gerrard's dead ball, moving it to one side so he could have a clear view of the midfielder's foot as it struck the ball. That was the only reason he was able to make the save. "Because I take free kicks, I know how to make the taker's life more difficult."

Penalties played a huge role in São Paulo's run to the 2006 Copa Libertadores. In the Round of 16 second leg, a derby against Palmeiras, the score was 2–2 on aggregate when São Paulo were awarded a penalty. As Ceni walked to the spot, Palmeiras forward Washington trash-talked him. Ceni ignored him, and scored with a *paradinha** to his natural side. The referee ordered a retake for encroachment and, eight minutes after the original penalty offence, Ceni went to the same side and scored again.

The quarterfinal against Estudiantes went to a shoot-out. It was 3–3 when São Paulo's Danilo missed the target. No problem for Ceni; he stopped the next two and São Paulo were in the semifinal. In the first leg at Mexican side Chivas, Ceni scored from the spot despite the efforts of opposition striker Adolfo Bautista, who walked with him to the spot saying how nervous he looked. Ceni saved a penalty in the second leg, when the game was goalless. São Paulo went on to win 3–0. So many penalties, so many saves; Ceni could do no wrong.

"There is no pressure on the goalkeeper, it's all on the guy who takes the penalty," Ceni explained. "It's about staying calm and controlling anxiety: that is more important than the technical part."

Paradinha, literally meaning "little stop," is a penalty in which the taker pauses mid run-up to encourage the goalkeeper to dive early. The man credited with inventing it is Pelé (see p 273).

On August 16, 2006, though, Ceni was nervous. It was the Libertadores final against Internacional, and once again he was taking a penalty. This time there was an added incentive: if he scored, it would take him above Chilavert as soccer's highest-scoring goalkeeper. He missed. "It was the most painful moment of my career." Internacional won 4–3 on aggregate.

Four days later, Ceni broke the record against Cruzeiro, scoring twice as São Paulo came back from two goals down to draw 2–2. Ceni gave Ramalho, the coach who had given him his first chance to score goals, his shirt.

The goals kept coming, and in 2011, Ceni scored number one hundred against Corinthians. He celebrated like mad and was feted as a national hero. "Ceni makes history and breaks the taboo," wrote *O Estado de S. Paulo*, while *Folha de S. Paulo* ran with the headline "*Rogério Cem*" (Portuguese for "one hundred").

Most fans in Brazil, even some São Paulo supporters, would accept that Ceni was a decent, though not outstanding, goalkeeper; and as a penalty taker his record stands up to scrutiny. Including a rotten run in 2013, when he scored only four out of his eight penalties, Ceni's career record from the spot was sixty penalties scored from seventy-eight, a conversion rate of 77%. That's slightly lower than the penalty average of 79% across the top five European leagues from seasons 2007/08 to 2012/13.

His legacy? Some goalkeepers in Brazil, like Atlético Goianiense's Marcio, now take penalties. And at São Paulo, if you arrive before training starts, you will see two players practicing free kicks. They are Denis and Leonardo, both reserve players. Neither is crazy. Both play in goal.

Ricardo's "crazy" theory was not holding up so far, so I decided to look closer to home. I spoke to two European goalkeepers whose teammates were among the world's best players and yet still they took on penalty duties. The first, somewhat surprisingly, was Alex Stepney, who started taking penalties in the 1973/74 season for Manchester United, despite the presence of George Best up front.

Stepney had scored in a preseason shoot-out when United had beaten Peñarol in a friendly tournament in Murcia; and he joined in, with some success, the penalty taking at the end of training sessions. Before the opening game of the season, captain Martin Buchan had asked coach Tommy Docherty who would be on penalty duty and he had replied, "Alex!"

"I have no idea why he said that, but I didn't question the manager and nor did anyone else," Stepney recalled.

United had lost three of their first five games that season and were awarded a penalty in the next one, against Leicester City at home. Stepney walked up to face Peter Shilton. "I don't remember being nervous at all, I just ran up and smacked it in the corner; no one went down the middle in those days." He scored, but United ended up losing 2–1. Five weeks later, Stepney became United's top scorer when he netted again from the spot, this time the winner against Birmingham.

"There was nothing crazy about me taking penalties, even though it was unheard of at the time," he reflected. "It was all about having the confidence to do it, and if you had that, why not take it? I've no idea why Georgie didn't want to take them, but it was never a problem for him, or any of the lads."

Not until the following February, that is (by which time Best had left the club), when with United struggling at the bottom of the table, Stepney missed a penalty in a goalless draw with Wolves. "That was it for me, I was done. Short and sweet but no more penalties, thank you very much."

Despite a burst of four wins in nine matches late in the season, United ended the season relegated. "Maybe we went down because the goalkeeper was the only one prepared to take the penalties, I don't know!" Stepney laughed. "It was unheard of in those days for a goalkeeper to be taking penalties but if the manager has confidence in you, what can you do?"

Stepney was not the only goalkeeper who became a penalty taker by accident. The same thing happened to one of Europe's most prolific keepers. Hans-Jörg Butt called himself a reluctant hero, and when we spoke he looked like one too, sat in an office, packed red files on every available shelf-space behind him, in his hometown of Oldenburg.

This is where he began his soccer career and now he was back, working as a sales executive for his family business, a loading-ramp manufacturer. With his blue buttoned-down shirt and wire-rimmed glasses, he certainly looked the part, but as he talked about eight-hour days in the office and long drives to meet customers, there was a wistfulness in his voice. It was only a year after he retired—he was on the bench for Bayern Munich's 2012 Champions League defeat on penalties—and he rarely gets to games now. "I still have friends at Bayern but mainly I follow like everyone else, through the media," he said. "Everything is still new for me in this business and I am just trying to learn about all the internal departments in the company."

The idea of Butt as a salesman is strange, especially when you consider his journey to become the Champions League's most prolific penalty-scoring goalkeeper.* He never wanted the role, never looked for it. At Oldenburg, where he played in the third division, he would join the players taking penalties after training, and always scored. After the club's main taker missed two penalties in a row, the coach told Butt that he would be taking the next one. He was twenty-one, there were around 5,000 fans watching. He wasn't nervous. He scored. "But I never asked to take penalties, never."

The same was true at his next club, Hamburg. Again, Butt was an assiduous trainer and by then had worked on his technique and developed the Goalkeeper-Dependent method, waiting for the keeper to make a move before deciding where to shoot. He soon graduated to first-choice penalty taker and because he (usually) scored, he never faced any complaints.

---

*Butt scored three goals in the competition, for three different clubs, Hamburg, Bayer Leverkusen and Bayern. Incredibly, all three goals were against the same team, Juventus, and twice against the same goalkeeper, Gigi Buffon.

He defined two key advantages that goalkeepers have over other players in penalty scenarios.

1. Knowing opposition goalkeeper patterns.

"It makes a huge difference to know how the mind of a goalkeeper works. We all know there is no chance of saving a perfectly struck penalty, but if a goalkeeper can anticipate a corner, he has more chance. Some goalkeepers have a preferred corner, others don't disguise movements so well. I was always conscious of who the goalkeeper was whenever I took a penalty. As I ran up, I would watch his whole body—but never his eyes, as that might make you distracted by the situation."

2. You have time to compose yourself.

"Goalkeepers are trained to focus on the moment, to handle the pressure in big situations. As a goalkeeper, you can 'switch on' very quickly and block out everything around you. For other players—a striker, for example—a lot of their game is instinctive, intuitive: the cross comes in and bang, it's a goal; they don't even know how they did it. So when they have time to overthink what they're going to do, it often fails."

Butt would use the walk from his goalmouth to the penalty spot as a time to compose himself and prepare for the penalty. It was all about focusing on the ball, and blocking everything out, just as if he was preparing to save a free kick. The one time he was made to wait around the penalty spot—when his teammate was being treated for an injury and other players were talking to him—he grew nervous and missed his kick. "After that, I would always wait in my half until I knew the coast was clear and I would walk straight to the spot, no distractions, and do my thing."

The jeopardy element, as Chilavert found, was not so much when an open-play penalty was saved and his goal was under threat, but after he scored. In May 2004, with his Hamburg side leading 2–1, Butt scored against Schalke and started running back to his goal. As he made his way into his own half, Schalke kicked off quickly and Mike Hanke hit a sixty-yard lob into Butt's goal. From 2–1 to 3–1 to 3–2, in twelve seconds. Butt laughed about it, but he was not so happy at the time. "The most important thing was we won the game, but I was angry that the referee had let this happen." When the game had restarted, there were clearly Hamburg players in the Schalke half—deliberately so, to allow Butt time to return—but the referee permitted the kick-off regardless. Butt was more annoyed that people thought Hanke scored because he was celebrating his goal. "I never celebrated," he said. "I always ran straight back to my position."

Butt was destroying my theory of crazy goalkeepers.

The more important the penalty, the greater his focus became. Butt scored thirty-two goals in all, none more important than a Champions League penalty against Juventus in Munich in December 2009. It was Matchday Six and Bayern, 1–0 down, had to win to qualify from the group. Butt had beaten Juventus goalkeeper Gigi Buffon from the spot before, for Leverkusen, but he knew this was crucial. "It was our last chance to qualify, and we were under pressure. The coach [Louis van Gaal] told me I should take the penalty if we had one; for him, the risk of criticism is high if the goalkeeper then misses, as most people think a goalkeeper is not as good with his feet as an outfield player." Butt scored, Bayern won the game 4–1, and went on to reach the Champions League final that season. Was that your best penalty? "The one that meant the most, yeah."

Like Ricardo, Butt was convinced that his experiences as a shooter helped him as a saver. "Yes, I had a good record at saving penalties, and I liked to receive analysis on where players preferred to shoot." Butt had a unique strategy: he would dummy early to dive one side, move back to the middle, and always return to the side where he made the original move. It worked many times, including, memorably, against Real Madrid's Luis Figo in a Champions League tie.

Why are so few goalkeepers taking penalties these days? "The general opinion is that a goalkeeper is not as good as an outfield player with his feet, and the risk is very high if you miss a penalty. As a coach, you have to think about those consequences if the penalty is missed."

Take that "running back to your own goal" scenario out of the equation, and Butt was surprised that more goalkeepers don't take penalties in a shoot-out. "There is no chance of an attacking threat, so I can see why that would work better. Plus, you are looking for five players, not just one."

As we have already seen, in shoot-outs you often need more than five. While the goalkeepers I spoke to agreed that taking penalties helped them when it comes to saving them, I wondered if the opposite was true: would it be possible for a goalkeeper to get better at scoring penalties if he saved a lot?

The best penalty record of active goalkeepers at time of writing belonged to Mickaël Landreau, who had saved sixteen spot kicks in his record-breaking 618 appearances in Ligue 1, but in shoot-outs was a specialist, saving twenty-three and conceding thirty-eight: that's a 62% scoring record against him. "Ever since I was little, I loved facing penalties," he said. Before matches, he received penalty data on his opponents but paid little attention to it: he preferred to visualize saving the penalty before it happened, and he relied on his instinct. "There's no secret: I've stopped players I did not know, and failed with players I did know. I love the fact that it's a boxing match, a duel, and that intimidation can play a role."

His story as a penalty expert who became a penalty taker can best be told through three games.

1. Bastia 0 Nantes 0, October 2, 1996, Ligue 1

Landreau was the baby of his family. His brother Vincent was twelve years older than him and a goalkeeper for the local village team in Arthon-en-Retz. Young Mickaël looked up to him and copied his style. Landreau could have played tennis at a high level, but chose soccer. At thirteen he joined the famous Nantes academy, where one of his first coaches was Christophe Lollichon.

Three years later, Landreau was fast-tracked after an injury crisis in the senior squad. The first two goalkeepers, David Marraud and Dominique Casagrande, were sidelined. Third-choice Eric Loussouarn was out of form and had become a liability. There was even a fourth choice, goalkeeping coach Jean-Louis Garcia, who played in a European Cup tie against Bayer Leverkusen. Coach Jean-Claude Suaudeau, one of the most successful in the French game, famously shouted after Loussouarn's latest calamity, "*Mercredi à Bastia, c'est le gamin qui joue!*" ("On Wednesday at Bastia, the kid plays!")

Landreau was seventeen years old. Nantes were struggling near the bottom of the table. In the dressing room before the game, his teammates were worried, and warned him that Bastia fans were notoriously unforgiving. "I felt comfortable and serene all day," he remembered. Sports director Robert Budzynski said Landreau had boosted the team's morale.

It was a tough game, in a fierce atmosphere. In the second half, Landreau saved a penalty from Lubomir Moravcik. He earned his team a point. "What calm he showed against a veteran like Moravcik. It was a special evening for anyone who saw him," said Budzynski.

The draw kick-started Nantes' season, as they beat Nice 7–0 in the next game. Landreau kept his place in the side for the next ten years. When he was nineteen, he was appointed club captain.

2. Paris Saint-Germain 2 Nantes 3, December 8, 2002, League Cup first round

Nantes had won successive French Cups in 1999 and 2000, and in both seasons had needed Landreau's help in penalty shoot-outs (against PSG and Gueugnon) to progress. Landreau had captained Nantes to the final in 2000, earning admirers throughout France for his gesture to losing captain Reginald Becque. It was the season that fourth division Calais had reached the final, and they were ahead at halftime. Only a last-minute penalty scored by Antoine Sibierski won the game for Nantes. Landreau went up to Becque and said, "I'm going to suggest something to you, but don't get the wrong idea, I'm not patronizing you. I think what you guys have achieved is exceptional, so I want you to come and lift the trophy with me." Becque spoke to his coach and teammates, and agreed.

In 2001, Nantes won the French league title. Landreau was a major part of that success, and he had impressed Sir Alex Ferguson after an outstanding performance in Nantes' 1–1 Champions League draw at Old Trafford in February 2002. He had also turned down a move to Barcelona, in summer 2001, because French players had a poor record at Camp Nou and, one year before a World Cup, Landreau wanted to be certain of a place in the France squad (after all that, he did not make it).

In this game against PSG, Nantes were leading a thrilling Cup tie at the Parc des Princes when Ronaldinho, in his second season in Europe, earned a penalty with five minutes left. Landreau had planned what he would do if this happened, and he took his place in the goal standing almost next to the right-hand goalpost. The whole of the left side of the goal was open for Ronaldinho. "I knew he was a good penalty taker and I wanted to confuse him," Landreau explained. "For me it was not about the striker's foot placing, it was more the run-up, the taker's positioning, how he took them in the past. But it was also a psychological duel; the more I saved, the more the opponents were scared of me. But the challenge is to convince the taker to hit the ball where you want them to."

As Ronaldinho began his run-up, Landreau pointed his left arm at the open space, and crouched as if ready to pounce into it. Ronaldinho was befuddled. Landreau ended up staying next to his post and Ronaldinho kicked the ball straight at him. "I tried something different and it worked," he said. "They called me a genius but it's nothing to do with that. You just have to take some chances."* Ronaldinho, stunned, stared open mouthed at Landreau after the save.

3. Nantes 1 Sochaux 1, April 16, 2004, League Cup final (Sochaux win 5–4 on penalties)

Nantes had beaten Auxerre 4–1 in a shoot-out in the semifinal, a game which Landreau's first coach, Lollichon, had watched alongside Petr Cech in the stadium. Lollichon used to take the fourteen-year-old Landreau to trampoline classes at seven o'clock on a Monday morning to improve his bounce. During the game, Lollichon gestured that Landreau was playing too deep and, spotting him in the stands, the goalkeeper adjusted his position. "Christophe was the coach who had the biggest impact on me," he said. Against Auxerre, Landreau was once again decisive, saving penalties from Djibril Cissé and Cyril Jeunechamp. He also took, and scored, the final penalty that clinched Nantes' place in the final. It was the first of his career.

The final ended 1–1 after extra time, and after five penalty kicks each, it was 3–3. Sudden death. Souleymane Diawara and Sylvain Armand both scored. 4–4. Max Flachez missed for Sochaux. Up stepped Landreau, taker number seven for his side, for the chance to win the Cup.

"I was sure that the kick I chose would be the most effective," said Landreau. "I thought Teddy Richert figured I would go hard to his right side. I had prepared for what I was going to do. I thought about it after the Auxerre game. I had taken my last one, and scored with it. Suddenly I was not only trying to save penalties, but now score them too. I am always looking for new

---

*In August 2013, former England goalkeeper Scott Carson, playing for Wigan Athletic, tried the same thing in a match against Bournemouth. The Bournemouth striker Brett Pitman, with almost the whole goal to aim for, rolled a weak shot into the space and Carson was able to make up the ground and save it.

ideas, to try new things. It's in my nature to push boundaries and to take risks."

And so Landreau, with the second penalty of his professional career, in the League Cup final at the Stade de France, tried a Panenka. "I disguised it well. There were over 80,000 fans in the stadium and the only one who wasn't fooled was Richert." The goalkeeper stood his ground and caught the penalty. In the next round of shots, Benoit Pedretti scored, and Pascal Delhommeau missed. Nantes had lost.

"I do feel responsible but I wasn't the only one who missed," Landreau said. "This kick won't change me, it fits my personality. I would never say I won't try it again. The aim is still to surprise the opponent. And I'm adamant that this is still the best way to score: nine out of ten times, a penalty down the middle will be a goal. I take responsibility for this miss but I don't feel I owe the club. I was part of the team, along with my pals, who got us into the final. The only thing that pissed me off was that we didn't win the trophy."

Crazy, then? Far from it. If anything, the likes of Chilavert, Ceni and Butt were the exact opposite: obsessive trainers promoted to their penalty roles on account of their extra work. Ricardo may have been right when he said he wasn't crazy, but he was wrong when he suggested that the others were.

PENALTY ICON—
ALEX MOLODETSKY

The story of Alex Molodetsky would never have become known if the *Komsomolskaya Pravda* newspaper had not run a competition in 1989 asking readers to send in their weirdest stories of achievement. The prize was the chance to appear in the *Guinness Book of World Records*, and while Molodetsky never made it into the book—he fell out with witnesses who wanted a cut of his future earnings as a result of their support—his story was soon picked up.

The following year, Russian magazine *Divo-90* told the tale: how the striker, playing for third division side Stroitel Poltava, once scored a penalty . . . with his head.

Molodetsky was a singing teacher and a choral conductor. He sang in the church choir, and played as a forward for Stroitel. He was twenty-five on August 13, 1971, when, during a training session, his coach came up to him and said, "If you can score a penalty with your head, you will go on to play for the Ukraine national team."

Molodetsky had felt the spirit of a powerful force around him ever since a recent church service, and he took his coach at his word. "Maybe he was joking but I took it seriously. I took a run from eight yards, and dived down to hit the stationary ball. At that moment, I felt intuitively that I would score. And so it happened. The ball went near the post and the goalkeeper could not reach it. After hitting it, for a short time I lost consciousness, and my teammates poured water on me."

His teammates, not knowing about his conversation with the coach, thought that Molodetsky had lost his footing and slipped and that the goalkeeper, concerned for his teammate, did not try to save it.

Molodetsky's achievement took on an apocryphal status because the only person in the Ukrainian archives who has ever verified it is Molodetsky himself. Later in the 1970s its influence seems to have reached Donetsk, where one day an unknown player turned up at Shakhtar's Kirsha training ground asking for a trial.

"He was a queer fish," recalled defender Viktor Zvyahintsev, who would go on to become one of the USSR's top referees. "His misfortune was that the first player he ran into was Vitaly Starukhin, our star player and the team joker."

Starukhin told the visitor that the first thing he had to do was write a letter of application to the head coach, and make sure he included all his contractual demands: he should ask for a three-room apartment and a Volga car (the most prestigious at the time). Then he started with the physical tests: first, load a wheelbarrow with grass and run fifty meters; second, take on Starukhin in a full-pitch one-on-one challenge. "Vitaly dribbled round him so many times the poor guy almost turned blue. We had to stop him because we thought he would have a heart attack," laughed Zvyahintsev.

The final challenge from Starukhin invoked Molodetsky's heroics. He told the stranger that he had to score a penalty—with his head. The player changed his mind and decided that Shakhtar was maybe not the club for him.

Between his soccer and singing, Molodetsky found time for

one more hobby: listening to radio transmissions from across the world. His mistake, he told *Segodnya*, was that he told his friends what he had heard on the BBC and the Voice of America. In 1976, an unfamiliar car pulled up outside his house, and before he knew it, Molodetsky was in Poltava Mental Hospital. "I went through hell with eight months of forced treatment," he said. "They made me incapable, disabled, and then sent me to Dnipropetrovsk Mental Hospital. There were dangerous criminals and dissidents in the clinic, who were drugged up and turned into vegetables. They accused me of organizing a spy network, and I still don't know how I survived. My sports background must have helped."

Molodetsky returned to the Church when he was released, and spent thirteen years as a musician at Poltava Cathedral. The church music helped him recover from his ordeal.

On his release from Dnipropetrovsk, Molodetsky developed another passion: calculating predictive algorithms. The walls in the small house he shared with his mother were covered in paper with mysterious equations on them. "It's a universal algorithm," he said. "If you put this in your computer, you can predict the weather, determine the optimal place to drill for oil, or predict future earthquakes." He also developed a program for soccer clubs, which can produce "unique data that will help players never lose."

The problem was that Molodetsky could not afford a computer. When he wrote to Ukrainian president Leonid Kuchma requesting a loan and mentioning his headed penalty, the response from the State Committee of Ukraine was not what he wanted. No money, said the letter. And it called his headed goal "a circus trick." That upset him more than the financial rejection.

CHAPTER 8

THE SEARCH FOR JUSTICE

Referees have more in common with players than you might think. Every decision they make on the pitch is closely scrutinized; they are under pressure to perform in big games; and if they make a mistake, they can expect a battering in the media. Despite these shared responsibilities, there is often a clear lack of support from players, and clubs, for officials.

"In a way we are in a special group, included in what is called the big football family by words, but not really by actions," explained Tom Henning Øvrebo, a former international referee who, given his day job as a clinical psychologist in Oslo, seemed to be a good person to ask about the psychology of decision making under pressure.

"Football is a lot of psychology with emotions and conflicts and communication and so it's not a disadvantage for me to have a theoretical background in psychology," he said. "It helps to understand the different reactions of players and yourself, but you still feel the same pressure, and you still make the same mistakes as everyone else."

Øvrebo made mistakes in one game in particular and, he added with a rueful smile, it's the game he is most famous for. It was the

2009 Champions League semifinal second leg between Chelsea and Barcelona at Stamford Bridge. The first leg had ended goalless. Chelsea scored an early goal at home, but because of the away goal rule were only ever an equalizer away from elimination. They kept on pushing forward and had their first shout for a penalty after 25 minutes when Dani Alves brought down Florent Malouda. Øvrebo awarded a free kick on the edge of the area. More would follow:

26 minutes: Didier Drogba went down under pressure from Eric Abidal. No penalty.

56 minutes: Yaya Touré tackled Drogba in the area. No penalty.

82 minutes: Gerard Piqué appeared to handle the ball in the area after a shot by Nicolas Anelka. No penalty.

95 minutes: Samuel Eto'o appeared to handle the ball in the area after a shot by Michael Ballack. No penalty.

By then, Andrés Iniesta had equalized for Barcelona—a rasping drive from the edge of the area after 92 minutes—and the succession of decisions against them was too much for some of the Chelsea players. Ballack ran fifty yards to remonstrate with Øvrebo after the Eto'o call, and was photographed, arms aloft and mouth open wide, appealing to the referee right under his nose. "Body language is so important for a referee and you look at the pictures of that moment and I did not look in control," Øvrebo commented. "I was not at ease at that moment."

He was sitting in his office, which has his name and "Psykolog" on the door, in a posh district of central Oslo when he said this, and could not have looked more at ease. He rents the office from a local health provider that specializes in helping teenagers cope with pregnancy, which explains why the waiting-room had tasteful pictures of female nudes on the walls, and jars filled with condoms placed on every surface.

Øvrebo spends most of his week here but for two afternoons he works on the mental conditioning of athletes at the Olympic training center. He had just come from there and was running a little late. I wasn't expecting him to wear all black, but it was briefly disconcerting to see him wearing jeans, a pink T-shirt and Converse trainers.

He is also on the corporate speaking circuit, giving lectures to companies and sports teams about stress management. "Stress is not objective, it's purely subjective," he told me. "So a stress is only something that you perceive as an individual, and coping with it is all about how you cope with that as an individual. I explain that and give them coping strategies to deal with it."

Was he stressed during that Chelsea–Barcelona game? "Well, the body language was not good. In my experience, it's not the decision itself that gets you into trouble but the way you sell it, if you like. The way you sell it will to a large extent be influenced by your body language, your posture, your eye contact; sometimes you can smile a little, but obviously not if it's a controversial penalty. That would not go down well."

Most of Øvrebo's decisions against Chelsea were, to a neutral, understandable. At least four of them were fifty-fifty decisions, which, if he was not 100 percent sure about them, he could not have given. The only one that seemed more definite was the Piqué handball. By then, the crowd was vociferously hostile toward Øvrebo and the players were openly showing their displeasure.

I wondered if Øvrebo had heard about the academic study in which forty qualified referees watched forty-seven incidents from a 1998/99 game between Liverpool and Leicester.* Twenty watched with crowd noise, the other twenty without. The referees with the crowd noise awarded fewer fouls than those without the noise. Øvrebo had seen the paper and found it interesting. "You try your best not to be influenced by fans or players

---

* Nevill, Webb & Watts, "Improved training of football referees and the decline in home advantage post WW2" (*Psychology of Sport and Exercise*).

or coaches or the media but of course we are human as well and sometimes it's maybe hard to avoid it, though I'm not saying we are always influenced in a direction that supporters want us to be. It can go the other way."

This is what I feel happened against Barcelona. Øvrebo was under pressure from the fans, who felt he was against him, and from the players, who felt the same. So when Piqué handled the ball near the end of the game, Øvrebo made a quick decision to show his authority. At that point he risked losing control of the game, so it might have felt more important to appear decisive than to be right. It was his only mistake, but then it only needs to be one mistake for people to remember.

I presented my theory to Øvrebo. "I can answer this not as a referee but as a psychologist: maybe the decision can go a bit in the other direction, to show 'I'm not influenced by the spectators.' If you say 'I shall not be influenced by the crowd, I will be extra strong,' it will still influence you one way or another."

So you were trying to be strong, to stamp your authority?

"Yes, it's fair to say that I tried to be, to have a strict line."

And if the same incident had happened after 20 minutes, before that hostile atmosphere had developed?

"Unfortunately we will never know! I could have and I could not have, that's the fascinating thing about refereeing. It's all about the heat of the moment."

Øvrebo has worked in the controlled environment of that study as well. He once took charge of a World Cup qualifier between Georgia and Turkey that was played behind closed doors because of previous crowd trouble. "It was a special experience but it felt strange to get no feedback after every decision you made. Normally you have references, this time there were none."

He wondered whether England's penalty record would improve if you removed the perceived "stress triggers" for the players. "If you take out the spectators and the media, would England win, or would it be the same?" he asked. It was a very good question.

The aftermath of the Barcelona game was challenging for Øvrebo. On the final whistle, Drogba shouted "It's a fucking disgrace!" into a TV camera and followed Øvrebo down the tunnel. Neither man has revealed what happened next but Drogba was reported to have struck the wall inches from Øvrebo's face. "People are very curious but I'm not going to stir that up again," he said.

Chelsea fans sent Øvrebo hate mail and UEFA smuggled him out of England in disguise. Drogba received a four-match ban for his outburst, and José Bosingwa, who called Øvrebo "a thief," was banned for three games.

"I took a lot of positives out of the experience when it comes to dealing with the stress and pressure for myself," Øvrebo added. "Being able to stand up to scrutiny like that, deal with it afterward and know what to expect, it is helpful for the rest of my life and in other areas. So I haven't put it away completely. I see it as a useful experience, one that can still help me." He joked to the Norwegian press that if he lost his job, he could always write a book about it.

Øvrebo thought it would have helped him to speak publicly after the game, to explain his decisions and, who knows, maybe admit he had made a mistake. After all, once referees become the story, they are already under more pressure. "If a star player missed a penalty in a big tournament, the easiest thing for him to do, instead of ignoring the media, is release a statement. That will end the story, which always lasts longer when no one is allowed to talk."

UEFA doesn't allow any of its officials to speak to the press after matches, apparently to avoid the danger of misinterpretations (or mistranslations) across different cultures. Øvrebo found that frustrating, especially as in Norway he had been known to admit to the odd mistake. "I did not have anything against talking about the incidents at the time, but UEFA were very restrictive on that, and did not want us to express our opinion on situations. When I've done it here, the media accept it, and the fans accept it. It might make headlines on Monday, but by Tuesday it's quiet again. If you don't speak, the experts queue up to criticize you on Tuesday, Wednesday and Thursday."

This was a similar strategy for failure to the one Geir Jordet introduced to the Holland Under-21 team, and it made sense. It would take some pressure off referees to know there is a plan in case of a bad call. "If you're scared," Øvrebo added, "you might think too much about the consequences and not have the courage to take the difficult decision, which might be the right one."

UEFA employs a psychologist to work with referees before major tournaments and has in the past engaged a Swiss consultancy firm to conduct two-year voluntary courses aimed at improving referees in three key areas: "emotional control skills, concentration skills, and capacity to communicate both within the referee team and with players and coaches." The aim is to reduce the number of refereeing mistakes, but it's impossible to eliminate them for good. "Referees' mistakes are part of football," said Øvrebo. "If you get rid of them, you lose part of the drama of football. And then you're left with a big question: are the pictures that you see really the truth of what happened? Sometimes two people can see the same image and come to different conclusions. What do you do then?"

Øvrebo was fortunate to have the psychological grounding to cope with the firestorm that followed. Anders Frisk was not so lucky: he retired after receiving death threats from Chelsea fans one month after the tempestuous 2005 Champions League tie against Barcelona in which Drogba was sent off and José Mourinho accused Frank Rijkaard of visiting the referee at halftime.

Øvrebo went the other way. He was due to quit as an international referee at the end of that season but stayed on for one more year, hoping to earn a call-up from UEFA for the 2010 World Cup. He made the long-list of fourteen names but was not one of the ten men who went to South Africa.

As Øvrebo drove me around Oslo city center in his battered red Vauxhall, on his way to pick up his son from soccer practice, he insisted he had no regrets about his performance at Stamford Bridge that night. "I took a lot from it, and you don't get anywhere by trying to change what's happened."

Spoken like a true *psykolog.*

I reminded him of the spoof story run by Spanish newspaper *AS* on Día de los Santos Inocentes, their April Fool's Day equivalent, which had Øvrebo quitting soccer to become a monk. "In my search for spirituality, I hope to recover the personal peace that I lost on that fateful night at Stamford Bridge," the paper quoted him as saying. He was even pictured (Photoshopped, rather) in a monk's outfit.

He thought it was funny at the time, and he laughed again. "I had no problem with it. But then again, my soul is at peace."

Øvrebo had a point about the media: in what other walk of life can one man be so publicly vilified and not be allowed the right to reply? In the case of Scottish referee Ian Foote, he did reply. But he had to wait eight years before doing so.

"*Ah, ce n'est pas possible! Ce n'est pas possible! C'est quand même pas croyable qu'il accorde le pénalty là-dessus. Mais c'est invraisemblable, à trois . . . deux minutes de la fin de la partie. Alors là, je n'ai vraiment pas peur de le dire: 'Mr. Foote, vous êtes un salaud!'*"

("Ah, this is not possible! It's not possible! It's unbelievable that he's given a penalty there. But it can't be happening, what, three . . . two minutes from the end of the game. So I'm not afraid to say this: 'Mr. Foote, you are a bastard!'")

That's how commentator Thierry Rolland, covering the World Cup qualifier between Bulgaria and France in October 1976, reported a late penalty awarded in Sofia on public TV station Antenne2, France's equivalent of the BBC. The score was 2–2 and referee Ian Foote gave the decision after Hristo Bonev had taken a tumble in the box. Foote had already allowed Pavel Panov's goal for Bulgaria to stand even though it had looked offside, and he'd failed to award France a penalty for a clear foul on Michel Platini.

Bonev stepped up to take the penalty for Bulgaria. As Rolland described it: "*A côté! A côté! Et bien, il y a un bon Dieu, croyez-moi! Quel scandale cet arbitrage, c'est invraisemblable. Je n'ai jamais vu un individu pareil. Il devrait être en prison, pas sur un terrain de football!*" ("It's wide! Wide! Well, there is a God, believe me! This referee is scandalous, it's unbelievable. I have never seen anyone like him. He should be in prison, not on a soccer pitch!")

Rolland was France's most famous commentator, and first covered Les Bleus in 1955. In Platini's words, "His was the voice of passion," while for Zinedine Zidane, "When you heard that voice, you knew it was football time." He was friends with the France players in the 1970s, and would often join the team for a jog on away trips. He spent six years studying in England and proudly described himself as "the only Frenchman who can appreciate cricket." And he liked his routine: for every away game, he would demand that a copy of *L'Equipe* be left on his hotel bed, along with the name of the best local Italian restaurant (even when he wasn't in Italy). He would only pick up the paper after he had phoned his wife.

After this particular outburst, Rolland was in trouble. The France players might have agreed with him—Marius Trésor had wanted to strangle Foote, and said that he would have been sent off if the referee had understood French—but the board members at Antenne2 called a disciplinary meeting. On the day they met, *France Soir* ran a picture of Foote under the headline "The Most Hated Man in France." *L'Equipe* had a cartoon of a masked Foote pointing his whistle like a gun at Platini.

Rolland was not taken off the air but was warned about his future conduct. He was helped by the fact that the Bulgaria–France match was played on a Saturday and none of the station directors was in the office on the Sunday. The timing saved Rolland: by the Monday, every paper was describing Foote as "the bastard that almost made the France team lose." And on the

Tuesday, the station received two full sacks of mail with letters written to back Rolland. By Wednesday, there were six sacks. Rolland claimed he received nearly two million letters of support. "It's a world record response for any TV program," he said.

Eight years later, in 1984, Foote appeared on French TV show *Telefoot* and sheepishly watched each of the controversial incidents again. On the penalty he didn't award to France he commented, "I was well behind the play but I would say that was a fifty-fifty decision."

On Bulgaria's offside goal: "I would agree that the player looks offside but the linesman gave no signal. I would say it's partly my fault, yes, partly. The referee carries the can as he is the man who makes the final decision."

On the late penalty award: "In the position I was in, it appeared to me he was brought down by two French players. I would argue with you even now about that one, he could have been tripped, though I would say there is some doubt. Because TV cameras are higher, the view you see is not the same as at ground level."

In 1987, Rolland and Foote were reunited when the Scot sportingly agreed to referee the first half of a Variety Club charity match Rolland had organized. In charge of the second half was Ali Bin Nasser, the Tunisian referee who missed Diego Maradona's handball against England in the 1986 World Cup. "Honestly, Jean-Michel," Rolland had said to his cocommentator Jean-Michel Larqué during that game, "do you not think someone other than a Tunisian should be refereeing a game of this magnitude?"

Rolland had commentated on nine European Championships, thirteen World Cups and over 1,300 matches when he died in June 2012. "He was not a journalist but a narrator, a storyteller, an actor. And, above all, a fan," wrote *France Football* a few days later. The magazine would go on to publish the full transcript of Rolland's tearful soliloquy after France won the 1998 World Cup on home soil. It is a wonderful piece of drama, and begins "After seeing that, I can now die happy . . ."

Rolland told a different story about Foote. He claimed in 2000 that back in 1976 Foote had feared for his own safety. " 'If France win this game, I won't get out of this stadium alive,' he told me," said Rolland. "If you've never felt physically afraid, I'd call you a liar, so I respected that." In the intervening twenty-four years, the commentator added, strangers would ask him about "*le salaud*" at least once a week.

There's nothing new about trying to trick a referee. "The referees are deceived, and so is nearly everybody else," wrote an anonymous referee in *Cassell's Saturday Journal*, published in December 1892. The official remembered a game—this was before goals had nets in them—when one team kept appealing for goals when the ball had sneaked around the outside of the post.

"You know very well that last shot was not a goal," the referee told one of the players.

"Of course I do," came the response. "But I didn't know that you did, and nothing is lost by appealing."

Appeals do not always work, though. As Tom Henning Øvrebo (almost) put it, the more a team appeals for a penalty, the less likely the referee might be to award it. According to one academic study, referees are less likely to give a second penalty to a team that has already won a penalty, and more likely to award a penalty to a team that has conceded one.[*] (The odd thing about this study was that the 115 participants were made up of referees—fifty-seven—and players—fifty-eight—who must have viewed the match, a 1999 La Liga game between Rayo Vallecano and Real Madrid, from differing viewpoints.)

Another study backed up those findings after looking at 12,902 games from the Bundesliga.[†] There were 441 matches in which more than one penalty was awarded—far more than the

[*] Plessner & Betsch, "Sequential effects in important referee decisions: the case of penalties in soccer" (*Journal of Sport and Exercise Psychology*).

[†] Schwarz, "Compensating tendencies in penalty kick decisions of referees in professional football" (*Journal of Sports Sciences*).

expected number—and the conclusion was that "there are considerably more matches in which each team is awarded one penalty than would be expected on the basis of independent penalty-kick decisions."

The lot of the referee is best summed up by a third study, and that's the one I mentioned to Øvrebo. Overseen by Professor Alan Nevill at the University of Wolverhampton's School of Sport, Performing Arts and Leisure, the purpose of the study ("Improved training of football referees and the decline in home advantage post WW2") was to evaluate the role of crowd noise in acting as a cue for officials to take decisions. The main finding was that the referees who watched games with crowd noise awarded fewer fouls to the home side. The more significant finding, for me at least, was that, even though the referees were all qualified, not a single incident resulted in a unanimous decision.

Despite their differing views, you'd hope that most would have avoided the mistake Japanese referee Toshimitsu Yoshida made in the 2006 World Cup play-off match between Uzbekistan and Bahrain. The winner of the tie would face Trinidad & Tobago in another play-off for a place in Germany, and Uzbekistan were 1–0 up when Yoshida awarded a penalty.

The penalty taker, Server Djeparov, scored from the spot, but Yoshida had noticed an encroachment by Uzbek players. Instead of awarding a retake, he gave a free kick to Bahrain. "If that penalty had counted, we were so dominant that I think we would have won 3–0 or 4–0," said Uzbekistan's English coach Bob Houghton. "Everyone was very angry and it was a tragedy for the country. I remember leaving the pitch at halftime. I saw the fourth official and said to him, 'What the hell is that?' and he said, 'It's a new rule.' I then saw the head of the Uzbek referee commission and I asked him why he had not told us about this new rule because he already had told us about a couple of minor changes previously. He just said, 'I don't think that is right,' and soon we were on the phone to FIFA."

Uzbekistan had won the game 1–0, but they protested to

FIFA, demanded a 3–0 forfeit, and were stunned by the response. FIFA annulled the result and ordered a replay. It was the first time a World Cup qualifier had been replayed. Bahrain scored early on and the first leg finished 1–1. A 0–0 draw in the second leg saw Bahrain go through on away goals.

In the play-off against Trinidad & Tobago, the boot was on the other foot when Colombian referee Oscar Julian Ruiz chalked off a last-minute Ahmed Hassan goal for a clear shove on goalkeeper Kelvin Jack. Hussain Ali Baba was sent off for his protests and home fans ripped seats and threw them on to the pitch. Bahrain even appealed unsuccessfully to FIFA.

As for Yoshida, his mistake earned him a lifetime ban as an international referee. One Japanese blogger referred to Yoshida and three colleagues as the "Fantastic Four," handing them Marvel nicknames that referred to their most characteristic mistakes: Hiroyoshi "Flaming Red Card" Takayama, Masaaki "Invisible Foul" Iemoto, Yuichi "Stretch the Truth" Nishimura, and Toshimitsu "The Thing" Yoshida.

In 2008, Iemoto was suspended for six months after some bizarre calls in a season-opening Japanese Super Cup game between Sanfrecce and Kashima Antlers. One Japanese writer had heard rumors before the game—their equivalent of the Community Shield—that Sanfrecce would win on penalties after a 2–2 draw, and he wrote as much on his Web site before kick-off. Three players were sent off, and when Sanfrecce's late penalty, generously given, was saved, Iemoto ordered a retake. The game ended 2–2. In the shoot-out, two more Sanfrecce penalties were retaken (both had been missed and were subsequently scored) and they won the game. Kashima fans stormed the pitch to protest but their players calmed them down so they could appeal through official channels. Some fans sent a copy of the article that had correctly predicted the game's outcome to the Japanese FA, and the Japanese soccer league. They never received a reply.

Every team has had an awful decision that becomes a reference for all refereeing mistakes that go against them. The injustice is what keeps us coming back for more. French ethnologist Christian Bromberger wrote that soccer's "deep structure represents the uncertain fate of man in the world of today." He compared soccer to a democracy where nobodies can become stars, and stated that the ritualistic images—of the substitutes' bench, the league table, and the top scorers' chart—provide comfort in the maelstrom of our lives. As he put it, "There is a special place occupied by uncertainty and chance due to complicated techniques involved, and the devastatingly powerful role of the referee who must immediately penalize offences which might not be spotted. Football therefore embodies an image of today's world which is consistent and contradictory, celebrating individual and collective merit but also underlining the role of luck and cheating in the achievement which may laugh in the face of merit. Failure and misfortune are only psychologically acceptable if they can be explained away in terms of third party action, injustice or fate."[*]

That is certainly the case for English soccer fans who, with the help of a complicit and scapegoat-hungry media, have managed to pin most recent international tournament eliminations, even those lost in a shoot-out, on a referee.

Figure 25: England excuses since 1986

Tournament	Referee	Reason
WC 1986	Ali Bin Nasser	Allowed Hand of God goal
WC 1990	José Ramirez Wright	Booked Paul Gascoigne
WC 1998	Kim Milton Neilsen	Sent off David Beckham
Euro 2004	Urs Meier	Disallowed Sol Campbell goal
WC 2006	Horacio Elizondo	Sent off Wayne Rooney
WC 2010	Jorge Larrionda	Disallowed Frank Lampard goal after ball crossed line

---

[*]Bromberger, "Football passion and the World Cup: why so much sound and fury?," in Sugden & Tomlinson (eds), *Hosts and Champions*, pp 281–90.

Four of those defeats came after shoot-outs, but none was the fault of England or their players; no, instead it was a decision that was made up to an hour before the shoot-out started that the media blamed for the loss. England know better than most that it's easy to blame the referee, and easier still when there are penalties involved.

At least none of England's losses carried a whiff of suspicion, which is more than can be said after Italy lost its 2002 World Cup match to hosts South Korea. Referee Byron Moreno awarded the Koreans a debatable penalty (saved by Gigi Buffon), disallowed a Damiano Tomassi goal that would have won the game for Italy, and then sent off striker Francesco Totti in extra time for diving. South Korea won 2–1. Had referee Moreno had a bad day? Or did his performance make more sense when the Ecuadorean FA banned him for twenty games after he played thirteen minutes of injury-time in a league match during which Liga de Quito scored twice to beat Barcelona 4–3?

During his suspension, he appeared on Italian TV station RAI's *Stupido Hotel* carrying a briefcase stuffed with bank-notes,* before claiming his decisions had been right. Moreno had been portrayed in Italian cartoons as a Korean robot, while one town in Sicily named their public toilets after him. "I don't think I was the major cause of Italy's World Cup exit, and I don't need to apologize," he said. "I've always fought against dishonest players and dangerous play. After the Portugal v. USA match I was marked 8.5 out of ten and I got an even better mark for the Italy v. Korea match. The Italians were looking for excuses." *Stupido* brought in former international José Altafini to interview Moreno; the chat ended with Altafini pouring a bucket of cold water over him.

Moreno denied that the Quito controversy was linked to his desire to enter politics. After the World Cup, he was running for

---

*Moreno was playing the role of a billionaire trying to revive the fortunes of a disgraced hotel by throwing an amazing party.

election for Quito city council under the slogan "Byron Moreno waves a red card to corruption." In that same game he had given Quito two penalties, sent off two Barcelona players, and disallowed a goal. He insisted he was not using it as a vote-winning ruse. He went on to lose the election and was alienated from soccer, much to the disappointment of his daughter Mishele, who, as a nine-year-old, had vowed to follow in his footsteps as a referee. "I would love to be able to call the police so that all the bad men will be put in prison for all the things they've done to Daddy," she said.

It didn't quite work out like that. Instead, Daddy ended up in prison after he was caught at New York's JFK Airport in September 2010 with over six kilograms of heroin, worth around $750,000, strapped to his stomach, back and legs. He pleaded guilty, was sentenced to thirty months in jail and served twenty-six of them before his release in December 2012. He returned to Ecuador and assisted Guayaquil's head narcotics prosecutor Monica Rivera in her investigations.

Moreno's is not the only story of a referee abusing his power through the penalty kick. The two penalties that fourth division SC Paderborn were awarded in their 4–2 German Cup win over Hamburg in August 2004 seemed dubious—as did Emile Mpenza's red card—but the full significance only emerged the following January, when referee Robert Hoyzer admitted he had received €67,000 and a TV set to try to fix nine games. Sports bar owner Ante Sapina, the man behind the scam, had made €750,000 from the Paderborn game alone. By then, Hamburg coach Klaus Toppmöller had been fired, in part for the humiliating upset.

Spanish referee Emilio Guruceta remains a controversial figure in Barcelona though he was never found guilty, at least in Spain, of any wrongdoing. He took charge of the 1970 Spanish Cup quarterfinal second leg between Real Madrid and Barcelona at Camp Nou. Madrid had won the first leg 2–0 and were 1–0 down in Barcelona when Joaquim Rife tackled Manolo Velazquez outside the box, only for his momentum to carry him into the area. Guruceta gave a penalty and Barcelona's players walked off in protest. Eladio was sent off for his complaints and Amancio scored from the spot. It soon became a political protest: the crowd sang anti-Madrid songs and saw the decision as the latest in a long line of injustices at the hands of Francoist authorities. They threw bottles and other missiles on to the pitch and Guruceta called time on the game five minutes early. He and his linesmen spent the night in police custody for their own safety. Barcelona's point had been made, and as historian Duncan Shaw put it, five years before Franco's death Barcelona showed it "could serve as a popular pole of resistance, occasionally violent, to the Franco regime."

Shaw investigated "Asunto Guruceta" (the Guruceta Affair) as part of his PhD thesis* and could find no evidence of any payment—even if Guruceta had bought himself a new BMW one week after the game. And yet the referee was not always innocent: he was later found guilty of receiving bribes to help Anderlecht beat Nottingham Forest in the 1984 UEFA Cup semifinal. He died before the case went to trial, in a car crash in 1987, on his way to referee Osasuna against Real Madrid.

Many years later, Spanish soccer writer Phil Ball sat next to one of Guruceta's linesmen while watching a game in a San Sebastian hotel bar. A fuse had blown so in the darkness the pair had a bizarre conversation in which the linesman, whom Ball suspected of being drunk, said that he had kept his flag down. "[That night] we were the three most famous people in Spain. Guru didn't want that, he just wanted to be a respected ref." As he left the bar, he mumbled, "*Le jodieron, sabes? Y no hizo nada.*" ("They got him, you know? And he didn't do anything.")

In Greece, a suspiciously manipulated refereeing "error" is called a *papoutselio*, in honor of Stratos Papoutselis, whose decision to award Olympiakos a penalty against Panathinaikos in

---

* "The political instrumentalization of professional football in Francoist Spain, 1939–1975."

December 1996 is said to have changed the course of Greek soccer history. Olympiakos had not won the title for nine seasons, and when Predrag Djordjevic scored after Giannis Kalitzakis brought down Ilia Ivic, apparently outside the area, the 1–0 win kick-started Olympiakos's period of dominance. They would go on to win seven titles in a row, and fifteen of the next seventeen.

Panathinaikos, who had two players, Kalitzakis (for his post-penalty protests) and Thanasis Kolitsidakis, sent off in the same game, released a statement ridiculing the officials. "There was a football crime that happened at the usual place, at Karaiskakis Stadium. This time Panathinaikos was the victim of the massacre . . . Instead of playing football every Sunday in Greece, why don't they just legally decree the title goes to Olympiakos now? It's a shame to bother all the other teams."

Papoutselis never spoke about the game. He refereed for one last season, in 1998, without controversy, and returned to Greek soccer in summer 2013, passing his exams to become a referees' observer, starting out in the Greek second division.

The first official from a World Cup final to face public approbation for a penalty decision was Edgardo Codesal, who cheered as much as anyone when Argentina beat West Germany 3–2 in 1986. The thirty-five-year-old Mexican, though he was born in Uruguay, was in the stands at the Estadio Azteca in Mexico that hot June afternoon. His grandfather was born in Argentina and his brother lived there. He felt connected to the country, and cried tears of joy when Diego Maradona lifted the trophy.

Codesal's father José Maria had been a referee at the 1966 World Cup in England, and he ran the line for the semfinal between West Germany and Soviet Union. Codesal Jr. was a qualified gynecologist and a highly rated referee whose dreams came true when he was picked for the 1990 World Cup. He took charge of Italy's 1–0 win over USA, awarding a penalty missed by Gianluca Vialli, and blew for two penalties when England beat Cameroon 3–2 in the quarterfinal. FIFA observers gave him an average rating of 8.5 for his performances, and he was put in charge of the final, a repeat of the 1986 clash between Argentina and West Germany.

The night before the game, Maradona received a knock on his bedroom door. It was Julio Grondona, head of the Argentine FA, complaining about the appointment of Codesal. "Diego, we are lost," he reportedly said. Maradona told him to leave, and did not tell his teammates about the conversation. The next day, when the Italian fans booed the Argentine national anthem, Codesal told Maradona to ignore them and "show them what you can do."

Instead, Codesal showed what he could do. The game descended into anarchy after the referee sent off Argentine substitute Pedro Monzón for a high tackle on Jürgen Klinsmann, who did not help his opponent with an exaggerated post-challenge triple-roll. Worse was to come after 85 minutes: Lothar Matthäus played through Rudi Völler who, tightly marked by Roberto Sensini, fell to the ground in the area. Codesal had rejected Gabriel Calderón's claims after a similar clash with Klaus Augenthaler, but this time he awarded a penalty.

Codesal had not taken the time to remember his father's advice: "Don't ever give a penalty if you think you will have to explain it a thousand times."

Andreas Brehme, with his right foot, scored. This was significant because four years earlier, in a shoot-out against Mexico, Brehme had scored with his left foot. Normally Matthäus was West Germany's nominated taker but the pair agreed that Brehme would take this one. "You need to have two or three penalty takers in the team so if one is not confident, you send the one who is confident," Brehme said. He had no idea why he took the penalty against Mexico with his left foot: "Normally I took them with my right foot, and I didn't really practice them in training. You just need courage to take the responsibility. Was Lothar not confident at that moment? I don't know, you have to ask him!"

So I did. Matthäus told me that his new boots had been bothering him, and he felt more comfortable with Brehme taking it. The feeling in Germany that he bottled it still lingers.*

Two minutes later, Codesal sent off another Argentine, Gustavo Dezotti, for grabbing Jürgen Kohler around the neck and wrestling him to the ground in an effort to get the ball off him for a throw-in. Codesal ran over and, theatrical as you like, brandished his second red of the game. "The referee has been physically manhandled by five players and if Argentina continue like this, FIFA will have to ban them from the next World Cup! Surely you can't have this in the final!" said John Motson, commentating on the game for the BBC.

Codesal never refereed again. When he returned to Mexico after the game, he was confronted by hordes of journalists. "I was brave and honest, like I always am," he said. "The foul was Argentina's fault, not mine. I'm calm and happy."

Codesal had been supporting Argentina throughout the tournament and he told *El Gráfico* one week later, "Argentina was my favorite in the final, but a referee has no feelings when he is out there on the pitch."

Nine years later, he remained convinced that his decision had been the correct one. "I have no doubt," he told *Olé*. "The referees don't have to look for intent, they have to look for contact. This is what I saw: the Argentine tried to get to the ball first but he stretched his leg and tackled the German. It was a penalty. I was convinced at the time and I have not changed my mind since. For me, it's a closed case."

The case, actually, was just beginning. Soon after that interview, Humberto Rojano, the former president of the Mexican

* Matthäus told me that his penalty record depended on how he was playing at the time. One of his most famous spot kicks was in the 1984 German Cup final, his last game for Borussia Mönchengladbach. Bayern Munich, the team he was set to join, were the opponents. The game finished 1–1 and Matthäus stepped up to take the first penalty. He hit it over the crossbar. "I hadn't played well in the game but I had scored every penalty I took for the team that season. But my confidence was affected by my performance, I made a mistake, and it was the main story of the game."

Referees' Association, went public on how Codesal had been appointed. He spoke of a meeting he'd had with Javier Arriaga, former head of the Mexican FA's Referees' Commission and a key figure in FIFA's Referees' Commission in 1990. Arriaga also happened to be Codesal's father-in-law. "He said there were three candidates for the final but he wanted Codesal, who was his son-in-law, and he was called by the authorities," Rojano explained. "They explained to him that Argentina didn't have to win and that if Codesal accepted that, he would be the referee. That's how Codesal became the referee." Arriaga had wanted to come good on a promise he had made to José Maria, Codesal's father, before he died in 1979.

FIFA president João Havelange was not a fan of Maradona: the pair had publicly clashed before the tournament, when the Argentine complained at how little of FIFA's vast profits from the tournament filtered down to the players. "If he isn't happy, he doesn't have to come," Havelange responded. The Brazilian was also furious that Maradona claimed the draw was fixed to give Italy an easy group and Argentina a difficult one.

"I can't fight alone against them," Maradona said after the game. "I thought this dark hand was not that strong, but I was wrong, we saw it. Codesal wanted to make them happy; a referee who didn't see the foul on Calderón, but saw the foul on Völler. It was the best solution for German problems: to invent a penalty."

"I know the Argentines still hate me and that hurts," Codesal said. "I love them, and it hurts that I made them suffer. I would have liked Argentina to win their third World Cup back in 1990. If I were God, I would change things, but I'm not God. I do know that in fifty years, they still won't forgive me."

By 2011, over twenty years after the incident, Codesal's stance had hardened against the continued hostility from the losing nation. "I admire the Argentine for their will to win, but they have not learnt to lose, they just can't accept it," he said. "Someone told them that they lost because I was the referee, and they believed it. When Maradona uses his hand to score, that's intelligent; but if they don't win, it's because someone stole from them."

This is what is so wonderful, and so frustrating, about referees, about soccer, about sport: the consistency and the contradictions. One minute, officials get it right; the next, they don't. Tom Henning Øvrebo told me that any decision he made at one point in the match could be totally different at another point. Context is everything.

Charles Corver, the referee in charge of the France v. West Germany World Cup semifinal in Seville in 1982, is convinced that it is harder to referee now than it was thirty years ago. "Everybody thinks football is better now but I don't agree. Maybe it is quicker and more dynamic but it is also more unsporting. It's not fair like it was. Players don't show respectful behavior, and they cheat."*

Those words resonated with me when I watched *Piłkarski Poker* (Poker Soccer), a Polish film released in 1989 about an ex-player-turned-referee, Jan Laguna, who was proud of the fact he had never fixed a game in his career. On the final day of the season, he came under pressure from club chairmen to set up a cooperative to fix the league table. Laguna claimed to oppose the idea, but he bluffed the chairmen, took their money and dictated the results to his liking.

The film was loosely based on the events of May 9, 1982, one of the most controversial days in the history of Polish soccer. It was the last day of the Polish first division and the issues it encapsulated—right and wrong, glory and greed, bluff and counterbluff—centered on one controversial penalty.

---

* Manchester City coach Manuel Pellegrini agreed with this comment in an outspoken press conference in January 2014 when he admitted that all players in the Premier League, including his own, try to con referees. "They [players] are always trying to take advantage for their team, so it is very difficult for officials and I respect them. It is very difficult to be a referee. Players play too quickly and are always trying to cheat because football is cheating," he said.

With two games left to play, the title race was down to two teams. Śląsk Wroclaw were three points ahead of Widzew Łódź, and (because it was only two points for a win) needed two more to be certain of success. On the penultimate weekend, Śląsk wobbled, losing 3–1 at Stal Mielec while Widzew beat Arka Gdynia 2–0.

One game left and one point in it; but because of their head-to-head record with Widzew, Śląsk needed to win at home to Wisla Krakow to finish on top. Widzew needed to win at Ruch Chorzow and hope Śląsk dropped points. Ruch, meanwhile, were fighting to avoid relegation for the first time in their history and had plenty riding on their game.

An investigation by *Gazeta Wyborca* journalist Artur Brzozowski thirty years later revealed what had long been suspected: Wisla took money from both sides—from Śląsk to lose and from Widzew to win—while Śląsk was alleged to have paid referee Alojzy Jarguz to help them. Śląsk paid Wisla PLZ500,000 (PLZ100,000 of which was handed to one of the players' wives in the loo before kick-off), while Widzew paid more, knowing they would be flush with funds from the imminent sale of Zbigniew Boniek to Juventus that summer.

As the five o'clock kick-off approached, Śląsk's stadium was unusually full: the capacity was 15,000 but at least 20,000 fans had crammed their way in. A banner, "Welcome, Polish Champions of 1982," hung from the stands, and club officials had organized a celebratory banquet after the game.

Śląsk had five players in the Poland team but their best player, Tadeusz Pawlowski, had not been part of the prematch training camp in Sycow. Instead he had stayed behind in Wroclaw, to manage "Operation Wisla" with some other senior players. Some club officials told Śląsk coach Jan Califski that the game was too important just to be played on the pitch. "They said they would handle it but I never asked what they meant," he said. One source told Brzozowski that Śląsk were struggling to find any money for Wisla, until a businessman friend of center back Pavel Krol lent the club PLZ400,000.

The Śląsk game kicked off at five on the dot. Just as they'd planned, Widzew kicked off eight minutes later. Śląsk created little in the first half but for a while it didn't matter because Ruch had taken the lead in Chorzow. Marek Filipczak soon equalized for Widzew and attention turned back to Wroclaw.

At halftime it was goalless, and Śląsk players were anxious. "Some of them thought Wisla would hand us this game on a plate, but that was not going to happen," said Califski. "We told them at the break that it was clear Wisla did not want to lose the game, but they remained unconvinced. We couldn't get it into their heads."

Six minutes into the second half, Śląsk's script changed. Piotr Skrobowski scored for Wisla, converting captain Andrzej Iwan's cross. Iwan knew some of Śląsk's players from international duty and he reportedly approached Pawlowski during the game to ask for a million zlotys to lose it. "All I have [to offer] is my gold wedding ring," replied the Śląsk forward.

Śląsk had chances but Wisla goalkeeper Janusz Adamczyk was saving everything. They had not counted on Jarguz, the referee. With seven minutes left—and by now Widzew were winning 3–1 in Chorzow—he awarded a dubious penalty for a push on defender Roman Wojcicki. Jarguz had been spotted having dinner with a Śląsk vice president on the night before the game.

Before the game kicked off, Pawlowski had agreed with Zdzislaw Kapka, his childhood friend and now an opponent, where he would kick a penalty if Śląsk got one. Before the kick, he caught Kapka's eye and the pair shared a nod. The agreed spot was low to the goalkeeper's left. Pawlowski kicked it there, but he was a victim of "Piłkarski Poker." He had been bluffed; Adamczyk knew where he was going, and made a comfortable save.

"Kapka cheated Pawlowski," said one Śląsk player. "Some things were agreed before the game and it was clear that changed on the pitch."

Even coach Califski felt that a deal had taken place. "That penalty showed that Pawlowski trusted in the agreement to the very end. It's a shame because had we scored then, I think we would have had enough time to win the game."

Wisla's players, led by Kapka, furiously denied the charges: "They messed it up. We never fixed games. This sport is about interrupting others, not helping them win. They can only blame themselves. They had a penalty, which Pawlowski missed. They should blame themselves, not make up fanciful stories."

Jarguz, the referee, put forward another twist on the concept of Piłkarski Poker: that as well as paying Wisla to lose the game, some of the Śląsk players had also been paid off by Widzew to lose it. "Śląsk had half the national team and Wisla was so weak we couldn't believe it," Jarguz told *Magazyn Fútbol*. "I knew what was going on but I couldn't find any evidence. Instead, I had to take part in the circus. I wanted to prevent the game from being fixed—so at the end, when Śląsk had a corner, the cross came in and I blew for a penalty."

Jarguz was suspicious when it was the Śląsk players, and not the Wisla players, who demanded to know what the decision was for. "I awarded it anyway. Pawlowski missed it, the fans were ready to kill them. They all say they're clean . . . but I prefer to stay silent."

When Jarguz blew the final whistle, Śląsk had somehow lost the game 1–0. They had allegedly paid off their opponents, the referee, even done a deal on where they would take a penalty, but had still fallen short. "We played normally throughout the season and the one time we tried to fix a game, we lost," said one player.

But had some of their players also profited from the loss? Midfielder Ryszard Tarasiewicz was surprised to be taken off early in the second half, and he noticed some of his teammates had new cars shortly after the match. "We all know the game was played in strange conditions. It was humiliating. I just wanted to win the game, but not all of us felt the same way. Some of them bought a Polonez or a Lada, but they lost their place in history forever."

Pawlowski had been one of the best players in Śląsk's history, but he never recovered from that penalty. He cried in the dressing room and in the aftermath, had his car burned and his children bullied. "I was accused of missing the penalty on purpose and taking money from Wisla." He strongly denied both accusations, and insists that Kapka tricked him.

That summer, Pawlowski was due to move to France to join Lens, but the club mysteriously lost his passport so the deal never happened. He was relegated to the bench, and once when he was told to warm up, during a European Cup tie against CSKA Moscow, an official ran down from the VIP section and told the coach not to bring him on. Eventually, Pawlowski got hold of his passport and completed a move to Austria Vienna.

He still gets recognized in Wroclaw whenever he returns, and is always asked about that penalty on May 9, 1982, the one that could have won Śląsk the title. He has a stock answer: "Yes, I took the penalty, but it's a shame you don't remember that I was also top scorer for Śląsk in the first division and in the European Cup."

Pawlowski has never forgiven Kapka, his old friend from their time together with Poland Under-18s. "We knew each other well, but from that game onward, we never spoke to each other again," he said. "And we never will."

As for Corver, he told me that in his day, he was one of the best referees in the world. "I had the experience and the personality to cope with anything," he said. "I quickly made it clear to the players that I knew everything and I was strict early on so they knew not to protest to me." And what advice would he give referees now to cope with the diving and cheating in the modern game? "The modern referee needs five things: one, good physical condition; two, let the players know that you have a personality; three, do not be afraid to take unpopular decisions; four, take the unpopular decisions; and finally, have courage—be strong!"

At least the pure action of the penalty—one player, one goalkeeper, one ball, one kick—is a simple one for the referee to judge. But even that has proved tough to uphold. Take the first penalty in World Cup history, which was, if anything, a precursor to the drama and controversy that would ensue.

On July 19, 1930, with Argentina leading Mexico 3–0, referee Ulises Saucedo awarded a penalty to Argentina, which Fernando Paternoster ended up hitting straight at goalkeeper Oscar Bonfiglio. It seemed a strange decision, odder still when according to *La Nación* Saucedo counted out sixteen steps for the kick, not twelve. Saucedo was not a qualified referee. He was Bolivia head coach, and his side ended up bottom of Group B after losing 4–0 to both Yugoslavia and Brazil. One of his linesmen, Constantin Radulescu, was also on other business: he was Romania coach (they finished second in Group C, beating Peru 3–1 but losing 4–0 to Uruguay).

The Argentine version of the penalty is that Paternoster felt Saucedo had made a mistake in awarding the penalty and missed it on purpose. Thirty years later, Paternoster was coaching Ecuadorean side Emelec and took them on tour for some friendly matches in Mexico. After one game, Bonfiglio approached him and reminded him of their clash in 1930. They embraced. Paternoster's son Fernando is convinced that the penalty was not missed on purpose. It made little difference to the outcome: Argentina won 6–3.

In Holland in the 1950s, there was then a bizarre rule that increased the pressure on referees: if a team disagreed with the referee's penalty decision, it could file a protest within five minutes of the final whistle. A penalty would then be taken, and only after that would a "protest committee" rule whether the complaint was just or not.

It happened in October 1957, when Feyenoord were leading Ajax 2–1 in Amsterdam. Late on, there was a scramble in the Feyenoord box and Ajax appealed for a handball against defender Kees Rijvers. Referee Bronckhorst saw a hand strike the ball, but thought it belonged to Feyenoord goalkeeper Teun van Pelt. No penalty. Ajax protested, and so, ten minutes after the game, Ajax striker Ger van Mourik faced van Pelt from the penalty spot, and scored. Did that make it 2–2? No. The committee still had to rule on the decision, and when it did, it found in Feyenoord's favor. The game ended 2–1. The law was abolished in 1959.

More recently, referees were at the center of an ethical storm over penalties in Brazil. When Neymar was at Santos, his love of the *paradinha*—the "little stop" in the run-up—caused an outcry that went all the way to FIFA.

It started on February 7, 2010, when Santos beat São Paulo 2–1 with their first goal coming from the spot. Neymar ran up to the ball, placed his standing foot next to it, cocked his kicking foot back as though ready to strike and waited one, two seconds; São Paulo goalkeeper Rogério Ceni dived to his right, and Neymar rolled the ball to his left. Ceni was furious. "I told Neymar to do it as often as possible in Brazil as when he moved to Europe there is no way they would let him do it there," Ceni said.

The chief problem with Neymar's kick, it was generally agreed, was that it was more of a *paradona* (a big stop) than a *paradinha*. His pause was a long one, far longer than that of Pelé, the man credited with inventing the *paradinha*. Also, at Santos, it was Dalmo, a defender, and not Pelé who was the first-choice penalty taker. After training, Dalmo used to practice his penalties against reserve goalkeeper Lalá, and he worked on the dummy move that would become the *paradinha*. "Pelé used to watch and then he copied Dalmo," said Lalá.

Pelé was reported to have scored with a *paradinha* in a 1961 friendly against Sheffield Wednesday, but the first confirmed *paradinha* came on February 6, 1962, in a friendly against River Plate. Santos lost 2–1 but more significant was that referee Aurelio Bossolino disallowed Pelé's penalty. The ball had gone in, but the goal was ruled out for ungentlemanly conduct and River Plate were awarded a free kick.

Brazil were on the receiving end of an unintended *paradinha* in the 1938 World Cup semifinal against Italy, whose striker Silvio Piola won a penalty with his side already one goal up. As

Giuseppe Meazza began his run-up, his shorts started to fall down and he stopped midrun to hold up the elastic. He had to stop one more time to preserve his dignity before striking the ball past the chuckling Brazil goalkeeper Walter. The goal was allowed, and Italy won 2–1.

In Brazil, no referee dared disallow a Pelé penalty, but his *paradinha* was ruled out twice more in matches: against Argentine side Racing in 1964 and Napoli in 1972.

In November 1969, Santos needed to beat Vasco da Gama to win the Brazilian championship. For three months anticipation had been building as Pelé's goal tally moved through the 990s and on to 999. Vasco were determined not to be the victims of Pelé's thousandth goal and did all they could to keep him out: Andrada, an Argentine goalkeeper nicknamed El Gato (The Cat), made one miraculous save from close range, and later in the first half the crossbar saved him. When Santos scored, it was an own goal by Vasco defender Renê, desperate to cut out a cross before Pelé could get to it.

With a quarter of an hour left to play, Pelé had his chance: 65,000 fans chanted his name after Fernando brought him down in the box for a penalty. But he wasn't the team's regular penalty taker; that was Carlos Alberto, the team captain. The two men met in the area and Carlos Alberto ordered Pelé to take it. "Now my only concern was not to miss the goal," Pelé recalled. "I set the ball down. Everything was quiet. And when I looked back, I was shocked. I saw the whole team of Santos there by the midfield." Pelé's teammates had abandoned their positions. As Brazilian writer Celso de Campos Jr. put it, "In reverence, they positioned themselves no longer as players, but as simple spectators of that historical moment."

Pelé was as nervous as he had ever been. His legs started shaking.

Andrada knew what was coming. When Pelé paused midrun, Andrada dived forward, knowing that there might still be time to commit himself to one side after Pelé had struck the ball. It almost worked: Pelé went to his natural side, Andrada touched the ball but could not stop it. "I never wanted to save anything as much as I did that penalty," he remembered. Pelé had scored goal number one thousand with a *paradinha*.

It was his last touch of the game. Fans invaded the pitch, carried him shoulder-high in celebration, and once the pitch was cleared he was subbed off for Jair Bala. He went to the dressing room still holding the ball with which he scored, which he now calls "my most fond souvenir."

Forty years later, Pelé joined the coaches, players and referees wading into the Neymar–Ceni debate. "Players stop for too long now, it wasn't like that when I was playing," he said. Internacional's Uruguayan coach Jorge Fossati called it "illegal and bordering on cowardly," while ex-referee Arnaldo Cézar Coelho claimed every *paradinha* should be retaken because the goalkeeper is forced to move too early.

The chief problem was, as always, consistency and contradiction: some Brazilian referees allowed the *paradinha*, others didn't. Palmeiras goalkeeper Marcos was fuming when Atlético Paranaense's Alan Bahia beat him from the spot with a *paradinha* one week after his teammate Alex Mineiro had his *paradinha* disallowed against Náutico by another referee. "Where is the consistency?" he asked. "The same rules need to apply for everyone."

And so, in May 2010, in direct response to the Neymar–Ceni fall-out, FIFA made another change to the penalty regulations, ruling that players could change pace, but crucially not stop, on their way to strike the ball. "Don't FIFA have other things to worry about?" asked Neymar, who missed four of his next eight penalties. The rule change came too late for Ceni who, despite his fury at Neymar's original cheek, a few weeks later tried a *paradinha* against Botafogo. He missed.

PENALTY ICON—
BRANDI CHASTAIN

Brandi Chastain remembers the silence. There were 90,185 fans watching her walk to the penalty spot in the Rose Bowl, Pasadena, and all she could hear was her own breathing. It was July 10, 1999, and after USA goalkeeper Briana Scurry had saved Liu Ying's effort (jumping off her line a little early had helped), Chastain was taking USA's fifth kick to win the World Cup final shoot-out against China.

She should not have been there. Chastain was the team's regular penalty taker but had hit a right-footed penalty against the crossbar in a defeat to China, in a friendly, three months earlier. When assistant coach Lauren Gregg had drawn up the USA list, she put Chastain in sixth place. Tony DiCicco, the coach, moved her up to fifth. He also asked her, during the break before the shoot-out, to take the penalty with her left foot.

Chastain was the only true two-footed player in the side. Her father would watch her knock a ball against a wall for hours with both feet, until she was just as good with her left as her right. Her grandfather would reward her when she played in junior games, paying her a dollar for every goal, and $1.50 for every assist.

Every player had practiced penalties in training, and DiCicco had liked Chastain's left-footers: they were more precise, and harder to read, than her right-footed kicks, which would always go to the same side, the goalkeeper's left. "It got to the point that goalkeepers knew where she would kick," said DiCicco, figuring that the change of kicking foot would surprise China's Gao Hong.

"I didn't think anything of it at the time," Chastain said. "I was always ambidextrous, and so it felt normal to use both feet. When I injured my right ankle, I used my left foot to drive the ball a lot more."

Chastain did not suffer from self-doubt like the team's star player Mia Hamm. Hamm did not want to take a penalty. She had asked Gregg if Shannon MacMillan, the other striker, could take one instead. Hamm had recently become soccer's highest-scoring international player—in the men's and women's game—but was on a four-game goal drought and terrified of missing. She still can't remember taking her penalty, USA's fourth; she passed out after the game and was sick all night, the anxiety of being USA's face of the tournament finally taking its toll. (Hamm would later meet her husband, former baseball player Nomar Garciaparra, at a promotional event at Harvard where the pair had a penalty shoot-out. Hamm won 4–3 and Nomar broke the ice telling her that he had let her win.)

Chastain had already been given the nickname "Hollywood" by her teammates and she thrived on the big occasion. "Brandi wants to have the responsibility on her," said DiCicco. "Some players are afraid of failure, they don't want the role. Brandi wants it. She wants the spotlight. That's the type of player you want in penalty kicks."

She had made sacrifices to get to this point: reconstructive surgery on both knees, which kept her out for almost two years, a period spent playing for Shiroki Serena in Japan, as well as four years out of the national side between 1992 and 1996. She played in the 1996 Olympic gold-winning final with a torn knee ligament. Oh, and she agreed to move from striker to full back just to earn a place in the team.

She had also missed USA's best chance against China, slipping and failing to shoot when Gao had punched a corner straight to her. Would that affect her nerves? There were forty million Americans watching on television—it remains a record for a women's sporting event, and for any soccer match in the USA. Would that affect her nerves? Team USA wanted the tournament to prove there was a market for a professional women's league in the country, and winning the final would make that much more likely. Would that affect her nerves?

No. She was not nervous. In the center circle, she decided where she wanted to kick the ball: to her natural side, as hard as she could. "I didn't mind if it went high or low, I just wanted to aim for that corner, and strike it hard." As she made the walk, she kept her eyes down. "Don't look at the goalkeeper, don't look at the goalkeeper," she said to herself. Back in March, Gao had unnerved Chastain by walking off her line and standing right in front of her before the missed penalty. "I didn't want her to have that edge on me again."

Then, the penalty. "It was complete slow-motion between my foot and the net. I've been in a car accident before, not a serious one, and just before it happened, everything went slow, but there's nothing you could do to change it. It seemed to take forever, and while it traveled, everything was so quiet and still and slow. And when it hit the net: an explosion! Noise, cheering, cameras, teammates, everything." Chastain had hit it high to the goalkeeper's left, just like usual. Gao dived the right way, but could not reach it.

Before her teammates jumped on her, Chastain fell to her knees and ripped off her shirt, waving it around her head. Five years earlier, in the same stadium, on another baking hot day, Roberto Baggio had missed a penalty for Italy that won Brazil the World Cup; just like then, the postpenalty image was captured and shown around the world. This time, the tears were of joy.

"It was definitely not premeditated," she said of the moment she took off her shirt to celebrate in her black sports bra. "Come on, I'm a left-back in a World Cup final, I'm hardly thinking this game will be my moment. It was a combination of things: joy, relief, satisfaction, the desire to do well for your team, your country, your family—those are emotions that you carry around every day for years, and finally I could let it all out. Put all those things together and what you get is insanity."

She is happy to talk about the sports bra moment, "because it always comes back to women's soccer." Chastain believes the victory changed the social fabric for women athletes in USA. "The number of young girls playing athletic activities is up 500 percent from when I was a kid." She is encouraging it, setting up the Bay Area Women's Sports Initiative, introducing disadvantaged eight- to ten-year-olds to sports to help them understand the value of exercise, decision making, communication and leadership.

She remembers meeting an eighty-nine-year-old man who was transfixed by the game, even though it was his first experience of watching soccer; and the pregnant woman whose daughter, now fourteen, is playing soccer. "This moment created so many reactions for different reasons, but it just shows how sport touches people."

It was genius from DiCicco to put Chastain fifth and ask her to kick with her left foot. She acknowledges that, too, but still, it was her nerve that held, her "wrong" foot that scored the winning penalty. With that kick, Chastain became a match winner, a role model and a pioneer. "The moment was life affirming. It was scary, invigorating and fulfilling. All your hopes and fears are distilled into this one moment. It's unique in life."

And if she hadn't taken off her shirt to celebrate, would the legacy of the 1999 triumph be so present today? "I would like to think the answer to that is yes." She hesitates. "But maybe not."

CHAPTER 9

THE ART OF KICKING

"Plusieurs disciplines" is how Christophe Lollichon, Chelsea's goalkeeping coach, put it. Shad Forsythe, when he was the German national team's performance manager, had his team practice archery—"one shot is all you get"—watch-making and rugby. The idea that other sports can help improve performance is no longer laughed at in the insular world of modern soccer.

I have been to several sports conferences alongside soccer coaches listening to leaders from *"plusieurs disciplines"* talk about innovative approaches to enhancing elite performance: these have included performance directors in skiing, hockey, swimming and acrobatics. From all of them I learned something that could be used in a soccer environment, and with that spirit of *"plusieurs disciplines"* in mind, I wanted to ask some outstanding sporting individuals from outside soccer what penalty takers could learn from their own sports. I started with an English coach who had won the World Cup.

By any standards, the crop of talent in Southampton's academy class of 2004 was something special. It contained players who would go on to light up the Premier League—the likes of Nathan

Dyer, Theo Walcott and Gareth Bale. One morning in spring 2005, the club's then director of sport, Sir Clive Woodward, paid a visit to training to test their skills from the penalty spot.

Woodward had made the leap into soccer from rugby union where, as coach of the England team, he oversaw the dramatic victory in the 2003 World Cup final against Australia, won by a last-minute drop goal by Jonny Wilkinson. In the rugby world, he specialized in using other disciplines to improve his players: first at Henley, then London Irish, and then England, who were ranked only sixth in the world on his appointment in 1997.

Woodward thought creatively and took the best advice from other sports to make his players better: gymnasts to improve flexibility, darts players to improve throwing straight at line-outs, cricket slip-catching machines to sharpen reactions, and even the Royal Marines to improve the team ethic. He wanted to do something similar at Southampton.

That morning at the academy, he set up four cameras focusing on the space between the edge of the eighteen-yard box and the goal line. One camera was facing the goal, the other behind the goal, and there were two on either side. He hung down two ropes from the crossbar, around three feet inside each post, and asked each player to take ten penalties. There was no goalkeeper to face, just the ropes hanging down, and the aim was to hit as many balls as they could between the rope and the post. These were good young players, remember, stars of the future, but their score? "It was not good," Woodward said.

The other coaches at Southampton wondered what on earth Woodward was trying to achieve with all the cameras, laptops and technology, but the players themselves soon found out. Two days later, they attended a video analysis session where a few players were shown taking their ten penalties. Not one time was their run-up, foot position or body shape the same. "Everything was different," Woodward remembered, "but to kick a stationary ball, you need to have the same routine, to do the same things over and over again."

Like Lollichon, I am convinced that soccer can learn a lot from other sports and that penalty takers (and goalkeepers) in particular can improve their records by studying other disciplines. That's why I felt that speaking to Woodward, a man whose greatest success had come partly as a result of learning from areas away from his sport, would be a good place to start.

I started by asking him if he could tell me about the secrets behind Wilkinson's success; I thought maybe that would reveal a lesson England players could take into their next major tournament. As it turned out, Woodward ended up delivering a passionate treatise on the ills of modern soccer, explained why England regularly failed from the spot, argued that soccer coaches feel threatened by change, and provided a one-stop solution to all future England penalty problems. And this all happened at a meeting in his London office before most people in the city had eaten their breakfast.

There are two things that Wilkinson focused on during his kick: the target, and his foot position. This all came down to technique, the result of hours and hours of purposeful practice, so that when the pressure kick came, his routine was unchanging.

Wilkinson was famous for taking his time lining up his kicks. He would shuffle his feet, clasp his hands in front of him and never take his eyes away from the posts. In fact, during that period he was actually looking for a marker between the posts, a target like someone's bobble hat, an umbrella, or a bright top in the crowd. "He wants a tiny little target to aim for, and that's what he's looking for during that preparation time," Woodward said. "Once he's found that, you can see that he then becomes ready to kick."

Wilkinson honed his method by trying to kick the ball against a single post from various points along the try line as far back as the corner flag. "It was amazing to watch him," said Woodward. "If he was on his game, he would get seven or eight out of ten, just kicking the ball at one post. Unbelievable."

So for Wilkinson it was all about keeping the same routine,

and practicing it, though I'm not sure finding a target in the crowd would work from the penalty spot, as a goalkeeper would read the search too easily. Woodward preached the same message, and was clearly frustrated when I told him that England's penalty practice sessions at the 2006 World Cup seemed to be based on a group of players standing with balls at their feet on the edge of the area, taking a kick whenever there was an opportunity. "Yes, it was 'my go, your go, let's all go,'" he said. "I would do it differently. At the end of every training session, I would make every player take a penalty, and incentivize them: 'You're not leaving till you've all scored.' Or choose five players and say the same to them.

"Not just that: I would get them to replicate the conditions. So wait five minutes after the end of training to take the penalties. Make them wait in the center circle and do the walk. Have a referee or a coach blow a whistle. The training sessions are the time you need to coach this stuff, so when it happens in the game, the players are rehearsed, prepared and know what to expect and what to do. The notion you can't practice is complete anathema to me."

Woodward's coaching philosophy is based on T-CUP, Thinking Correctly Under Pressure, and the idea that you can train smart for any eventuality fits the penalty model. "I wouldn't just practice one penalty: make them retake one sometimes, as that can happen in a real game too.

"And the nearer you get to big tournaments and big games, it's an absolute no-no, you don't change a thing. This is my big thing in sport: you must do everything that you normally do. It's not the time to bring in anything new."

Does that mean England shouldn't practice penalties at a major tournament?

"It means they should be doing it all year round. If you only start when you're at the tournament, you're making it a big thing. That's been a problem for us in the past. Yes, practice at a World Cup, but make sure you've been doing it all the time anyway."

Woodward had another idea, and he was convinced it would help England in tournament soccer. "This would be great fun, and we can start it from next week: every Premier League game should end with a shoot-out, no matter what the score. It should be just for English players to take penalties, but the crowd would stay behind to watch it, the TV cameras would love it, you would replicate everything, and it would normalize it for players." The same thing happened in Yugoslav soccer at the end of drawn games in the late 1980s, just a few years before Red Star Belgrade won the European Cup on penalties.

The more Woodward talked, the more passionate he became; he jumped out of his chair to impersonate Alan Shearer eye-balling a referee before he blows his whistle. But he really got going when I brought up an issue that touched a nerve: should a coach take responsibility for a missed penalty?

"This whole thing is about coaches, not players," he said. "It was conservative [at Southampton] mainly because high-profile coaches say you can't coach penalties, because they don't understand how to. Coaching is all about how your players perform under pressure: there are so many things you should be coaching the players to do. I don't like the word 'psychology.' The coach is a psychologist: if you practice properly, you will be mentally strong. If you don't, you can have as many psychologists as you like, but if you're not used to doing it, you will fail.

"Look at Cristiano Ronaldo and his free kicks. You can't just think, 'The guy's a genius.' There's more to it than that. He has great technique, the same routine, approach to the ball, he's not just crossing his fingers. He spends hours practicing that. To me, this stuff is so basic and yet we have this blockage, and that is the coaching world at a senior level."

Woodward claimed he suffered no resistance to his methods during his year at Southampton, even though he heard the same refrain again and again: you can't practice penalties. "The reason is because they don't know how to coach to kick a penalty; most don't know how to coach to kick a football. When you come back to it, it comes down to you exposing them in terms of what's right and wrong, and that's the real issue."

The players, on the other hand, loved Woodward's video approach and wanted to get better. "None of them want to miss penalties, they want to be coached," he insisted. Woodward felt that in soccer, the better the player, the likelier the coach was to back off and feel that he couldn't improve him. But the best players demand the best sessions, the best technology; they demand to be coached.

Woodward has set up a company that develops software for sports professionals. The software is called "Captured," and it's all about capturing thoughts and knowledge for each discipline—golf, tennis, basketball, any sport—to improve the athlete. "Knowledge, knowledge, knowledge: once you have all that, you can create your 'Winning Moves,'" he said.

"Captured" taps into Woodward's passion for creating a culture of education for athletes. It allows them, and their coaches, to build two databases, one for knowledge and another for practice, from which they can improve training methods and, in a pared-down way, evaluate the requirements for winning performance. These "Winning Moves" are the "Captured" results that emerge once all the data around your sport, the mass of knowledge via video, audio, written notes, is inputted. The system takes that knowledge and from it works out how to increase your chances of success.* Woodward launched "Captured" at the 2014

---

* Woodward showed me the detailed level of information in the "Captured book" of Amy Williams, who won gold in the skeleton at the 2010 Winter Olympics. Her Knowledge chapters were broken down into several mini-chapters: "Positional features"; "Bony articulations, soft tissue and range of motion"; "Pronation"; "The Windlass mechanism"; "Barefoot training"; "The push track"; "Start" and "Acceleration." Within each minichapter were several other headings, featuring personal thoughts, expert recommendations, best- and worst-practice videos and academic studies focused on every aspect of her sport. The result: a handful of "Winning Moves" that encapsulated, in a few sentences, how she became the first individual British gold medalist in a Winter Olympics for thirty years. In 2014 in Sochi, another British athlete, Lizzy Yarnold, succeeded Williams in winning skeleton gold.

Sochi Winter Olympics, and the International Olympic Committee gave every competing athlete access to the software on a free smartphone. As an educational tool, he told me, the athletes absolutely loved it.

So what would be the Winning Moves for the penalty taker? Woodward gave me four:

1. The placement of your nonkicking foot. Get that right and it's your best winning move.

2. The part of the ball you strike.

3. Find the bobble-hat—make an unequivocal decision about where to hit the ball.

4. Make it your absolute routine, especially if you are not used to taking penalties. So if you have to take one at a tournament, you know what you will do.

Woodward was sitting behind the goal at Wembley in 1996 when England's penalty complex began. He watched the shoot-out defeat to Germany with his young son, and he remains a huge soccer fan who still thinks about what might have been. He turned down the chance to run a lower-league soccer club from top to bottom to take on the job as performance director for Team GB's successful London Olympics campaign.

He knows that England aren't just unlucky when it comes to the shoot-out. "It's becoming a national stigma and we deserve it," he said. "We don't deserve to win because we are arrogant to think we can turn up with players who have never taken a penalty in their lives before to do it."

And the reason is because of the coaches and not the players?

"There's a big body of football people who are terrified of it, who are saying, 'You can't coach this.' That's the most ridiculous thing I've ever heard! I think the FA should employ a specialist penalty kicking coach. And listen: it wouldn't just make them better penalty takers but better footballers. The whole team should be doing it. This is about striking a dead ball, but if you strike a dead ball well, you will be able to strike a moving ball better too. It's about improving players across the board. You just need to set up a program, appoint the right specialist and say to him, 'Right, your job is to make sure we don't miss a penalty in the World Cup.' That's what we did with the rugby team—and we won the World Cup."

My next port of call was Thierry Omeyer, the handball goalkeeper whose name had stuck in my mind ever since Christophe Lollichon had described his reflexes as "exceptional." No player has won more trophies in his sport than the Frenchman, who burst on to the scene as a penalty-saving specialist for Selestat after keeping out an effort from then France captain Jackson Richardson when he was eighteen. Since then, Omeyer has become the iconic figure in France's dominant handball team, winning two Olympic gold medals (2008, 2012), three World Cups (2001, 2009, 2011) and two European Championships (2006 and 2010).

When Lollichon told me he wanted to discuss his methods with Omeyer, I wondered what he might learn. There are obvious differences between soccer and handball, of course—the "foot" and "hand" give that away, but also the size of the goal (in handball it's three meters by two meters) and the distance of the shooter (seven meters) are smaller. Players stand behind a line, not a spot, and are allowed to dummy before they shoot. Essentially, though, the duel is the same: the shooter is up against the goalkeeper and is expected to score.

"When I was younger, I used to move around the goal a lot to try and distract the shooter, like Jerzy Dudek used to do for Liverpool, but that doesn't suit me now," Omeyer said. "These days, I try and enter his mind. I try and trick him, force him into shooting where I want him to go." That might involve shifting his balance to one side, or throwing up a leg to misdirect the shooter when he knows a feint is coming. And after seventeen years in handball, there aren't many players he doesn't know about. "A lot of penalties come up during matches—much more than in football—and the relationship between the shooter and goalkeeper across the teams evolves during the season. A part of the story has already been written in previous games, and that will inform your movements in the next game. But more than technique, of course the battle is in the mind. It's all psychological."

Omeyer was talking just after his last game for German club THW Kiel, where he had spent the past seven years. In that time, Kiel won four German titles, three Champions League titles, and two league, Champions League and Cup trebles. After his last match in June 2013, 10,000 fans inside the Sparkassen Arena chanted "Titi! Titi!" for over an hour while waiting for Omeyer to address them. "It was very emotional for me," he said. A few days later, he was the fifth player, and first goalkeeper, to be inducted into Kiel's Hall of Fame.

Omeyer is a soccer fan and concentrates when a penalty is awarded. He is always looking for a new tactic that might give him an edge. Before Euro 2012, he spent a day at the France national team's training center, working with coach Franck Raviot, consultant Fabien Barthez, and goalkeepers Hugo Lloris and Steve Mandanda. "When I saw how big the goal was, and saw them all diving around, I was very impressed," he said. The feeling would probably be mutual, given that in handball the ball reaches speeds of up to 100 kilometers per hour.

So is there anything goalkeepers can learn from his methods to improve their penalty record? "I take into account the players I will be facing in the next match, with a one-hour video session in the week leading up to the game," Omeyer told me. That will be followed by specific training to ensure he knows what to do on game day.

That plan worked to perfection in France's 2008 Olympic semifinal against Croatia. Omeyer studied the video and noticed that Mirza Dzomba, at the time the best penalty taker in the world, would only go for two options: either a midheight fast shot or a *chabala*, the equivalent of a Panenka, over the goalkeeper's head. Omeyer spent hours training with France shooter Luc Abalo, who would copy Dzomba's style. France won the semifinal 25–23, and Omeyer saved two Dzomba penalties.

He's always remembered that the pressure was on the shooter, and psychologically, that gave him the advantage. "If you are feeling good in your mind, then you are feeling good on the pitch," he said. "On days when you are hot, you keep out every ball, shots and penalties, like you're something out of *The Matrix*. On those days, you are putting your stamp on the game."

I asked who his favorite goalkeeper in soccer was, and though he had not (yet) spoken to Lollichon, I was not surprised by the answer. "It's Petr Cech," he said. "I like his technique, the work he puts into his game, his confidence and the respect he gets from everyone else. When Chelsea won the Champions League, I hope all the players said, 'Thank you, Petr.' I like that idea." I hope Lollichon did track down Omeyer: they would get on well.

As a younger reporter, I went through a phase of asking strikers what was in their mind before they took a shot, what their thought process was as they made a certain run and completed a certain move. I stopped asking when the same answer—"Nothing, it's just instinct, innit?"—came back again and again.

But with penalties, it is different. There is time between the award of the penalty and its execution, time for the mind to play an important role. And time—especially if it's a shoot-out—for commentators or pundits to say something fatuous like "Well, you can't practice for this kind of moment." Try telling that to the darts player who throws a hundred treble-twenties a day, the snooker player who cuts the black into the bottom pocket over and over again, or the golfer who spends hours, daily, on his putting.

The ability to control your mind in the build-up to these shots, in all these sports, can be decisive. As Geir Jordet suggested, and Gareth Southgate confirmed, that phase in the shoot-out when players wait in the center circle before their kick can determine what state of mind they will be in when they take their penalty.

Dr. Michael Anderson, who runs the Cognition and Brain Sciences Unit at Cambridge University, knows this all too well. Dr. Anderson ran a study looking at the effect of over thinking in sports performance (the official term is "verbal overshadowing in motor skill").* He brought eighty golfers into his Memory Control Laboratory, half of whom were novices and the other half good-level club players with handicaps of below 16. He set up a putting green and counted how many putts each group needed to hole three consecutive six-foot putts.

Twenty novices and twenty club players were then told to spend five minutes writing down any and every detail they could about their putts. This group were the verbalizers. The other forty players, the nonverbalizers, were given images with absolutely no relation to golf to match up for the same amount of time: a distraction task. When the time had elapsed, the golfers were told to repeat the exercise of holing three putts in a row.

The results for the novices in each group barely changed, but for the higher-standard players it was a different story. The non-verbalizers, who had not focused on golf in the downtime, needed ten putts to complete the putting task. The verbalizers, on the other hand, needed twenty-one putts. "It showed us that thinking hard about something can be detrimental," Dr. Anderson explained. "It's not thinking while you're doing the putt, or taking a penalty, that's the problem: it's the thinking *between* the actions." It was also significant that the affected group was the skilled as opposed to the unskilled one. Anderson said the results are the same in other pursuits, like wine tasting or witness recognition in criminal cases.

Could this be a clue to help players cope with the trauma of Jordet's Phase 2 stressor? In the center circle, should they, or

---

* Flegal & Anderson, "Overthinking skilled motor performance: or why those who teach can't do" (*Psychonomic Bulletin & Review*).

even could they, focus on a nonsoccer memory? Anderson's speciality is in the suppression of negative memories and how the brain responds to them. I told him that Jordet's results showed England were less likely to score in shoot-outs than other teams because of their previous record. Is there a way for players to suppress the memories of previous penalty defeats to help them in the shoot-out? "Yes, you can train people to get better at not thinking about things," he said.

How? This could be the answer to England's problems!

Anderson has data on over three thousand subjects who have been tested on recalling and suppressing memories; sometimes those memories are prompted by cards with random words on them, sometimes pictures, and sometimes negative memories (for example, a picture of an ex-girlfriend's car). Before he began, he calculated the baseline figure for memory retrieval—essentially the recall of a something or someone based on a reminder trigger—which was 80%. That figure rose to 95% when his subjects were asked to recall something, and dropped to 65% when asked to suppress it. So there is a way to suppress memories.

He identified two strategies to follow, though pointed out that in real life we are more likely to use a combination of these processes rather than one or the other.

1. Thought substitution. In an effort not to think about the reminder, you generate a different thought entirely by self-distraction.

2. Direct suppression. In an effort not to think about the reminder, you push it out of your mind, which operates in a fundamentally different way in the brain to self-distraction.

I was surprised to learn that it was not only players who missed traumatic penalties—like Gareth Southgate, Michael Kutzop, Robert Pires and Daniele Massaro—who blanked them out. Many were unable to recall scored ones too, including Mia

Hamm in the 1999 Women's World Cup final, and Fabio Grosso, whose kick won the 2006 World Cup final. This is what Paul Breitner said about the penalty he took to equalize in the 1974 World Cup final against Holland: "There are only two minutes from that final that I can't remember: between the referee blowing for [our] penalty to the moment that Holland kicked off again after we had made it 1–1. I can only explain it like this: I was so focused on the situation and blocked out all the outside influences. In moments like that, you can't think about what you're doing. Otherwise you run up and trip over yourself. If you take another look at Johan Neeskens' penalty, you'll see what I mean. Neeskens just thumped it because he was completely unprepared to take a penalty after one minute of the game. It was different with me. It was like I was in a trance, scoring the penalty was like a bodily reaction. I just did it without thinking."*

"In the penalty scenario," said Anderson, "the situation is the reminder and surrounding the players—the goal, the pitch, the players gathering in the center circle—are the cues that elicit the recall of the last failure. But to suppress that is an effortful process that requires attention and could detract from the ability to do something else well."

Former professional golfer Andrew Coltart needs no reminding that the mind can play tricks on elite sportsmen. Coltart had won two tournaments and was a European Tour regular when he was selected as one of European captain Mark James's wildcards for the Ryder Cup in Brookline, USA, in 1999. His misfortune was to be drawn in the singles against Tiger

---

* Breitner also did it because no one else wanted to. He has famously said that "everyone else was shitting themselves" and that the team had no designated taker. "I even got the impression that some guys hoped we didn't get a penalty so it wouldn't come up." Breitner only realized the enormity of his achievement when he watched the full match the following morning. "As I saw myself go to the penalty spot, within seconds I was soaked through with sweat, and I felt sick. 'This is mad,' I said to my wife. For an hour I just sat there thinking about the madness I had put myself through, and what might have happened had I missed."

Woods. He lost 3&2, but it was his reaction after the tournament that came to define his career. "I wanted to sustain the level I was at, and in an effort to get better, I put more pressure on myself," he said.

Coltart hoped that he might play in another four or five Ryder Cups, so he set about improving his game and focusing on his weaknesses. "When you do that too much, you focus more on what is wrong than what is right, and maybe I should have consolidated my game and strengthened what was already strong." His results dropped, his ranking dipped, and the pressure became even greater.

He knew there was nothing wrong with his technique. "None of this is about technique. If you're good enough to play in the Ryder Cup, you're good enough to win tournaments; just like if you're good enough to play football for your country, you should damn well have the technique to score a penalty. What makes an athlete win titles is not technique; it's how he handles adversity, how he deals with the pressure, how he copes with his status in the team or in the rankings—all that is mental. When that pressure comes, it's fight or flight, and I failed because I wasn't great at it."

Coltart saw a succession of sports psychologists to help him out of his rut and one gave him a stark choice. "Here's the deal," he said. "Let's work together and I will take 25 percent of your four biggest prize checks for the next year." That deal had its own psychological effect: Coltart, who jokingly called himself a naturally tight Scot, was so uncomfortable with the prospect of paying out, he used it as another excuse for underperforming.

By 2004, he had dropped below the top 115 players in the money-list, which is the cut-off for full playing and qualification privileges for the European Tour. "What got me in the end was the pain of failing was so great that I tricked myself into feeling no pain, and then there was no fire," he said. "I did care but because I didn't want to be too hurt, I subconsciously underperformed. At that point, it became self-fulfilling: I thought I would fail so I did."

Does this fear of failure exist for penalty takers who miss a penalty? I wondered.

"There is more bravado and ego in football, so a player may well step up because he'd rather do that than admit he's terrified," said Coltart. "The penalty is not so much about practicing under pressure: these guys know already how to block out the crowd, how to breathe, that kind of thing—so it's not as simple as thinking positively. It's about mental strength. The mind plays a ridiculous part: even if someone said something to you ten years ago, when the crunch is on, your brain has the ability to pull that up and throw it in front of you. So how will you react then?

"I was always intrigued by soldiers who would dive in and save one of their own under a hail of bullets and then say, 'I just let the training kick in.' Meanwhile, I would brick myself if I had a five-iron to the green and there was a water hazard on the right."

Coltart also emphasized the importance of a failure strategy: just as the data said that one in five penalties will be missed (and therefore should be expected) so the success rate of holing a ten-foot putt is not as high as you might think from watching golf on television. In fact, once a putt is eight feet or more in length, the chances of a European Tour professional missing it become greater than holing it. We would expect it to be holed because the higher-ranked players we watch in a tournament's latter rounds on TV hole them more often, but the breakdown over the whole tour is surprising.

Figure 26: Putting success

Putt Length	Converted	Missed*
Six feet	63.5%	36.5%
Eight feet	48.1%	51.9%
Ten feet	36.3%	63.7%
Twelve feet	28.6%	71.4%

* Data factors in all European Tour events in 2013, provided by Chris Sells at strokeaverage.com.

Coltart might have benefited if Dave Alred had been coaching golf when he was still playing. Alred was the kicking coach whom Woodward employed to help England win the rugby World Cup in 2003, and though he still coaches rugby players at Bath, Dublin, Toulon and Cardiff, he now has another passion: golf. He plays off a handicap of 3, a fact he revealed to me with no pleasure at all, focusing instead on the troublesome shoulder-throw at the top of his backswing (even a gadget that shows his swing path can't stop him doing it).

Alred moved into golf because, as he put it, "I lost the art of being frustrated." Just as Coltart lost his fire, Alred felt that he had coached kicking for so long that he was no longer managing his athletes' learning. "How can you empathize with someone learning something new and getting into an ugly zone when you don't have that yourself?" He had always been a talented kicker, playing for Bath and Bristol and then in American football with the Minnesota Vikings. But he wanted to challenge his own learning, and the similarities with golf were clear. "It is about the one-shot moment," he said. "You're the only one who is striking that ball, not your teammates; it's all on you."

One of his first clients was Luke Donald, who was ranked 32 when they started working together after a trial week training camp in Miami in January 2010. Alred gave Donald a new competitive practice regimen, improved his posture and body language and taught him visualization to create an air of inevitability about his shots. "You have to rehearse all that, it's about the processes that involve a certain mindset." Over the next eighteen months, Donald won six tournaments and had three top-eleven finishes in the majors. He became world number one in May 2011 and stayed there for forty weeks. (Donald was ranked second in the world when the pair went their separate ways in September 2012. "He wanted to go in a different direction," Alred said. And he did: over the next twelve months he dropped to number 15 in the world.)

Alred stated that you can't learn anything by watching from

the stands, you have to participate. When he went on a fact-finding mission to study kicking in Aussie Rules football, he embedded himself with the West Coast Eagles and was so indispensable that now, when golf commitments allow, he coaches them. He learned from West Coast Eagles players first: he was amazed at how high the players could jump to catch the ball. So he watched them train, and later taught the England backs the same technique. The players were awkward at first and the move, a one-handed jump with a high leading knee, was nicknamed the "Bambi Jump." But within a few months, England were becoming dominant in aerial play and Ben Cohen—"he made his career out of overhead catching on the run"—scored a try against France after a one-legged high-knee jump. Even then, no one realized this was a revolutionary new aspect of the game which deserved a closer look. "That's the big difference with golf," Alred said. "In the golf industry, if someone swings their club in a new way and gets compression on the ball, then the world and his brother will want to know how he's doing it."

We met at a driving-range in Bristol on an autumnal Friday evening and watched golfers hitting balls all over the place. Alred pointed out a few decent hitters. "The majority are fun-loving hackers, but if you hit so many balls every night, then you'd eventually get it right. Technique is such an important thing: you have to ask yourself, 'Is it repeatable? Can it withstand pressure? Is this shot repeatable under pressure?'"

And so we come to penalties. Alred has worked in soccer: first at Newcastle United, when Jonny Wilkinson, whom he still coaches after fourteen years together, was playing for the local rugby side, and at five other Premier League clubs. He was impressed by the soccer players' skills—"some of them can get that ball to make them a cup of tea"—but disappointed by their attitude. He claimed too few players stayed behind to improve themselves and that senior players didn't encourage younger ones to put in extra training. "They say there is no changing-room bully mentality in football, but I think it still exists," he said. "In three of the six Premier League clubs I have worked in, I have witnessed it first-hand."

One comment made by an England international with over fifty appearances has stuck with him, and he repeated it at least three times during our conversation. "He told me that the skill of getting on in football is to never let them see what you can't do. It's frightening!" The same player once came in on a day off to work with Alred, and the next morning was reprimanded by his coach. "He got a bollocking for it! He'd have been better off getting pissed in the pub! But this guy always said: 'Don't get caught doing the things you can't do. It's the skill of hiding your weaknesses.' Then we come unstuck because we can't hide in penalties. That whole culture needs to change."

The first thing Alred would try to improve is the players' technique. Not enough players, he believed, work specifically on their kicking technique, just as golfers work day in, day out on their swing. "They need to try to kick more efficiently in terms of power application, and in essence, to kick with their body, rather than the leg being the sole source of power. Once the technique is starting to become more grooved, then time should be spent matching their intention with the shot. That means aiming for specific spots in the net, and even if you hit them, only counting it if the shot is struck perfectly. A scuff, or mishit, would not count, even if the ball ends up in the right area."

Then, add some pressure to training. "For example, at any point in a training match, blow the whistle, penalty. One chance, one shot. Pressure. Carry on, and then, another penalty. Hit the hot spot. Pressure. At the end of the game, put two goalkeepers in goal, and get players to drive the ball to score. That will teach them to put power and accuracy on their shots. And if you score ten in a row in practice, then in the game, you will be more confident."

The real secrets behind Alred's methods are in a vault at Loughborough University library where his PhD thesis, "Performing under Pressure," is under lock and key. He won't make it publicly available, with good reason: everyone might steal his methods. There are two techniques that he did confirm were in the thesis:

1. J- and C-shape.

Alred realized that the rugby player who wrapped his foot around the ball and curled it in one direction was very talented. He would have an advantage on one side of the pitch, but a much tougher kick on the other side. So he focused on a way of teaching players to kick straight, and it's all about body shape. The C-shaped kicker curls his foot around the ball and swings around it in his follow-through; the final movement of the J-shaped kicker's follow-through straightens out. "If your muscles tighten, then the shape changes from a J-shape to more of a C-shape; if you keep the posture and discipline the body movement, you get the J-shape." And which is better, the J or the C? "The J, absolutely." George Ford (Bath and England), Johnny Sexton (Racing Metro and Ireland) and Wilkinson (Toulon and England) kicked with a J-shape and so, after working with Alred, did Joe Cole. "I remember a magnificent shot from Joe, a run-through half-volley on his left foot, straight into the top corner," said Alred. "He could have been mistaken for Ronaldo."

2. Top Pocket.

This is another coaching tool developed, and indeed trade-marked, by Alred which is a kinesthetic map that measures the feel for the shot. "It's a way of measuring the ball so you know how much energy has escaped. The perfect shot has no energy leaks." Alred believed the tool could also fast-track the development of two-footed kicking and reduce the risk of soft-tissue injury. This required slow-motion video analysis as well, but the idea that you can measure something so intuitive is unique in soccer. "Managed skilfully," he said, "it is the ultimate model of implicit learning."

*

Alred then surprised me by flashing up a scene on his laptop from a movie I'd recently seen as part of my own penalty research. "I've added subtitles to give it my own twist," he said. It was from *A Fistful of Dollars*, the sequence when Clint Eastwood, whose character has no name, kills four Baxter brothers for shooting and laughing at his mule. "My mule don't like people laughing," Eastwood said. "He gets the crazy idea you're laughing at him. Now if you apologize like I know you're going to, I might convince him that you really didn't mean it." The brothers stayed silent. Eastwood shot them all.

I watched Alred's interpretation of the scene. As Eastwood, a stranger, walked into the new town, he took in everything around him. Alred's notes flashed up above the movie: "Dislocated Expectations: Plan, Rehearse, Visualize." It was quickly apparent that the atmosphere was hostile and unpredictable.

"Wide attention focus: Controlled, Total Awareness, Prepared."

As he approached the four brothers, his head up, his back was straight and his gaze unwavering.

"Confident, Purposeful, Inevitable: Create Inevitability by Practicing."

When Eastwood saw an extra brother sitting on a nearby fence, he revised his plan.

"Ready for Everything, Aggravation will not Impact Performance."

Then, the preshot routine.

"Total Focus on Relevant Cues."

As the brothers lay dead on the ground outside the sheriff's house, the final caption on Alred's screen flashed up.

"Revised Plan Successfully Executed: are you an Apology or a Gunslinger?"

"Are you a gunslinger?" he asked me, laughing, as we headed out to the car park for an impromptu kicking lesson.

It's all about pushing your best power source, your center of gravity, "your pillar," toward the target. I leaned into my first shot and dragged the ball right of the target. "Wrapping!" shouted Alred. "Don't do it!" The next shot was straighter but scuffed. "Keep your pillar straight!" I don't think I have ever hit anything as sweetly as my third shot: hard, low, on target, and with my body upright and following through. It felt good. "That's it!" he shouted. "Did you feel that? No energy escaped the ball with that one; you know it yourself and can measure it."

Then a mistake. Not the one I made back in 1997, when I beat Packie Bonner and arrogantly thought I had cracked the mystery of penalties. No, more like one that Dr. Anderson, from his Memory Control Laboratory in Cambridge, would have set for his analysis. I verbalized my task, mumbling to myself, "Yes, that felt good, now let's do it again." But my next kick was the opposite of that: scuffed, sliced and horribly wide.

"Waaaghh, you jacked it! No jacking!"

I had no idea what Alred meant, but on my next kick, I tried to suppress my negativity. I visualized the ball hitting its target. I slowed down my preshot routine. I didn't want the frustration, and the memory, of my last bad shot to impact my next one.

I took a deep breath, kept my body straight, and as I struck the ball, I hit through it. Bang! It was a decent hit, and if there had been a goalkeeper in the way, I doubt he could have stopped it. Alred had been watching my body shape, the spin of the ball and its flight path, and my follow-through. "Good!" he shouted. "If the others were two or three out, that was one-eighth out. Not perfect, but getting there. Now you just need to hit ten in a row, and practice every day. Then you'll start to get it." Before then, he might have to work on my mind a little more.

Doug Blevins knew he wanted to have a career in American football when he was four years old. He loved the Dallas Cowboys and would always stay awake for the Monday-night games, no matter how late they finished. Blevins dreamed of a career in American football. The only obstacle was that he was born with cerebral palsy and could not walk.

When he was twelve, he started writing letters to people in the game—Cowboys coach Tom Landry, Hall of Famer Roger Staubach, kicker Bob Agajanian. They all wrote back, and it was then that Blevins realized that kicking was a neglected part of the game. He started recording matches, noting what worked in the techniques of successful kickers, what was going wrong with the failed kicks. He could spot an error within seconds; you could pause a kick at point of contact and he would know whether it would be successful or not. He started working with kickers in high school, graduated to a college, and then began a correspondence with New York Jets' General Manager Dick Steinberg. The Jets hired him as a kicking consultant and, finally, Blevins had his career in American football.

Now he wanted more: it was not just about being in American football, it was about being the best. He wanted to make his mark. One of his kickers at the Jets, Brian Hansen, spent the 1995 off-season working on his game in Minnesota. There, he met a graduate called Adam Vinatieri who could kick well, but was inconsistent. Hansen gave him Blevins's business card, and two days later they met at the airport in Tennessee. "I thought someone was making a big joke," Vinatieri later told *Sports Illustrated*. "Here is this handicapped guy being wheeled around by his wife. I'm like, 'Seriously, where's Blevins at?'"

The pair spent months improving Vinatieri's kicking and by the time he joined Amsterdam Admirals in spring 1996, he was a brilliant kicker. The fact that Blevins has never kicked a ball in his life helped him. He had no "perfect kick" ideal, and could tailor a successful kick to whatever individual quirks a kicker had. Vinatieri signed for New England Patriots that same summer, and was their kicker when they reached the Super Bowl in his rookie season.

The Vinatieri story does not quite end there. He spent ten years at New England, and in 2002 helped them win their first ever Super Bowl with a last-gasp forty-eight-yard field goal to beat the St. Louis Rams 20–17. Two years later, he repeated the feat: in front of a TV audience of 144 million, he kicked a forty-one-yard field goal with four seconds left to beat Carolina Panthers 32–29. Vinatieri was the first kicker to decide two Super Bowls, and always he acknowledged the influence of Doug Blevins. "I wouldn't be here without him."

When I caught up with Blevins, he was running an off-season kicking camp with some college kids whose dream was to become the next Adam Vinatieri. Blevins has already developed ten graduates who now play in the NFL, but was not sure any of his current crop would make it. He was working with one player, very talented, a natural kicker, but any time an NFL coach came to scout him, he couldn't do it.

"Is he English, by any chance?" I asked. Blevins laughed with a throaty rasp.

"I actually worked with an English guy once, when I was helping the teams in NFL Europe," he told me. "His name was Clive Allen. Do you know him? What a kicker he was!"

I grew up watching Clive Allen score goals wherever he played in London: first at QPR, then Crystal Palace, Spurs, Chelsea, West Ham and Millwall (but famously not Arsenal: he joined them for over £1 million in 1980 but soon after moved to Palace). When he signed for American football side London Monarchs in 1997, it was seen as a gimmick, but in fact Allen was successful. He scored all six of his field goals, and when I asked him about it, he said it was all down to one man.

"I remember Doug, what an amazing coach he was," Allen said. "He had never kicked a ball in his life, but knew exactly what I was doing wrong, and how I had to correct my technique to suit the change of sport. I was surprised when I saw him in a wheelchair but it didn't take long for me to realize he was an expert in his field. It helped that mentally I was strong for the pressure moments, but I never missed a field goal for the Monarchs. Doug has to take big credit for that."

Blevins worked on a leg-lock routine so at the point of contact between foot and ball, the knee of the kicking leg was locked. "If it's 98.9% straight, it's not enough," he said. It doesn't feel natural and it needs a lot of practice, but there is a reason behind it: "In NFL you want explosiveness and lift, and for that you need leg speed, and the lock is the best way to get it."

Blevins has branched out into coaching other sports. He was working with college-level basketball players, focusing on their jump shooting, and with golfers. I wondered if his skills could transfer to penalties as well. "Sure they can!" he said. "I can look at a guy take one kick, and almost instantaneously can see what he's doing wrong and what he needs to do."

He also worked on athletes' psychology. This is crucial in American football, where the role of the kicker is purely to come on and either punt or kick for a three-point field goal or one-point conversion. They often train apart from the group because of this speciality. "I teach the psychological aspect a lot," Blevins added. "The starting-point is that if you are mechanically sound and technically sound, that will breed confidence. Then there is body language: I tell my young guys, 'When you walk off the field, look the same whether you made it or missed it.' From a young age, they need to have a short memory, because if they missed a field goal with three minutes to go, they might need to take another with one minute to go. And that might be to win the game."

So what can soccer, and particularly penalty takers, learn from American football?

"You absolutely have to channel the same techniques and have the same mental tools to be successful. You get one chance to make the shot and once it's done, you can't change it."

Now Blevins is coaching other sports, it's not such a great leap to switch over to soccer. I asked if he would consider it. "Of course! I feel like I'm the best in the world at what I do, and if I didn't then I shouldn't be doing it. My numbers reflect that. I can improve these athletes."

Sir Dave Brailsford was in the middle of moving house, and like many outstanding managers, was not quite so good at managing himself. "I can control other people's lives much better than I can my own," he shrugged. One thing he hadn't done in preparation for his move was what he tells all his charges, as head of Team Sky and formerly of British Cycling, to do as a matter of course: analyze the demands of the event. He repeated it like a mantra. "Analyze the demands of the event. Any discipline, that's what you need to do. Analyze the demands of the event."

So how would that work in the case of a penalty shoot-out? Brailsford would gather as much information as he could—from psychologists, sports scientists, performance analysts, ex-players, current players and any other experts—and work out the trends from the findings. In England's case, they would be that high expectations play havoc with the players' nerves, the weight of history has its own burden, and often the nonregular penalty takers miss in the shoot-out; there are also correlations between rushing after the referee has blown his whistle, players turning their backs on the goalkeeper, and the goalkeepers' slightly below average saving record from penalties.

"So you need to analyze the demands of the event," Brailsford repeated. "We'll say, let's practice taking penalties after running for 120 minutes. We need to understand the physiological demands of that: what are they? Would it be better to maintain a warmed-up status, keep the body in optimal condition, or to stand there crapping yourself with your arms around your teammates? Is a fresh player more accurate than a fatigued player? You could work it all out."

I mentioned Geir Jordet's finding that the more shoot-outs you lose, the less likely you are to score in the next one. His cycling team almost suffered from a similar "linking" issue at the London Olympics. In the first cycling event of the competition, the men's road race, gold medal hope Mark Cavendish finished twenty-ninth as the rest of the field had sussed out Team GB's tactics, which had worked at the World Championship the previous year. "As a professional, what you did with your last touch should have no bearing on your next touch," he said, "but it does.

So when you don't win an event, like Cavendish at the Olympics, we had to remind the guys that will have no bearing on what Bradley Wiggins was going to do, or what Chris Froome was going to do." The reminders worked: two days later, Wiggins won gold and Froome bronze in the men's time trial.

I suggested that England have been a little unlucky in that three times, key penalty takers have not been around to take part in the shoot-out. In 1990 against West Germany, Paul Gascoigne was in no shape to take a penalty. In 1998 against Argentina, David Beckham had been sent off, as was Wayne Rooney in 2006, when Beckham had also gone off injured.

Not relevant, said Brailsford. It's part of the manager's job to build in the what-if factors. "If someone has just got booked and is too hyped up and on edge, then take them out of the picture. But you need to have a Plan B or a Plan C no matter what. If someone is slightly injured, then you make a decision. It needs hard work and detailed thinking beforehand."

When he had the dual role in charge of Team Sky and British Cycling, Brailsford was at an advantage. In 2012, for example, he was able to ask Geraint Thomas to tailor his race program so he would peak at the Olympics, even though that involved him missing the Tour de France. The decision paid off: Thomas was part of the GB team that broke the world record in the men's team pursuit Olympic final. The equivalent would be the England coach also managing Manchester United, and balancing both priorities easily. Such is the delicate balance between the FA and Premier League clubs, it's hard to imagine any England coach phoning a club manager to put in a request for a certain player to practice more penalties.

Brailsford knows all about dealing with the pressure of expectation. After Wiggins won the 2012 Tour de France, the pressure on Team GB was sky-high, but you'd never have guessed it. Brailsford watched as the gold medals rolled in—the hosts won eight of the eighteen events—but more success leads to more pressure. Team Sky then won the 2013 Tour de France, Chris

Froome carrying on from where Wiggins left off, and that left Brailsford wrestling with how to manage expectations.

"We've thought about this and there are two ways to do it. One, we say, 'We won the Tour again and now, blimey, we have to defend our title, as if we lose it will be a disaster.' Or we can say, 'Wasn't it brilliant to win it once, we won it for a second time, now we want to win it again, and that might be in 2014 or 2015.' There is a different psychology to that: one is looking backward, defending the title, and the other is looking forward, to win it again."

Brailsford is a soccer fan and is as frustrated as anyone with the repeated failures of the national team. The only time he sounded less than convincing was when I asked him, "Why do England lose on penalties?"

"I would imagine failure . . . one of the big challenges that's perceived . . . the more the whole penalty shoot-out scenario develops, the more the media play it up. We make it way more stressful than it could be," he stuttered.

So what would you say to the players just before a shoot-out?

"Right," he said. "We've thought this through, guys. Forget what happened in the match, whether we feel cheated or lucky to be here. The moment that whistle blows, it's all over. You might as well think this is a different game. This is nothing to do with football anymore. Whatever happened in that match is irrelevant now. I want you to completely stop and start afresh with a new approach. It's like this: we were playing dominoes, now we're playing table-tennis. We know we have left no stone unturned to be prepared. We are ready to go. So let's go and do it!"

I was convinced by his up-and-at-'em rhetoric—I felt hyped and psyched—but unfortunately there wasn't a ball or a goal, nor a table-tennis table, in sight. Brailsford is a polymath, he is inspiring. I was far from surprised when England coach Roy Hodgson arranged for him to address the England squad before the 2014 World Cup in Brazil. Perhaps that will be his first step to working in soccer in the future.

He was certainly interested in the success of Spain's national team, and wondered what advantage the team had, given that most of its players came from Barcelona and Real Madrid, and therefore knew each other and their moves so well. He wondered if there was an analytics model to measure the performance of England players to compare their output for club and country; that way coaches might be able to replicate players' best club form for the national team.

"Analyze the demands of the event." When he started with Team Sky, their competitors laughed at his fixation on the phrase. Analyzing road racing, where everyone is subject to variables in weather and other conditions, was one thing, but in the velodrome, where the variables are fewer, there was less competitive advantage to be found. Brailsford found it. "When it came down to it, and we ran all the numbers, of course you can control it and improve it." And what did the others think of you after that? "Probably that we were a bunch of idiots."

Brailsford was being diplomatic when he said that some sports rely too much on conventional wisdom. It seemed pretty obvious that he was talking about soccer. "Penalties are still seen as a bit of an after-thought. But with any game you play, you can optimize your chances of winning."

He then came up with a theory so simple, I wondered why no one had mentioned it before. "You need strong people and strong management and you know what, actually I will take the responsibility myself and make the decision for you." Brailsford knew that at moments of extreme pressure, the first thing to go was an athlete's decision-making ability. "The decision they will make will be an emotional one which will be irrational. But at this moment, you want a logical response."

Brailsford is brilliant at delegating but this was proof he also micromanages. You can't imagine Sven-Göran Eriksson, for example, telling David Beckham where to aim his penalty. But in Brailsford's scenario, he has watched every player take penalties in training; he has assessed every facet of his game and knows his strengths and preferences. So before the game, Brailsford would say: "You must know that if it goes to penalties, I want you to kick the ball there."

"That way," he explained, "the player can go out knowing what he has to do. He has one less thing to worry about. He can now focus on the process, not the outcome. There is no point when he will go, 'Oh shit, what do I do now?' He's done it in practice over and over again. He's worked on the routine, every day, so it's natural for him. Place the ball well, take fourteen steps, three deep breaths, two steps to the side, wait for the whistle, and then breathe again. That's the thought process you develop for every single player."

You make it sound so easy, I said.

"It's a penalty!" he laughed. "It is easy!"

APPENDIX I:

THE BIRTH OF THE PENALTY KICK

There are no shops in Milford. There's not a post office or a school. It's five minutes from Armagh, in Northern Ireland, and it's the kind of place you could drive through without even realizing it exists. But stop there, walk around, and the stories quickly emerge: how Milford House, the big house on the hill, lies empty and derelict; how the man who built it in 1864, Robert Garmany McCrum, invented and patented double-damask linen (patterned on both sides) and supplied napkins and tablecloths to the British Admiralty, the American Navy and the Canadian Parliament; how he's also said to have invented the electric kettle and the dishwasher, but never got around to patenting them; and how he built the five roads that make up the village, to house the thousand workers in his booming cotton-mill factory.

The final road to be built was William Street. It was completed in 1911 and could have been named after RG's father or his son. The red-bricked terraced houses on William Street overlook the village green. It used to be the soccer pitch where Milford FC played. And it was where William McCrum, RG's son, invented the penalty kick.

McCrum was goalkeeper for Milford FC, who finished bottom in the Irish Championship's inaugural season in 1890. He conceded sixty-two goals in ten games. McCrum, known as "Master Willie," was a free spirit, an amateur actor and inveterate gambler, but with a conscience: he hated the violent defending in front of him. Referees only gave indirect free kicks for fouls in the penalty area, and it was no deterrent at all. Some tackles even ended in death.*

McCrum felt the whole team should pay for an individual offence, and in 1890 submitted a proposal to the Irish FA to introduce penalty kicks into the laws of the game. IFA general secretary Jack Reid, McCrum's friend and also a striker for Cliftonville and Northern Ireland, submitted it to the International Football Board and it was initially met with a storm of protest. Players were offended by "the Irishman's motion," as it became known, and the suggestion that any fouls might be deliberate. Because McCrum was an amateur thespian, he was accused of being selfish: only a goalkeeper, it was said, could have come up with this supreme moment of drama and self-sacrifice that makes the goalkeeper the star of the show.

The mood changed in February 1891, after Stoke City were denied a clear equalizer in the last minute of an FA Cup tie when a Notts County defender punched the ball off the goal line. Stoke could not score from the subsequent indirect free kick. On June 2, at the next IFB meeting held at the Alexandra Hotel in Bath Street, Glasgow, the English FA backed the proposal and the penalty kick was born. In the minutes of that meeting, the penalty is referred to as a "Kick from the Penalty Mark."

The early regulations stated that a penalty could be given for one of three offences—tripping, holding or deliberate handball—within twelve yards of the goal line, stretching across the pitch.

---

* In 1898, Enderby defender Henry Moore was found guilty of manslaughter for tackling Aylestone forward John Briggs by kneeing him in the back and throwing him into the goalkeeper; Briggs died of internal injuries a few days later.

The penalty could be taken from any point twelve yards from the goal line. This distance was logical, as the line marking the penalty area was eighteen yards from goal, and the line marking the goal area six yards. The goalkeeper was able to stand up to six yards from his goal line. And if a penalty was awarded, the team did not have to accept it: famously, Corinthians felt the penalty law was a slur on fair play, and would refuse to take spot kicks.

That moralistic view was copied in Holland, where in a match between two gentlemen clubs from Haarlem, HFC, and The Hague, HVV, a penalty was awarded, much to the disgust of HVV goalkeeper de Groot, who refused to stand in the goal for the kick. The referee ordered the penalty to be taken anyway, but the HFC captain refused.

For McCrum, the invention barely registered amid the ingenuity that ran through the family. Up at the house, RG had installed his own petrol pumps to service the three cars the family owned; he diverted water from the nearby Callan River to a self-made water tank so the six Turkish baths could be filled; and at a time when no one thought it would catch on, Milford House was the first in Ireland to use electricity.

R. G. McCrum had amassed a fortune of £55,000 (£4.75 million in today's money) when he died in 1915. Unfortunately Willie, and his sister Harriette, had no business acumen and within one generation—but also because of the 1929 Wall Street Crash—the money was gone. William did not squander it all on the good life, he was incredibly generous too, and thought nothing of funding his fellow scout Robert Gwynne, the son of his head gardener, to stay in London to become a musician.* He

---

* Gwynne was, like McCrum, a member of the Milford Scout Troop and was a talented singer. McCrum sent him to London, paid for his music tuition, and he had a successful career as an opera singer. He came back to Milford dressed as a gentleman and married to a Lafian princess from the Nigerian state of Nasarawa. McCrum, Captain of the Milford Scout Troop and County Commissioner for the Scouts in County Armagh, once said of the scouts, "They may be mill boys but they are the best kind of gentlemen."

also funded Thomas Stringer's trip to Switzerland for treatment when he caught tuberculosis; when he died, William paid over the odds to ensure his body could be brought back for burial. Harriette, meanwhile, was fluent in Russian, Italian and Japanese and once shared correspondence with Joséf Stalin.

Perhaps more astonishing is the fact that McCrum's story emerged only relatively recently, when property developers put in plans to build houses on the site of the original Milford FC pitch. Locals were up in arms and in 1997 established the Milford Community Development Association to save the site. By this time the village was a shadow of the hub it had been: the factories closed in 1980, the R. G. McCrum Institute, a community center from where Master Willie ran the cricket and badminton teams and the drama society, closed in the 1970s, and the Manor House School, which was in Milford House, closed in 1965; it then became a hospital, which closed in 1988.

Local historian Joe McManus led the fight to save the green. He proved McCrum's invention by interviewing two locals who corroborated the story: Stephen Hyde, whose great-uncle Henry Hyde played alongside McCrum, and Kieran McAuley, whose great-grandfather Harry was part of the team. McManus sent the interviews to FIFA, and in 2001, the game's governing body verified that McCrum had invented the penalty. The village green was saved. It is now called William McCrum Park and has a bust of Master Willie at its center.

A penalty kick away from the green, a discreet house in William Street is filled to overflowing with treasures from the original Milford House: crystal glasses that belonged to RG, Harriette's wedding dress, an old cigar-box that belonged to Master Willie. The house has five rooms and every one is a shrine to Milford House. Its curator is Stephen McManus, Joe's son, who for three years slept on a sofa as his bedroom was chock-full of Milford memorabilia. "I find it hard to explain to people why Milford House is empty, derelict and gone to ruin," McManus told me with a crack in his voice. "There is no logic to it. The current owners refuse to do anything with the house, even though we are trying to get the funding to restore it to its original glory."

The eerie quiet in the village reflects the state of Milford House. It could, and should, be a thriving tourist spot; it's a beautiful Victorian house with an extraordinary story to tell, and a unique place in history. Instead, it sits there empty and rotting, occasionally victim to thieves, who have stolen radiators, banisters and even a fountain from the grounds.

Developers built new houses on the three sides around William McCrum Park, which, by design or not, has trees planted eight meters apart all the way around. The trees are the perfect distance apart to form makeshift goals. Six goals for each side, twenty-four goals in all—that's a lot of penalties to go round. Master Willie would be horrified by the current state of Milford House, but he might have chuckled at that.

APPENDIX II:

THE ORIGINS OF THE PENALTY SHOOT-OUT

It sounds like the start of a bad bar-room joke: there's a Spaniard, a German and an Israeli. The Spaniard was general manager of CF Cádiz, the German a former referee who took charge of over a thousand games, and the Israeli a soccer administrator who spent forty-seven years working for his country's FA. And each of them thinks he was the one who invented the penalty shoot-out.

The question of who actually invented the shoot-out persists to this day. All three men have strong cases, so let's look at the candidates.

The Spaniard: Rafael Ballester

Ballester worked for Spanish side CF Cádiz but his breakthrough came when he wrote an article for local paper *Diario de Cádiz* in 1962 bemoaning the fact that drawn matches were being decided by a coin toss. In every summer since 1955, Cádiz had hosted the prestigious preseason tournament for the Ramon de Carranza Trophy. The organizers asked Ballester to come up with a solution in case of a tie, because a replay was impossible.

Ballester suggested a shoot-out, so when, on Sunday, September 2, 1962, Barcelona and Real Zaragoza drew the final, it had all been agreed. One team would take five penalties in succession, and the other team would follow suit. Barcelona went first and scored three times. Zaragoza also scored three. There was no plan for what happened when the shoot-out ended in a tie.

Laszlo Kubala, the former Barcelona forward who was then coach, argued that five more kicks be taken by the five outfield players who had not yet taken one. Zaragoza, whose team was not as talented as Barcelona, vetoed that idea and suggested the same five players kick again. That's what they did: this time, Barcelona scored all five. For Zaragoza, their Brazilian forward Duca missed.

There seems no doubt this was Ballester's idea, and the execution was close to the shoot-out's current form. But the Spanish authorities never developed the idea further, and the concept existed only in this tournament. By the time the next final was drawn, it was 1983, and the format was by then in regular use. The next five times the Ramon de Carranza Trophy went to penalties, though—in 1983, 1985, 1986, 1993 and 1994—the same team won the shoot-out: Cádiz CF.

"Whenever I see penalties I remember my father," said Ballester's son, also called Rafael. "It's good that draws have been decided this way for so many years. I just wish he had patented the idea."

The German: Karl Wald

Wald got his refereeing license in 1936 and officiated in the lower south German leagues before he was promoted to Oberliga Süd, the highest division before the Bundesliga was created in 1963. He didn't get to referee any Bundesliga games because he was overage at forty-nine, but he was a linesman for the game between Bayern Munich and Eintracht Frankfurt in 1965 (Bayern, with Franz Beckenbauer, Gerd Müller and Sepp Maier in the side, won 2–0).

That season, Liverpool had beaten FC Cologne in the European Cup quarterfinal after the two legs were drawn and the English side went through after a plastic disc (one side red, for Liverpool, the other white, for Cologne) was twice tossed after the first effort landed on the muddy pitch on its side. "Tossing a coin had nothing to do with sport and wasn't a sporting way to decide the winner. It wasn't a proper victory," Wald explained before his death in July 2011.

Wald retired as a professional referee in 1969, after over a thousand games and recognition with the referee's "golden badge of honor." One year later, on May 30, 1970, he stood up at the Bavarian Football Federation's annual meeting and raised the idea of the penalty shoot-out. He had already trialed it at youth and amateur matches, and players and fans liked it. The BFF president Hans Huber immediately opposed it but the other members voted in favor and the board implemented it for the 1970/71 season.

The German FA quickly followed suit and the shoot-out was first used in an official game on December 23, 1970, when Schalke beat Wolfsburg in the German Cup. Wald's format was much more like today's: teams taking alternate penalties, the referee standing level to the spot, and sudden death if the scores were level after five kicks apiece.

Again, there seems no doubt that Wald was the man who had the shoot-out idea ratified by the German FA. His grandson Thorsten Schacht has set up a Web site in his honor, his hometown of Penzberg commemorated his achievement in 2007, and the German press report as fact that Wald convinced FIFA to adopt his shoot-out idea. After England managed to score only one penalty in their 2006 shoot-out against Portugal, German paper *TAZ* took particular delight: "In Gelsenkirchen, England reached a new realm of ridiculousness. The inventors of football messed up something that a German had invented."

The only overt sign of recognition that Wald could claim from

FIFA, though, was a Christmas card from its president, Sepp Blatter, sent every year from 2001 onward.

The Israeli: Yosef Dagan

If there was a job going at the Israeli FA in the second half of the twentieth century, chances are Yosef Dagan filled it. He was general secretary, head of foreign relations, team manager, managing director—all roles he filled in his forty-seven years at the federation. But his lasting legacy to the game may well have been one that did not actually benefit his home country.

His idea first took root in 1965, when he persuaded Israeli FA chairman Michael Almog to experiment with the shoot-out as a way of eliminating replays in Cup matches. Dagan only thought about pushing it on to the international stage after the 1968 Olympics, the first time Israel had qualified for the soccer tournament.

Israel won their first game 5–3, beating a Ghana side that had two players sent off by referee Michel Kitabdjian. After the final whistle, the French official was pushed and kicked by furious Ghana players, and the Israeli side helped usher him off the pitch. Israel faced Bulgaria in the quarterfinals and, thanks to a late equalizer from Joshua Feigenbaum, drew the game 1–1. The result was to be decided by the drawing of lots: two pieces of paper were placed in the straw hat of Olympic Games organizing committee president Pedro Ramirez Vázquez, and the referee, who happened to be Kitabdjian, drew out the winning team. The paper said: Bulgaria.

"We knew that was not the right way to decide a game and I already knew what was a sporting and fairer way to decide games that were drawn," Dagan told me. "Sport is about equality, and we have to give both teams a chance to decide the winner."

Dagan drafted an article with Almog that was published in the August 1969 edition of *FIFA News*. It said: "The drawing of lots is immoral and even cruel, it is unfair to the losing team and not honorable for the winner." The fact that FIFA even published it showed a mindset that was prepared to be persuaded.

Dagan then asked Koe Ewe Teik, a Malaysian referee and senior member of FIFA's Referees' Committee, to present it to the International Football Association Board. Dagan and Teik were colleagues and friends; they spent a lot of time together because at that time Israel was part of the Asian soccer confederation. "He was a very good friend of mine, and that relationship made the whole thing happen," Dagan said. "He really got it, and told the committee all the technical details of how it would work, where the players and officials would stand, that kind of thing."

The minutes of the IFAB meeting held in Inverness, Scotland, on June 27, 1970, show that the shoot-out was approved, though it was called "Kicks from the Penalty Mark." It's easy to see how Dagan was successful in dealing with the game's true power-brokers of the time: he was sociable and enthusiastic, keen to continue our conversation despite the busy afternoon he had lined up, organizing his eighty-sixth birthday party.

He even had the grace to apologize for England's terrible shoot-out record, and told me about his favorite Englishmen. "[Ex-FIFA president] Stanley Rous, he was a very good friend. He used to come over and give courses to our coaches and referees. I would spend two weeks with him practically as his servant. Walter Winterbottom, he was a great friend, and his wife and I still exchange Christmas cards. Bert Millichip, Geoffrey Thompson, very good friends. Bobby Robson, very nice man and a great friend. The one after him, also a good friend: what was his name again?"

What does he say to those England coaches who think penalties are a bad idea?

"If they have a better solution, let them tell me."

What about Wald, the German referee who claims he invented the shoot-out?

"What a cheek that is! This story is stupid, and I will tell you why. He said in Germany they used it in 1970, and in Israel we used it before then. But the first time in Germany, it was years after us. No way!"

And how does he feel when he watches a shoot-out now?

"It's not so much a matter of pride, but I do feel at least I contributed something to football."

Dagan received a diploma for his contribution to European soccer at the UEFA Congress in 2000—though that was for his work in Israel rather than with penalties.

To further confuse the issue, there are examples of shoot-outs being used to decide games in Europe before any of these three men claimed the invention as their own. Serie C side Treviso beat Maestrina 5–3 on penalties in the 1959 Coppa Italia first round, while Swiss side Ticno beat Geneva 3–2 in the 1960 Swiss Youth Cup quarterfinal.

Go back a little further, though, and the first recorded use of the shoot-out in a competitive match was actually in the first country to win the World Cup on penalties: Brazil. The Torneio Início was the traditional curtain-raiser to the State Championship season, in which sides in each state would play each other in a knockout tournament in a single day at the same venue. The format was similar to a preseason tournament in today's game—except the matches had to be shortened, to ensure that the knockout (known as *eliminatórias*, or *mata-mata*—kill-kill) left just one team standing.

The games lasted only ten minutes each half, so there were lots of draws. The first Torneio Início, in 1919, had the tiebreaker rule that the team with most corners would progress. If it was still a draw, then a coin toss or extra time would take place, depending on the state's local rules.

In 1942, the São Paulo State Federation added a new rule to boost interest in the competition. "Radical Rules Changes for This Year's Torneio Início" went the headline of daily paper *O Esporte* five days before the tournament kicked off at the Pacaembu Stadium on March 1. The paper explained:

The 1942 Torneio Início will feature suggestive news for local sport fans. Indeed, we'll have innovations never seen before in our capital, in the classic tournament that decides the one-day champion. Corners won't be used to decide a match anymore. If the game ends in a tie, each club will have to take three penalties; and if it's still a tie, the clubs will take three more penalties, this time alternate, and the game will be decided when one player misses and the other scores. The rules also say that, if there's still a tie after the last three penalties, a draw will be made to appoint the winner of the match. Apparently, fans will welcome the innovation from the local football directors. Players won't worry about corners, so we won't see that battle between forwards and defenders. Now we'll have the fight between the top penalty takers against the goalkeepers . . . Fans will have the opportunity to root for the better goalkeepers and the best scorers.

The key element to this shoot-out was that only one player from each team would take all three penalties. Of the ten games played on that day, one ended in a draw: the first-round game between Espanha and Comercial. The teams drew lots to shoot first, and Comercial forward Romeu was up first. He scored two from his three, his final effort saved by Espanha goalkeeper Nelson. Bemba, Espanha's taker of choice, scored his three and Espanha went through.

Gazeta Esportiva, the oldest newspaper in São Paulo, was not happy with the innovation. Under an illustration of a goalkeeper being bombarded with balls, and the headline "The Prestige of the Penalty Kick," the new format came under attack. "Why would you apply a penalty, the ultimate capital punishment in football, to settle a drawn game? It should only be used for a foul. Using it to decide a winner trivializes the penalty. The federation decided to adopt a system which is absurd, fairly illogical and truly irrational! Our fans cannot appreciate this penalty system. And hopefully they won't have to, for the good of the game and even for the prestige of the penalty kick, which can't be thrown into the mass grave of unnecessary things in this sport, so loved by so many."

In future seasons, the corner-count rule returned, but penalties still decided games in the event of corners tied. In 1943, São Paulo (through forward Bazzoni) beat Ypiranga (Rodrigues) 3–2 on penalties, while in 1944, four games were settled on the corner-count. There was another change in 1945: the number of penalties increased from three to five, still with only one player taking them. On March 25, Ypiranga forward Garro scored his five out of five—an impressive achievement—while Portuguesa's Lorico scored only four.

So what does all this mean? Ballester, Wald and Dagan all thought they were right, and, at least in their own countries, they were. Ballester introduced the shoot-out to Spain, while Wald's intervention convinced the German FA to go with it. Dagan had the contacts to have more influence on a global level and is right to claim the credit for getting it ratified by FIFA. He couldn't have done that without the assistance of Koe Ewe Teik, the one figure in the story who barely gets a look-in. He was the one who pushed the idea over the finishing-line. But it was the Brazilians who got there first.

BIBLIOGRAPHY

Newspapers and magazines

11 Freunde
ABC
Active
AD
AS
Clarin
Daily Mail
De Groene Amsterdammer
De Volkskrant
Die Tageszeitung
Divo-90
El Confidencial
El Gráfico
El Mundo Deportivo
El País
ESPNFC.com
FIFA News
Filathlos
Folha de S. Paulo
France Football
France Soir
Gazeta Esportiva
Gazeta Wyborca
Gazzetta dello Sport

Guardian
Het Parool
Humo
Johan
JotDown
Kicker
La Nación
L'Equipe
Magazyn Fútbol
Marca
Mirror
Munich Merkur
New York Times Soccer Blog
NRC
O Esporte
O Estado de S. Paulo
Olé
Panenka
Perfil
Segodnya
So Foot
Sports Illustrated
Süddeutsche Zeitung
Sun
TAZ
The Blizzard
The Times
Trouw
Universo Fútbol
Vima
Voz de Galicia
When Saturday Comes

TV, film, radio and other media

11 Metri
Arena
COPE Radio
France-Allemagne
Injury Time
La Séance (Canal Plus)

Number 10
Piłkarski Poker
Punto Pelota
Sfide (RAI)
Stupido Hotel (RAI)
Telefoot
Un temps d'avance (Canal Plus)

Books

Andersson, P., Ayton, P. & Schmidt, C. (eds), *Myths and Facts about Football: The Economics and Psychology of the World's Greatest Sport* (Cambridge Scholars Press, 2008)

Anthony, A., *On Penalties* (Yellow Jersey, 2000)

Auclair, T., *Thierry Henry: Lonely at the Top: A Biography* (Macmillan, 2012)

Baggio, R., *Una Porta nel Cielo: Un Autobiografia* (Lìmina, 2005)

Balague, G., *A Season on the Brink: A Portrait of Rafael Benitez's Liverpool* (Orion, 2006)

Ball, P., *White Storm: 101 Years of Real Madrid* (Mainstream, 2003)

Beilock, S., *Choke: The Secret to Performing under Pressure* (Constable & Robinson, 2011)

Bergkamp, D. & Winner, D., *Stillness & Speed, My Story* (Atria Books, 2013)

Brown, P., *Goal-Post: Victorian Football* (Goal-Post, 2012)

Coyle, D., *The Talent Code: Greatness Isn't Born, It's Grown* (Arrow, 2009)

De Campos Jr., C., *As Joias do Rei Pelé* (Realejo, 2013)

—— *São Marcos de Palestra Itália* (Realejo, 2012)

Downing, D., *Best of Enemies: England v. Germany* (Bloomsbury, 2000)

Fisher, Dr. A., *Radical Frontiers in the Spaghetti Western: Politics, Violence and Popular Italian Cinema* (IB Tauris, 2011)

Froese, Dr. G., *Sportpsychologische Einflussfaktoren der Leistung von Elfmeterschützen* (Dr. Kovac, 2012)

Gerrard, S., *Gerrard: My Autobiography* (Bantam, 2007)

Hašek, J., *The Good Soldier Sveijk* (Penguin Classics, 2005)

Hawkey, I., *Feet of the Chameleon: The Story of African Football* (Portico, 2011)

Hiddema, B., *Cruijff! Van Jopie tot Johan* (Luitingh-Sijtoff, 1996)

Hunter, G., *Spain: The Inside Story of La Roja's Historic Treble* (BackPage Press, 2013)

Huybrechets, C., *Rik De Saedeleer: Duivelse Memoires* (Borgerhoff & Lamberigts, 2011)

Kuper, S., *The Football Men: Up Close with the Giants of the Modern Game* (Simon & Schuster, 2011)

—— & Szymanski, S., *Soccernomics: Why England Loses, Why Spain, Germany, and Brazil Win, and Why the US, Japan, Australia, Turkey—and even Iraq—are Destined to Become the Kings of the World's Most Popular Sport* (HarperSport, 2010)

Levinsky, S., *Maradona: Rebelde con Causa* (LibrosEnRed, 2001)

Llamazares, J., *Tanta pasión para nada* (Alfaguara, 2011)

Longman, J., *Girls of Summer: The U.S. Women's Soccer Team and How It Changed the World* (Harper Perennial, 2001)

McManus, J., *Milford: The Home of the Penalty Kick, Red Bricks, and Golden Memories; A Village History* (Inglewood Press, 2002)

Michiels, K. & Raes, F., *Ik, Rik Coppens* (Uitgeverij Houtekiet, 2005)

Miller, C., *He Always Puts It to the Right: A History of the Penalty Kick* (Victor Gollancz, 1998)

Palacios-Huerta, I., *Beautiful Game Theory: How Soccer Can Help Economics* (Princeton University Press, 2014)

Palermo, M., *Titan Del Gol y De La Vida* (Planeta, 2000)

Peters, Dr. S., *The Chimp Paradox: The Mind Management Program to Help You Achieve Success, Confidence, and Happiness* (Tarcher, 2013)

Pirlo, A., *Penso quindi gioco* (Mondadori, 2013)

Popa, G., *Poli nu piere și va trăi mereu* (Eurostampa, 2012)

Rooney, W., *The Way It Is: My Story* (HarperSport, 2007)

Sanders, R., *Beastly Fury: The Strange Birth of British Football* (Bantam, 2009)

Santoni, V. & Salimbeni, M., *L'Ascensione di Roberto Baggio* (Mattioli 1885, 2011)

Southgate, G. & Woodman, A., *Woody and Nord: A Football Friendship* (Penguin, 2004)

Sugden, J. & Tomlinson, A. (eds), *Hosts and Champions: Soccer Cultures, National Identities and the USA World Cup* (Arena, 1994)

Syed, M., *Bounce: The Myth of Talent and the Power of Practice* (Fourth Estate, 2011)

Van der Steen, H., *Penalty! Het trauma van Oranje* (Tirion Uitgevers, 2004)

Vergouw, G., *De Laatste Minuut* (Elsevier, 2006)

—— *De Strafschop* (Elsevier, 2003)

———— *Oranje wereldkampioen* (Holland Business Publications, 2010)

Wangerin, D., *Soccer in a Football World: The Story of America's Forgotten Game* (Temple University Press, 2008)

Wilson, J., *The Outsider: A History of the Goalkeeper* (Orion, 2012)

Winner, D., *Brilliant Orange* (Bloomsbury, 2001)

Academic papers

Bar-Eli, M., Azar, O. H., Ritov, I., Keidar-Levin, Y. & Schein, G. (2007), "Action bias among elite soccer goalkeepers: the case of penalty kicks," *Journal of Economic Psychology*, 28, 606–21

Baumeister, R. F., Bratslavsky, E., Finkenauer, C. & Vohs, K. D. (2001), "Bad is stronger than good," *Review of General Psychology*, 5, 323–70

Crowley, L., Hand, D. & Jeutter, R. (2000), "Playing the identity card: stereotypes in European football," *Soccer and Society*, vol. 1 no. 2, 107–28

Flegal, K. E. & Anderson, M. C. (2008), "Overthinking skilled motor performance: or why those who teach can't do," *Psychonomic Bulletin & Review*, 15 (5), 927–32

Jordet, G. (2009), "When superstars flop: public status and 'choking under pressure' in international soccer penalty shootouts," *Journal of Applied Sport Psychology*, vol. 21, issue 2, 125–30

———— (2009), "Why do English players fail in soccer penalty shoot-outs? A study of team status, self-regulation, and choking under pressure," *Journal of Sports Sciences*, vol. 27, issue 2, 97–106

————, Elferink-Gemse, M. T., Lemmink, K. A. P. M. & Visscher, C. (2006), "The 'Russian roulette' of soccer? Perceived control and anxiety in a major tournament penalty shootout," *International Journal of Sport Psychology*, 37, 281–98

————, Hartman, E., Visscher, C. & Lemmink, K. A. P. M. (2007), "Kicks from the penalty mark in soccer: the roles of stress, skill, and fatigue for kick outcomes," *Journal of Sports Sciences*, 25, 121–9

———— & Hartman, E. (2008), "Avoidance motivation and choking under pressure in soccer penalty shootouts," *Journal of Sport and Exercise Psychology*, 30, 452–9

————, Hartman, E. & Sigmundstad, E. (2009), "Temporal links to performing under pressure in international soccer penalty shootouts," *Psychology of Sport and Exercise*, vol. 10, issue 6, 621–7

————, Moll, T. & Pepping, G. (2010), "Emotional contagion in soccer penalty shootouts: celebration of individual success is associated with ultimate team success," *Journal of Sports Sciences*

────── & Elferink-Gemse, M. T. (2012), "Stress, coping and emotions on the world stage: the experience of participating in a major soccer penalty shoot-out," *Journal of Applied Sport Psychology*, 24, 73–91

──────, Hartman, E. & Vuljk, P. J. (2012), "Team history and choking under pressure in major soccer penalty shootouts," *British Journal of Psychology*, 103, 268–83.

McGarry, T. & Franks, I. M. (2000), "On winning the penalty shootout in soccer," *Journal of Sports Sciences*, vol. 18, issue 6, 401–9

Nevill, A., Webb, T. & Watts, T. (2013), "Improved training of football referees and the decline in home advantage post WW2," *Psychology of Sport and Exercise*, 14, 220–7

Palacios-Huerta, I. (2003), "Professionals play minimax," *Review of Economic Studies*, 70, 395–415

────── (2012), "Tournaments, fairness and the Prouhet-Thue-Morse sequence," *Economic Inquiry*, vol. 50, issue 3, 848–9

────── & Apesteguia, A. (2010), "Psychological pressure in competitive environments: evidence from a randomized natural experiment," *American Economic Review*, 100, 2548–64

Plessner, H. & Betsch, T., "Sequential effects in important referee decisions: the case of penalties in soccer," *Journal of Sport and Exercise Psychology*, 23, 254–9

Schwarz, W. (2011), "Compensating tendencies in penalty kick decisions of referees in professional football," *Journal of Sports Sciences*, 29(5), 441–7

Shaw, D. (1988), "The political instrumentalization of professional football in Francoist Spain, 1939–1975," PhD thesis—University of London

ACKNOWLEDGMENTS

A penalty may be one man against another, but I never felt I was on my own in putting this book together. David Luxton helped enormously in the early stages, and my editor Giles Elliott was brilliant in the later ones. I'd also like to thank Rebecca Winfield and, from Penguin USA, Patrick Nolan and Maxwell Reid for their support.

I was lucky enough to receive unstinting help from wonderfully talented colleagues I am proud to call my friends. Huge thanks are due to all of them: Gary Al-Smith, Peter Alegi, Marcus Alves, Philippe Auclair, Dr. Anthony Bale, David Barber, Marc Beauge, Sheridan Bird, Ned Boulting, Mads Gudim Burheim, Abby Burton, Tam Byrne, Ed Chamberlin, Melissa Chappell, Hikabwa Decius Chipande, Dermot Corrigan, Lawrence Donegan, Rob Draper, Fernando Duarte, John Duerden, Sorin Dumitrescu, Piers Edwards, Paul Ellis, Dion Fanning, Federico Farcomeni, Dr. Georg Froese, Yasunori Fujiwara, Stoyan Georgiev, Simon Gleave, Igor Goldes, Luke Gosset, James W. Grayson, Dirk Grosse, Christian Gruber, Paul Hansford, James Horncastle, Graham Hunter, David Jones, Geir Jordet, Tor-Kristian Karlsen, Mitchell Kaye, Auke Kok, Sergio Krithinas, Jakub Krzyzostaniak, Rémy Lacombe, Mark Ledsom, Gonçalo Lopes, Gabriele Marcotti, Jeroen Maris, Ken Matsushima, Stephen McManus, Paolo

Menicucci, Mohamed Moallim, Cahe Mota, Sydney Mungala, Ignacio Palacios-Huerta, Elena Papadopoulou, Pedro Proença, Bernie Reeves, Samantha Reilly, Cordula Reinhardt, Ronald Reng, Ofer Ronen-Abels, Emmanuel Roşu, Vasilis Sambrakos, Daan Schippers, Alex Sereda, Ellie Shoesmith, Matt Spiro, Tom Stockwell, Alex Stone, Gyuri Vergouw, Leo Verheul, Grant Wahl, Jonathan Wilson, David Winner and Michał Zachodny.

The following exceptional colleagues helped set up or translate interviews for *Twelve Yards*: Lorenzo Amuso, Federico Bassahun, Ronan Boscher, Ali Farhat, Kennedy Gondwe Jr., Karel Häring, Alex Holiga, Michael Oti Adjei and Darren Tulett.

I also received much-needed encouragement from friends and experts who read the book at various stages and helped with comments along the way. These include Annie Auerbach, Alex Bellos, Celso de Campos Jr., Massimo Cecchini, Marcus Christenson, James Eastham, Dave Farrar, Raphael Honigstein, Simon Kuper, Andrea Lyttleton, Mark Lyttleton, Ben Oakley and Darren Tulett.

Finally, to Annie, my inspiration, and Clemmy and Bibi, who reminded me that a penalty is only a penalty. I could not have done it without you.

INDEX

Note: Page numbers in *italics* refer to tables or illustrations. Page numbers followed by an "*n*" refer to notes at the bottom of the page.

INDEX